SINCE YOU WENT AWAY

Since You

WORLD WAR II
AMERICAN WOMEN

Went Away

LETTERS FROM
on the HOME FRONT

Edited by
Judy Barrett Litoff
David C. Smith

· UNIVERSITY PRESS OF KANSAS ·

This paperback edition is published by the University Press of Kansas (Lawrence, Kansas 66049), which was organized by the Kansas Board of Regents and is operated and funded by Emporia State University, Fort Hays State University, Kansas State University, Pittsburg State University, the University of Kansas, and Wichita State University, by arrangement with Oxford University Press, Inc.

Library of Congress Cataloging-in-Publication Data

Since you went away : World War II letters from American women on the home front / edited by Judy Barrett Litoff, David C. Smith.
p.   cm.   Includes index.

ISBN 0-7006-0714-5 (pbk.)

1. World War, 1939–1945—Women—United States—Correspondence.
2. World War, 1939–1945—United States.
3. Women—United States—Correspondence.
I. Litoff, Judy Barrett. II. Smith, David C. (David Clayton), 1929—
D810.W7S54   1991   940.53'15042'0922—dc20 [B]   90-20639

Printed in the United States of America

10 9 8 7 6 5 4 3 2 1

The paper used in this publication meets the minimum requirements of the American National Standard for Permanence of Paper for Printed Library Materials Z39.48-1984.

For
B.W.T. and C.E.T.

and
All the other World War II
letter writers

Foreword

WE ARE OFTEN ASKED HOW WE BECAME INTERESTED IN THE topic of women and letter writing during World War II. When we are most honest, we go back to our childhoods when one of us came of age in a small Maine town, dominated by the wartime milieu, and the other spent many happy hours in a small Georgia town during the postwar decade, listening to her father's old 78 records of big band wartime swing. We also sometimes talk about seminal courses taken and taught. In actuality, though, substantive work began about eight years ago when the two of us, longtime friends, began to write a book based on the World War II letters written by a young southern couple who were the aunt and uncle of one of us—Judy. That book, *Miss You: The World War II Letters of Barbara Wooddall Taylor and Charles E. Taylor* (Athens: University of Georgia Press, 1990), was based on thousands of pages of letters which these two individuals wrote to each other during the war years.

The letters written by Barbara Wooddall Taylor are extremely powerful documents. They chronicle a grand story of romance, making do, learning to cope with life, and "growing up" during wartime. We became convinced that Barbara Taylor's story was similar to those of other women during the war. But how could we be sure? What had happened to the more than six billion letters which were sent overseas during World War II?

While conducting the research for *Miss You,* we learned that the letters written by men in combat had often been carefully preserved by loved ones at home, donated to military and university archives, and made into many books. However, after conducting exhaustive searches, we did not locate any books based on the home-front letters of American women. Whenever we asked about the letters which women wrote, the response we most often heard was, "There aren't any letters from women. They were all destroyed. The men in combat were under orders not to keep personal materials." Yet the historian in each of us could not quite believe that this was true.

We were intrigued by the challenge presented to us as we began to consider possible ways to locate letters written by American women during the Second World War. We share the view, held by many scholars, that the private writings of American women are important documents which need to be retrieved and analyzed. We were and are convinced that the personal letters of women contain valuable information and insights which will benefit historians as they continue in their efforts to validate the "female experience" and to incorporate the meaning of this "experience" into their accounts of the past.

We decided to draft a brief author's query requesting information from anyone who had knowledge of letters written by women during the Second World War. It stated that we wanted to use the letters for a book we were preparing in commemoration of the forthcoming fiftieth anniversary of World War II. The query was sent, in the spring of 1988, to the editors of 1400 daily newspapers throughout the United States and to about 400 popular and professional periodicals and newsletters, including specialty publications for veterans, minorities, and women. Much to our delight, editors across the United States published our query. Newspapers, for example, often printed it on the letters to the editor page. Quite by chance, we had sent out the query a few weeks before Memorial Day. Many editors seized upon this coincidence and published it during Memorial Day weekend. Some newspapers even carried short feature articles about our project. Subsequently we wrote letters of inquiry to every state historical society and archive and to many large university archives as well as to more than 100 African-American organizations, institutions, and publications.

Today, some three and a half years later, our lives have been dramatically altered by our search for World War II letters written by women. Sweethearts, wives, mothers, stepmothers, mothers-in-law, grandmothers, daughters, sisters, aunts, nieces, the "girl next door," and just plain friends all have written letters which have been donated to us. In total, we have heard from 600 individuals from all fifty states, and we have collected 25,000 letters written by approximately 400 American women. *No one*, including ourselves, had any idea that such letters had survived the vicissitudes of war and the postwar years.

We have made a conscientious and concerted effort to secure letters written by women from a wide socioeconomic/ethnic/geographic cross-section of American life. We have been very successful in locating letters written by white, middle-class women, both rural and urban. We have good representation from persons of European descent as well as Mexican-American, Japanese-American, and Jewish women. However, we have not been as successful as we had hoped in locating letters from African-American women.

The history of the safekeeping and preservation of the 25,000 letters which we have collected is a story in and of itself. Some recipients simply wrote on the blank sides of the letters they received. Others carefully saved their letters and shipped them back to the United States in empty K-ration boxes. Occasionally, the letters have been organized into scrapbooks and even made into privately printed books. A few collections have been donated to archives. For the most part, however, the letters have remained hidden away in the attics and closets of private homes for the past fifty years.

Since the onset of the project in the spring of 1988, hardly a day has gone by that we have not heard from wartime letter writers. Letters have been sent to us in shoeboxes, a variety of corrugated containers, suitcases, and even a World War II ammunition box. In addition, wartime letter writers have sent us notes of encouragement, remembered us on our birthdays and on special holidays, and frequently telephoned us. They have visited us and we have visited them—from Maine to Mississippi. One letter writer even sent us a jar of homemade pepper jelly. For our part, we have kept the letter writers abreast of our work with a V-Mail newsletter which we have sent out every few months to all who have written to us.

We have become very close to "our" World War II letter writers. We have been saddened by the deaths of a few of our newly found friends, but we have also been heartened by the willingness of letter writers to share their wartime experiences with us. We have been especially gratified to learn that events which occurred half a century ago have continued to enhance their lives.

The letters in our collection are wonderfully compelling. And increasingly it has become clear to us that they are compelling because they were not originally written for everyone to read. They were directed to a small audience, usually a single reader. They were hurriedly written—sometimes during "lunch" breaks on the midnight shift—but with an intensity that makes them read like great literature.

We continue to be impressed with how well the letters were written. Students in our classrooms, with whom we have shared the letters, have been equally impressed with their literary quality. Whatever other conclusions one might draw from reading these letters, it is apparent to us that the quality of public education in the 1930s and 1940s was far superior to that of today.

We have organized the letters around themes which were of especial importance to the women who wrote them. These themes are very different from those which are emphasized in traditional accounts of World War II. We would have been unfair to the letter writers had we organized this book around the great events of the Second World War. Instead, the book focuses on the responses of women to the outbreak of war, courtship by mail, the varied experiences of war brides and war wives, and the challenges faced by female war workers. In addition, it provides examples of home-front responses to the demands created by the war. The book concludes with an examination of how women were affected by the sacrifices which led to victory and how they perceived the larger meaning of the war. We have also included a pictorial essay to illustrate the important role of the mail in sustaining morale both away and at home.

In the opening and closing chapters, we use single letters from different letter writers to probe the extraordinary nature of the events at the beginning and end of the war. The remaining chapters use several series of letters written by different women which focus on specific themes, and we have supplied biographical sketches for these women.

Because wartime letters were often hurriedly composed, the writers sometimes omitted words such as "it," "is," and "the." We have supplied missing words to ease readability. For the same reason, we have also added commas and apostrophes, and occasionally we have corrected spelling errors.

Wartime letter writers often penned very long letters. In fact, ten-page letters were not uncommon. In order to include a wide sampling of the available letters, we have provided abridged versions of many of them. We have indicated this by the use of ellipses.

The women who wrote the letters which are reprinted in this book lived in thirty-nine of the fifty states, and Washington, D.C. Nearly all of the letters which we have reprinted have been donated to us and are in our personal possession. We have indicated in the text when we have used letters from archives.

This book is not meant to be a book which celebrates war. It is, however, a celebration of the purposes for which the Second World War was fought. We offer it as a testimonial to the indomitable spirit of those who fought it, both at home and away.

Acknowledgments

THIS BOOK OWES MUCH TO THE NURTURE AND INSPIRATION WE received, decades ago, from Bell Wiley, Harvey Young, Gwil Roberts, and Paul Gates. The interchange of ideas which took place in their classrooms and seminars taught us to think of history in different and exciting ways. Their research and publications continue to provide impeccable standards by which we measure our own work.

Two prolific wartime letter writers, Barbara and Charles Taylor, have provided us help, love, and support over the last decade. The newspaper, magazine, and newsletter editors who carried our appeal for letters written by women also deserve special thanks. We feel extremely privileged to have had the opportunity to have read thousands of personal letters written during the Second World War. We offer this book as a token of our affection for the many letter writers who have shared their wartime experiences with us. For each letter printed in this book, there remain scores more which are equally moving and profound.

Archivists and librarians make up the infrastructure of history. No historian works well without their support. Even when they were unsuccessful in locating wartime correspondence for us, their letters of encouragement gave us the fortitude to continue.

Our colleagues are amused by us, shake their heads at our persistence, and yet they always help us to push ahead. At Bryant College, we are especially grateful to Mary Lyons, Jim Ingraham, Conny Sawyer, Bret McKenzie, Bob DiPrete, the many work-study students who spent tedious hours photocopying letters for us, and all the wonderful people who acted as porters, carrying boxes of letters from the parking lot to Judy's office. We would like to pay particular tribute to Debbie Winde, who has taken a personal interest in this project and who performed "above and beyond" at a time of incredible stress for us. To say thank you is not enough, but it will have to do in print. At the University of Maine, we wish to thank Dick Hale, Dick Blanke, Ed Schriver, Howard Segal, Bill Baker, Jerry Nadelhaft, Marli Weiner, Kathie Moring, and Suzanne Moulton. David Demeritt, Jr., provided witty and provocative comments which we usually took into consideration.

A wide community of scholars has demonstrated confidence in this project. They include Mary Giunta, Ray and Pat Browne, Randy Roberts, Martha Swain, Lee Kennett, Bill Tuttle, Malcolm Call, Larry Malley, Glenda Riley, and Judy Austin. We extend special thanks to our editor, Sheldon Meyer, and our agent, Gerry McCauley.

While awaiting the adventure of her first year at Georgetown University, Nadja Barrett Litoff devoted many summer days to this book. We hope that she learned a bit about the frustrations *and* fun of being a historian. We were buoyed by the enthusiastic response to our project from the eight-grade students at Moses Brown School, even though their classmate, Alyssa Barrett Litoff, was somewhat skeptical about our encroachment into her world.

When embarking on a joint endeavor of this type, one needs to have tolerance, trust, love, patience, fortitude, and a sense of humor. Because our families have these attributes, they are able to endure us and our work. The greatest of these is tolerance.

J.B.L.
D.C.S.

Contents

SINCE YOU WENT AWAY

October 1942

It is almost unbelievably breathtaking to be outside in these enchanted days. I have a secret feeling that so long as they last *you* are safe. That all life is suspended in some gold and orange spell. The fact that men are killing and being killed somehow cannot penetrate. I suppose that is essentially the trouble with a democracy such as ours. Democracy itself is an enchantment which lulls. And part of it is conscious. By that I mean the person within the spell deliberately puts painful sense awakenings from him in order that he may preserve his status.

Isabel A. Kidder of Durham, New Hampshire, to
Chaplain Maurice A. Kidder, c/o Postmaster, N.Y.

Chapter 1

Don't You Know
There's a War On?

THE POPULAR PHRASE "DON'T YOU KNOW THERE'S A WAR ON?" was often repeated throughout the United States as a reminder to citizens that the country was now a nation at war. The war had broken out in Europe in September 1939, and it had been raging in Asia since the mid-1930s. However, the United States avoided direct involvement in the conflict until the Japanese attacked Pearl Harbor on December 7, 1941.

For individual Americans, the sense of participation in the war became even stronger when loved ones departed for military service. Many children saw their fathers only in photographs, although letters from "Daddy" often arrived from faraway places. Of course, the families of those who had been drafted or had enlisted in the service before the events of Pearl Harbor were already well aware that, indeed, a war was on. As the pace of world events intensified, Americans increasingly turned to letter writing to bridge the miles that separated loved ones.

———————————— ✍ ————————————

The following letter was written by Lucille Mumm, whose husband, Carl, was stationed at Hickam Field in Oahu, Hawaii, when the war began. He had

3

been sent there for one year as a member of the Army Air Corps in early December 1940. The letter, written in a Christmas card, was sent to a college chum, Erman Southwick, and his wife, Flora. Lucille was evacuated after the Pearl Harbor attack and Carl went on to serve through the war in the South Pacific. Both died in the early 1980s.

Honolulu, Nov. 26[?] 1941

Dear Southwicks:

. . . Carl's birthday was last Saturday (22nd). I had a dinner for him at the club. There's a dinner dance there every Saturday night and the place is always alive with little dinner parties celebrating this and that. Our table was on the lanai next to the dance floor. There was an Hawaiian orchestra and a hula dancer who was the most graceful I've ever seen. The orchestra came over and played Happy Birthday to Carl when they saw the enormous cake I'd had made and decorated for the centerpiece. It was quite gay, with rosebuds, fancy dabs of icing here and there, and whatnot. The florist had banked rosebuds around it and trailed them out to the ends of the table. The only off-color note was the blue and gold of the placemats. The club furnishes them only in the Air Corps colors and I didn't realize it until it was too late to pick up any others.

I just love to give parties over here. There's no end to the flowers, odd foods—Chinese, Japanese, Hawaiian—table decorations, etc. that you can find if you just snoop around all the little curio shops. I've never had the opportunity, funds, or facilities, for party giving that I have here and I get such a kick out of it and will miss it all no end when the Army discards us. Everyone stopped by for a bite of cake and I had our little Filipino take both cake and ice cream to the orchestra. They beamed as only Hawaiians can with their gleaming white teeth and bronze skin. You'd love it all, Flora, and I certainly wish you could come over here on your "paint the town red" spree. . . .

Write us more about your new Intelligence job, Erman. It sounds interesting.

A very, very, Merry Christmas to you both.

Love, Lucille

Dorothea Taylor, a nurse from Mt. Carroll, Illinois, was living in Honolulu at the time of the Japanese attack on Pearl Harbor. She wrote the following letter to her brother, P. H. Taylor, of Gambier, Ohio, just a few hours after the bombing.*

---

*The letter of Dorothea L. Taylor is located in the Mary Dewhurst Miles Papers, Illinois State Historical Library, Springfield. Printed by permission of the Illinois State Historical Library.

Honolulu, Dec. 7, 1941

This morning was as delightful a Sunday morning as ever. There was a cool breeze, for rain had fallen in the night. I wakened about seven. There was the sound of heavy firing in the distance as there so often is when our brave defenders are practicing. I thought it peculiar the paper was not in the box. When I stepped up to the street to look at the ocean I noticed heavy black smoke, as from oil rising from the region of Pearl Harbor. My first thought was that an accident had set fire to one of the oil tanks, or worse still, aircraft, which did not amaze me as they are often shot for practice.

Calmly I sat down to my coffee and doughnuts to listen to the broadcast of the Salt Lake City Choir. The singing was interrupted by the announcer stating that a sporadic attack had been made on Pearl Harbor and one Japanese plane had been shot down. Civilians were forbidden to use the telephone or to go on the streets. We were advised to keep our radios on and bulletins would be given as fast as they came in. We were told to be calm and stay where we were, that everything was under control. The announcer had to repeat a number of times that this was a real attack, not practice maneuvers.

Bulletins and orders continued at intervals. All firemen were called to duty. All army and navy men told to report to their stations. Disaster wardens were sent to their districts and the meeting places named for each ward. Mine is at the Robert Louis Stevenson school, just down the steps from my gate. Explosions and anti-aircraft firing continued. I went to the top of the reservoir across the street where most of my frightened neighbors had congregated. With my binoculars I could see numerous large fires in Pearl Harbor and Hickam Field. It made me sick at heart to see all the oil going up in clouds of black smoke, for of what good will our ships and planes be without oil? The loss is already disastrous. I heard two shells whistle overhead. The fire siren sounded every few minutes. KGU announced a bomb had hit about 50 ft. from their building, and there were some other craters elsewhere. As a precaution I packed up all the valuable things in the apartment in small baggage, so it could be moved easily. I filled everything with water, inside and out, and Miss Davis did the same, and asked everyone to draw water into every container in their apartments. There was smoke raising from two large fires in Makiki district, about a mile away, but I have not yet learned what started them or how much damage was done. Governor Poindexter spoke on the radio at 11 a.m., but unfortunately that is just when my set went bad so I could not get any broadcasts. It has been acting up for some time, and has not been serviced for a year. I had to depend on my neighbor's radio for further bulletins. One bomb fell on a place on Lillian Street, about two miles from me. No one hurt.

Parachute troops were reported to have landed on St. Louis heights—a mostly bare steep hill, far from any military objectives—and guards were directed by radio to deal with them. I never learned whether the suspects were our own men who had to bail out of a plane or whether they were enemies. By mid-afternoon there was no more smoke from fires that I could see, which was a relief because the wind was blowing quite strongly all day, and still is.

Most of my time was spent trying to calm and divert these young navy wives. They have husbands on cruisers and destroyers and in the air force, but they cooked meals with each other and insisted I eat supper with them, which I did. They packed their suitcases and stayed at home. About three o'clock martial law was declared, so we now have to obey all orders and give an account of our every move. Two civilian men are left on the place and they were made Civilian Defense wardens and act as police in the neighborhood. Tonight there is a complete blackout. Millions of stars not otherwise seen make the heavens shine with a soft glow. I believe the moon rises about 10. I am sitting in my dressing-room closet with the door shut, and heavy green paper over the narrow high screened opening in the shower. Very little air gets in through the cracks, so I go out and cool off every few minutes. I am not excited, nor a bit afraid. I have plenty of food on hand. We were instructed to boil all our drinking water in case the open reservoirs had been meddled with.

I resort to my knitting when I get a little nervous. I am in the midst of Cronin's book *Keys to the Kingdom,* but it was hard to concentrate on any reading or study today. Now night has come, everything is silent and peaceful. It has been a tense day, and with no lights on, everyone seems to have retired. You people on the mainland have probably had a lot more news of this incident than I have while right on the spot. One announcement stated a naval battle was going on west of Oahu. It was said a Japanese ship flying the American flag with planes marked with U.S. insignia came within range and started all the trouble. It has been an Incident. We are all wondering what tomorrow will bring forth.

Most affectionately,   Dorothea

Ray Woods of Detroit, Michigan, left school after the eighth grade and joined the Civilian Conservation Corps. In 1940, he enlisted in the Navy and was assigned as a Seaman Second Class to the USS *Pennsylvania* which was berthed at Pearl Harbor in December 1941. He was wounded during the Japanese attack and spent about four weeks recuperating in the hospital. Although Ray's parents received a telegram from the government on December 11 informing them that he had been wounded, it was three weeks before they received any mail from their son. The Christmas season of 1941 was not a very happy time for the Woods family. The stresses created by the uncertainty of Ray's status and the outbreak of war were underscored in a letter which his sister-in-law, Alice Woods, wrote to him on December 21.

Garden City, Dec. 21, 1941

Dear Ray:

I'll write and write—just like you've answered my letter 'cause I think you *must* be getting better. I hope well enough to enjoy Christmas. It's raining here—imagine—Thursday is Christmas and no snow. I love rain—but not when it should be snowing. To me that's what makes it Christmas—the lights from the trees inside the houses reflecting on the snow. The creak of the tires on the cars riding by. The snow on your eye lashes—and the dear little children who pop you in the kisser with a snow ball when you least expect it.

I have a friend who loves dogs and every year she gets so many Christmas cards with dogs on them. This year you'd be surprised at the number of cards we've received with *boats* on them. Not because we like them so much tho,—it's because of you—you know we've talked about you so much—and believe me it's *all good!!*

I don't suppose you'd care for a card with a boat on it. Bet you're sorta fed up on 'em—right?

I hope you're not disappointed 'cause you didn't get a Christmas package—we don't know where you are, how you are, or if you are (sounds like that song "All Alone," doesn't it?) well enough to enjoy what we uns wanted to send you un.

Except for *you*—I've got my Christmas shopping done—Got a nice Paradise Fruit cake for your Ma and Pa. . . . How about you Ray? Could you enjoy one? Or would a plate of mushrooms fried in butter taste better—or perhaps a fried cheese sandwich? 'Member when you told me they were swell—and a couple of days later you confessed you didn't like them? You are a perfect liar—and a nice one!

Got to leave room for Leon [Alice's son].   Alice

Hi-Ya? Ma was knitting a sweater for the Red Cross and her knitting needle broke. I haven't much room to write anymore so, so-long. Leon.

Alice's second letter, written early in the New Year, expressed the elation which she and other family members felt upon finally receiving a letter from Ray.

Garden City, Jan. [?], 1942

Dear Ray:

I couldn't put down on paper *how* we felt when we received your letter (Dec. 29th). To say we were elated is putting it mild. It just seemed like a black cloud was suddenly lifted. Like hearing from someone we thought (and prayed not) didn't exist anymore. As soon as I got your letter I called your mother. . . . I'll send the letter to your mother just as soon as the kids read it.

Your Ma has only received *one* card from you and that was dated Dec. 8th and we thought that was before the bombing and hard telling what happened since then. We'll make *shore* you get the pictures we took on Christmas. . . .

They had a nice Christmas at your house—considering you weren't there— I mean of course it would have been perfect if you were home. I hope you got my last letter cause we thanked you for the gifts you bought. I have a lovely purse with a V on it (gloves to match) and it's gotta be Victory. . . .

I could talk and talk to you now that I know you're at least able to write. . . .

Alice

Clifton and Lillian Goodnight of Kentucky were living in Honolulu when Pearl Harbor was attacked. Among the letters of concern they received from stateside friends was one written by Vera Hicks of Los Angeles, California. Throughout the war years, the Goodnights opened their home to servicemen passing through or stationed in the area.*

Los Angeles, Dec. 13, 1941

Dear Folks:

To say we were all stunned to hear the terrible news of Sunday last over the air is putting it mildly. "God Bless us all," we are certainly in for it now it would seem. But soon as we get thoroughly awakened guess we will pay up in full. Up till now, of course, we do not know a thing about the general welfare of you all and we are hoping and praying you are all safe and reasonably calm. The last is a large order and we do hope it can be filled. We have had a few blackouts off and on a number of times, without explanation, but we are anxious to do anything we can do to help the cause.

Christmas spirit here is at a standstill. We are all sort of walking around in a daze. All stores are closed at 5 o'clock instead of 9:30 p.m. as a number of them had planned. New Year's football game called off and "Rose Tournament" too is going to be cancelled according to our radio news. . . .

Hope it won't be long now before we can get some authentic news from you.

Be of Good Cheer—
Always,   Vera Hicks

Richard Long met Rubye Seago in Lawrenceville, Virginia, in October 1940 when he went to register for the draft. They fell in love almost immediately and were married in 1943 at the "Little Church Around the Corner" in New York City. This letter from Rubye, written to Richard while he was in basic training at Camp Wheeler, Georgia, indicates the extraordinary way in which

---

*The letter of Vera Hicks is located in the Goodknight Collection, Kentucky Historical Society, Frankfort. Printed by permission of Kentucky Historical Society.

the Japanese attack on Pearl Harbor often disrupted the lives of young people in love.

Lawrenceville, Sunday Nite, Dec. 7, 1941

My Darling:

I know you feel exactly like I do right now. I've just been listening to the radio. I've never been so blue or heartsick as I am right this minute. Oh, my darling—if it were possible I'd charter a plane—do anything—just to see you for a few minutes. . . .

Honestly, Dick, if I don't get to see you I'm going to lose my mind. Isn't there *any* thing you can do? 'Cause if you don't do it now do you realize we may *never* see each other again? Of course you do—you realize how serious the situation is, even more then I. Darling, they *can't* take you—the finest, sweetest boy that ever lived and send you away—it just tears my heart out to think of it.

Everyone in town is talking war, war war! Everyone is sure it will be declared tomorrow. There are some sad hearts over this world tonite. And none sadder than mine. And your poor mother.

There isn't any use of me pretending to feel other than the way I do. It's too serious now. And you'd know I was pretending, if I tried to write a cheerful letter.

. . . Pete [a lodger in the Seago home] is in the bathroom crying her eyes out. I think she'd marry Jack tonite. I don't blame her. She'd have that much. It's better than not having anything—to remember. This is awful—I know I'm hurting you. And I can't help it. Every word is coming from my heart.

I love you, Dick, more than anybody in the world. You know it already, but I want to tell you again. And I'll always love you to the end of my life. I love you because you're fine and good and just the kind of man I always wanted to meet and love. You meet all the requirements, Darling.

I'd give everything I own, or ever hope to have, to see you right now. Isn't there anything we can do?

Please don't let anything happen without letting me know. Wire me or call me or something. If it's possible.

Forever yours,   Rubye

Barbara Wooddall Taylor of Fairburn, Georgia, was nineteen years old and working as a secretary at Twentieth Century-Fox Film Corporation in nearby Atlanta when she wrote the following letter to her future husband, Private Charles E. Taylor, stationed at Fort Leonard Wood, Missouri.*

*Reprinted from Judy Barrett Litoff, David C. Smith, Barbara Wooddall Taylor, and Charles E. Taylor, *Miss You: The World War II Letters of Barbara Wooddall Taylor and Charles E. Taylor* (Athens: University of Georgia Press, 1990). Reprinted by permission of Taylor Lawson.

Atlanta, Dec. 11, 1941

Dearest Charlie:

. . . Well, what about this WAR business. Oh, Charlie, will you still get your Christmas leave? You must get it because I'm counting big on being with you again. I hope I feel just the way I did the first night I had a date with you, remember? We had such a good time and I've never been so knocked for a loop. I remember exactly what I thought about you and I wonder if I will think it again when you come. We must be sure and we will be sure. . . .

A man here in the office just said that Italy had declared WAR on the U.S.A. What's going to happen to us? There is no doubt in my mind as to whom shall win this WAR, but how long will it take us? It makes you feel like getting the best of everything before it's all gone. Now I know that isn't the right way to feel, is it Charlie???

Charlie, please don't threaten me. I just want to wait until I see you and I already know what I'll say and do. I can hardly wait.

Must close now.

Sincerely,   Barbara

Eunice L. Hagen was a student at Carleton College in Northfield, Minnesota, at the time of Pearl Harbor. In a letter to her boyfriend, Maurice Beck, an Army private stationed in Ft. Belvoir, Virginia, she described the Carleton College response to the outbreak of war.

Carleton College
Northfield, Dec. 13, 1941

Dearest Maurice,

. . . Perhaps you'll be interested in hearing the developments on our campus in regard to these history making times. Last Sunday the first reports of Japanese bombings in Pearl Harbor and the Philippines came through about 2 p.m., and the N.Y. Philharmonic broadcast was interrupted intermittently from then on as were subsequent programs with various bulletins. . . . After Vespers (a weekly occurrence) that evening a special I.R.C. roundtable discussion was held in Great Hall and really was jammed with students. Four faculty members held forth for several hours with a very interesting, enlightening and objective discussion of the War from geographic, economic, political, and international aspects.

On Monday a scheduled chapel was held at a later time so we could all hear the President give his message to Congress. Every one seemed to be on edge and there was little overjoyousness evident.

During the course of the week, there have been, oh so many, great discussions. Also a number of the senior men have been making preparations for leaving. In fact, my friend who was in Brazil this summer, being a commissioned officer had reported to Ft. Snelling in St. Paul for his physical and may or may not be able to finish even the first semester which ends the latter part of January.

Of course, the Dean and Prexy are urging all to stay in college.

There seems to be no point in losing hope now, as our only hope for the future rests on our defeating the Japs. . . . Heaven help us, if we don't.

My thoughts are ever of you. Let's still hope for some future meeting.

Yours ever,   Eunice

For millions of Americans, the first real sense that "a war was on" occurred when a loved one departed for military service. Women often wrote poignant goodbye letters which described the heartache of parting.

Isabel Kidder and her two young children lived in Durham, New Hampshire, during the three years that her husband, Maurice, a chaplain in the Army, was stationed in Europe. She wrote this letter to him as he was awaiting shipment to England.

Durham, Oct. [?] 1942

The First Day:

My darling, I call this the first day, for it is the first day in which I do not know where you are. If your ship slipped out into the wideness of ocean last night, to-night, or tomorrow I shall not know until after the war probably. Maybe there will be many details which I shall never know, and that seems hard to bear. It must seem equally hard to you to feel that there are things which are going to happen to "we three" which you cannot know. But I shall attempt to write as many of them down as possible.

If you could see me now, pleased as punch because down in the cellar the fire is burning and it is of my creating. I am determined to master that imperturbable monster. Otherwise, it just isn't decent to have it there. But I say burning with a good deal of relief. For I was afraid it was roaring. My coal came this afternoon and I got a fire built. . . . But it got away from me. The house got so hot I shut all the radiators and opened the front door, and I felt as if I'd let the genie out of the bottle. . . .

This was one of October's perfect afternoons. We put our lunch in a bag—two peanut butter sandwiches apiece, an apple, two cookies, and a napkin full of those little bittersweet chocolate drops they put in cookies and took to the road. We went down . . . to the reservoir. It was enchanting there. We sat on yellow leaves in a group of little trees and watched the water spreading into pools below the dam. It made a rippling sound coming over the rocks around the bend, but right in front of us it was clear and still enough to reflect the trees. . . . Even the off-red of a glowing tree colored the water like the reflection of a fire. Everywhere the water-spiders glanced along over to surface and as we sat there thistledown was forever passing us and skimming out over the water. Joel [their six-year-old son] thought it was exactly like the milkweed fairies in *Fantasia*.

I could have stayed forever in a spell-bound world where I was young and you were there. . . .

Good night you nut.

Isabel

Sigrid Jensen of Caldwell, New Jersey, wrote the following letter to her Marine husband, Karl, shortly after he left for training. This letter has some strong resemblances to the first letter in Margaret Buell Wilder's novel, *Since You Went Away* (New York, 1943).

Caldwell, June 16, 1943

My Darling:

You've only been gone a few hours and already the house is waiting for you. I came back from driving you out to the avenue and began mentally putting away our life together to make room for the new one alone. The main difficulty was that there is too much of *you* here. Your magazines, your books, your ash receiver, your papers still where you dropped them last night, your clothes spilling out of your closet, and even your pajamas flung on the bed. But it wasn't till I picked up the shirt you'd worn last night that the feel of you was unbearable. Then this morning's dashing, and packing and tearing around and the ride out to the avenue and the 15 minutes I sat there in the car after your trolley car had disappeared in the distance all came back again—and snatches of our life together, some funny, some sad, some gay, some mad, were all there, between us forever and not to be wiped out. I stood there holding the shirt thinking it must go to the laundry. But I couldn't put it in the hamper. I couldn't even lay it down.

And that's what it was like. Except that no words can get down to the awful unreality and finalness of it, the knowledge in one's mind, still unaccepted by the senses. That you, the best-natured and most tolerant person in the world, should have to learn to hate and kill is just as incredible to me as the fact that the peculiar oneness of us as a family should be broken. . . .

I can't think any longer now. I'm groggy a bit—the weather's terrifically hot, and I hope, sleepy-making. It's not yet 10:15, but I'm going to bed— I'll pretend we're together, and that every once in a while I must nudge you to make you move over, or stop snoring! And if I dream about you, tomorrow will be a lovely day.

I love you,   Sigrid

Saidee R. Leach of Edgewood, Rhode Island, wrote her son, Douglas, a serial letter following his departure for South Bend, Indiana, where he was to undergo basic training as an ensign in the Naval Reserve at the University of Notre Dame.

Edgewood, Aug. 10, 1942

Dear Douglas,

Half past eight—it's dark outside and I'm hoping that you have had a good dinner and because you can't see the scenery, that you are dozing a bit and catching up on your sleep. I was glad for you that there were several whom you knew . . . for conversation helps pass the time.

You certainly had quite a send-off at the station and we shall go down to speed Tom [Douglas's best friend] on his way when he leaves. . . .

Your wonderful letter to us means more than you can ever know. It will be kept in my Bible beside my bed and when distance seems great and clouds dark, it will help to comfort and strengthen me as nothing else could. You have always been a dear son and brother and I know you will return to us the same trustworthy, lovable, Christian (I can't say boy, for I know your experiences will mature you) but to us you will always be "Our Boy." Your letter I know will help Dad over some of the rough places and will help Marilyn [Douglas's younger sister] to think over some things which have not as yet touched her. But I know that will come in time, if I but keep faith. God bless you always.

I shall be interested to know whether you were sorry not to have your light-weight trousers, whether you slept well and what kind of a dinner was served on the train. Also, are you using your electric razor?

I shan't write you every day, but I thought I would jot down a few lines each night and then when I receive your address I will have a letter all ready to send.

Lots of love from all of us,

Mother, Dad, and Marilyn

Geraldine S. Kiefaber began a serial letter to her Navy husband, Paul, shortly after he left for a tour of duty in the Canal Zone. At the time, the young couple had been married for four years, owned a home in Arlington, Virginia, and had a three-year-old son, Billy. During the two years that her husband was away, Geraldine received a monthly allotment check of $99. Through careful planning and frugal spending, she managed to maintain their home in Arlington.

Arlington, April 13, 1944

Dearest Paul:

. . . Surely liked that smile you gave us as the bus pulled out and hope it is with you a part of the time anyway. I hope to keep smiling too and I have Billy to help me over the bad spots. Please don't worry about us and when you can. advise us on anything we will do our best to follow it. . . .

When I got [Billy] ready for bed he said, "now that Daddy's gone I can sleep with you." He did sleep with me but I couldn't get to sleep because I didn't have you to warm me up. I thought of you trying to sleep on the bus and wondered how you were feeling as I watched the hands of the clock go round.

I was thinking of you today at one o'clock this time and wondered how you felt as you walked into camp. Wish we could be with you but as it isn't possible we will make out alone until things are right for us again. In the meantime good luck to you sailor.

All my love until tomorrow. . . .

Love & kisses, Jerry & Billy

Anna and Clinton Beadle of New Athens, Illinois, had been married for a little over three years when he was drafted in October 1944. Clinton had received three deferments because of his work in an oil refinery. When he left for the service, Anna and her two young children moved in with her sister, also a war wife who had two children and was expecting a third. Anna wrote Clinton two moving letters shortly after she sent him off to combat in the Pacific.

New Athens, Feb. 8, 1945

Oh Darling:

It's so much worse already than it ever was before. I know that with every minute you're going farther away from me. I figure that you are somewhere in Texas now, Darling. I don't suppose it will be possible for you to save my letters so o.k. Anything you want to do will be all right with me—as long as you're faithful.

Diana had a whooping cough shot today and has been pretty cross. She's way down under the cover again. I'll have to dig her out. One consideration, in a few months she won't need cover.

Harry got the camera out of the suitcase tonight and turned it past one of the pictures. It's on 13 now. You might say he is the most investigating child—to say the least.

I'm having trouble with the darned pens so I finally gave up after trying three of them.

Diana's feet are coming out the other end of the blanket.

I love you, darling. I don't know of any other way to put it except that same old time-worn phrase. But I *do*. And I always will. Nothing can change that. Not war, nor fire nor flood. You'll always be part of me and I you.

I just dug Diana out and she's already started down again.

The Dr. checked her good, lungs and throat and says her cough is evidently mucus from her nose. She weighed 17 lbs. 8 oz., and is 15½ inches long.

I don't seem to have anything further to write about except how much I love you. And you know all about that. So I think I'll try to find our bed under all the clothes and suitcases and then crawl in it.

I love you, darling. Love you, love you.

I wish that I could dream every night of you and our love.

Ever your own,   Ann

New Athens, Feb. 9, 1945

My Darling:

. . . Darling, you've never left my thoughts one instant in the past two days and nights. I miss you so terribly. I hope the fellows you're with are keeping you busy enough that you aren't missing us too much.

I love you so, darling. It hurts so much. Love shouldn't hurt this way. It was meant to be happiness but then it was nearly a hundred years ago that Sherman said, "War is Hell." . . .

Darling, I'm like you in that I can't think of anything to write about. You probably think I could write more about the children. But it's all routine day to day stuff to me and nothing of importance stands out. Oh, I do have an incident that happened yesterday.

Your mother ironed Harry's khaki overalls and he wanted to put them on right away. I said no. He didn't need to wear them. Well, when I came home from East St. Louis, he had them on. Your mother couldn't resist him—he told her—"My mother doesn't spank my Daddy when he puts his soldier pants on."

I'm going to sign off to save weight since this will go airmail. I love you, darling. And always will be your,

Ann

After the entry of the Untied States into the war, many young people found themselves contemplating an uncertain and daunting world. In the case of Dawn Dyer and Jack Sage of Sprague, Washington, it meant that they were forced to plan for their future at a time when they were uncertain of what the next day might bring. Dawn wrote this letter to Jack shortly after he left for Nevada where he was to undergo training with the Army Air Corps.

Sprague, Aug. 10, 1942

Dear Jack:

. . . I don't like the idea of being so unsettled about my future. But I spose everyone feels that way, too. We're really a lot better off tho' than the rest of the world. People here don't realize yet that we're in a war. I think we'll have to go thru some of the things Europe has gone through before we'll come to life and then it might be too late.

I really don't blame you for wanting to get into action but it really means a lot to me. Maybe I'm thinking too much of myself but it does help a lot to know where you are and that you're safe. But if that's what you want and if it will make you happy by all means do it. But don't go thinking no one cares 'cause I know they do and speaking for myself, I'm positive. I hope you realize that. I'm trying to make you believe it. I'm all but throwing myself at you to make you believe me.

Don't be discouraged. Just keep thinking that it will be over someday, and then we all can have a chance to build our futures and try to make the most of them. The younger generation will be the wiser for it and we can try to build for our children to live in (It seems funny to think that we will have children some day but I expect we all will). The world never stops growing even for wars, I guess. I hope my little bit of philosophy can cheer you up. We have to live for the future now.

All my love,   Dawn XXX

As loved ones departed to "far-flung fronts," children also came to understand that "a war was on." They wrote many unpretentious and innocent letters which undoubtedly buoyed the spirits of those who were stationed far from home.

Two-and-a-half-year-old Meredith Haselton of Athol, Massachusetts, "wrote" the following letter to her father while he was in boot camp. Meredith's scribblings were enclosed in her mother's May 25, 1944, letter to her husband with the comment, "Translation on other small sheet! That's what she was saying as she wrote this."

Dear Daddy:

Daddy's a good boy. Mummy's a good girl. Meri's a good girl, too. A letter to Daddy—

I'm doing it by myself. Thank you for the pretty card. Give Daddy a kiss, Here's a kiss from me.

I love Daddy. I'm all done now.

Meri

In June 1944, six-year-old Nancy Rae Bobeng of Chicago wrote a short V-Mail to her aunt, Lt. Florence E. Nelson, a member of the Army Nurse Corps who was stationed with the 8th Field Hospital in Europe.

Chicago, June 23, 1944

Dear Aunty Flo,

NO MORE PENCILS

NO MORE BOOKS

NO MORE TEACHER'S

SASSY LOOKS

I PASSED TO 1ST GRADE

MRS. BREEDE IS THE TEACHER

I LOVE YOU.

NANCY RAE

Ruth Erling of Pennock, Minnesota, was six years old when she began writing to her father, Bertil A. Erling, a Protestant chaplain with the Marines in the South Pacific.

Pennock, [?], 1943

Dear Daddy Berlie Erling

Are you very *lonesome?* Do you live in a house? Sunday we eat very good.

Ruth Erling

Pennock, [?] 1944

Dear Daddy

I got a loose tooth. We have only 10 pages left in our reading books. Helen tried to pull my tooth. We read about Pinocchio. We are all lonesome for you. I like the letter we got today.

Love, Ruth

Eleven-year-old Joan Corbin of New Haven, Connecticut, was visiting relatives in Maryland when she wrote a V-Mail letter to her uncle, Walter S. Kellogg, a lieutenant in the Navy who was serving in the North Atlantic.

New Haven, March 26, 1943

Dear Uncle Joe:

Is it fun on your boat? I hope so. I am in Maryland but am going home very soon.

It's very warm; 70 degrees to-day! We waded in the woods even!

I have made lips here. Mine! I have kissed them. You kiss them too. The love will carry.

I hope you will come home safely. I am telling God to keep you in His grace.

Please remember me. I won't forget you, or the job you are doing for your country.

Love, Joanie

Thirteen-year-old Charmaine Leavitt of Kalamazoo, Michigan, wrote to "the boy next door", Private Justin Slager, while he was stationed with the Army in North Africa.

Kalamazoo, Oct. 30, 1943

Dear Justin,

Last night at school I helped with the rationing. I had to tell the people where to go and what to do. And the other night I went to a Girl Scout party. We went on a scavenger hunt. I had to get a cigar butt, 3 cups of mud, a girl's finger nail, a picture of Bob Hope and a couple of other things.

In school this year I am taking Latin, Jr. Business, civics, English, Science, and Gym. And I don't like any of them. In Jr. Business all we ever do is to listen to Mr. Morris blow about his house, his wife and Sears and Roebuck.

Your dog sure looks lonely, all he ever does is to sit on your front porch.

My Grandmother and Grandfather are living with us again. They have been here about a week and a half.

Sincerely yours, Charmaine

Doris Vinje and Herrett "Polly" Wilson grew up together in the same neighborhood of Everett, Washington. Doris was sixteen years old when she wrote the following letter to Polly, who was then stationed with the Army in the Pacific.

Everett, July 9, 1943

Dear Polly,

. . . I will be a Senior next year and hope to graduate next spring.

I do not remember exactly when you left Everett, but it certainly has changed. . . . For one thing, there are new front steps at your house next door. Sharkey's gas station, on the northeast corner of Everett and Wetmare avenues, has been entirely removed. The house where Thompson's used to live has also been removed, and the men from the Telephone Company have started using it for a parking lot. . . .

Do you have your clarinet with you, or aren't you allowed to have such things? By the way, do you still write poems? Even your letter has some very poetic phrases in it. . . .

We had a Fourth of July parade on July 5. It was fairly good, and there was also a horse show.

Do many of the boys in your group attend church services when they are held? I mean, of course, when services are held, not when the boys are. Of what denominations are your chaplains?

Your mother mentioned that when you left you liked the 23rd Psalm. I hope that you are still keeping by it.

As one might say—I'll hang my close on this line.

Goodbye for now.

The girl next door,   Doris

Months before the Japanese attack on Pearl Harbor, the United States began preparing for war. As part of this preparation, Congress passed the Selective Service and Training Act in September 1940. Over the next year, almost one million men were drafted. These early draftees and their families and friends were directly affected by the conflict that was already raging overseas.

John Larson of Chicago, was one of the first men to be drafted. He was inducted into the Army on January 4, 1941, almost a year before Pearl Harbor. After basic training in New Mexico, he was posted to a coast artillery unit near Bremerton, Washington.

At first, John and his sweetheart, Marjorie Griffith, also of Chicago, had planned to marry when his one-year tour with the Army was completed. But it soon became clear to them that John's year in the service would, most likely, be extended. Consequently they were married on June 27, 1941. As it turned out, John remained in the Army a full five years, including assignments in both Europe and the Pacific.

Marjorie's prewar letters to John reflected the anxieties of many of the early draftees and their families. At this time, few people in the United States had experienced life in the military and the problems often brought about by new and different surroundings.

Chicago, Jan. 3, 1941

Dearest Jonathan:

. . . Over the heads of all the people who are at present praying this war will soon be over—we see the future, and in it, America will play a big role and the farmers—wouldn't it be a good idea to save what we can "now" so outside of what expenses we will have on furloughs, we might have a little to go and buy a piece of America. . . . Huh, Johnnie? . . .

John, do you get griped if I ask you such questions concerning your precious Army pay and what thou doest with it? I have no criticism to make. I just like to have my finger in all your pies, I guess. . . .

You too dream what we will do in our house. I will tell you a couple of things I've remembered. . . . I often wonder too how you and my idea of raising Peter and Patty [prospective names for children] will click. I think the Dad has a big part to play and so often they leave it all to the Mom. . . . I often think of the Army, "hope" and pray you will not be changed by association with a lot of men who indulge in coarseness to different degrees. I know you won't tho'. And I appreciate that you do not deceive me. . . .

Hello, it's almost 8 o'clock. I've shopped for Mom and my little self. Do you know I had to go to two stores in order to get Kleenex—all such paper commodities are getting scarce. No bathroom tissue, no wax paper, no paper napkins. Some stores still have a stock, so I got three boxes, and may get some more. If hay fever comes and [there is no] Kleenex, life will be beastly. . . .

Good Night, my Johnnie,
Marjorie Elizabeth

Chicago, Jan. 17, 1941

Dearest Private Jonathan:

. . . It seems to me, Dear, we are doing our share for the defense business. Look at all the stamps we buy—have bought and will buy. There's a lot of money. And we're separated in part and that's worse, so I feel real patriotic. . . .

By the way, when I think it over I know of several fellows who joined the Army and when they came back, they were just as stupid as when they went. I expect nothing of this sort from thee—Sir Private John Elmer Larson, 36000745 202nd Coast Artillery, A.A. Battery B. R.S.V.P., P.D.Q. and X.Y.Z. You are to shine bright and wonderful—head and shoulders above them all. In short you are to be (all from this one year's training) a super fine, super good, super intelligent, super big-minded, super well read, super well served, super super man.

Seriously, Dear—I love thee—and I'll be something by the time you

come back—if not a super super woman a nervous wreck with an anxious
eye for the mail man.
    Yours,   Marjorie Elizabeth

The Japanese attack on Pearl Harbor brought the war home to Marjorie and
John with an even greater immediacy.

                                                    Chicago, Dec. 30, 1941
    Hello my Johnnie Boy:
    How is my gunner today? . . . I was thinking—you say you dug your
guns in right in the people's front yards—imagine them having gone to the
expense of 20 cent grass seed last spring, and perhaps spending quite a time
trying to coax the little seeds to grow—then thee comest with thy gun and
it all goes to smash. We can chalk another grudge up to Hitler. . . .
    After the war started I tho't—heck—what's the sense of saving—we don't
know how much longer this will last. But that was rather silly—after all—it
can't last for ever. And altho' they say it will be a long war, God knows best
how long it will be. I hope so for all the men in charge. You say now I can
spend, and buy what I want. I would like a lot of things, and I could go
drizzle my money away on a bit of self-indulgence for which I'd not be any
better off for afterwards. I save all I can for the best and nicest things for
when you come home anyway. And more than all these little things I want
to be able to stand on my own feet. So that when you come home on furloughs, and you will a couple of times anyway, we will be able to pay our
own way, and not have to sponge off anyone else. And too, we will need
some to start out on. Radio programs and articles plead with people to spend
sparingly in view of past war hard times. We will be way behind, but if we
save a little it will not be too hard. . . . And when you come home to stay,
we will not be poverty stricken.
    By the way sweet—do keep writing to thy folks so they know you are
allrite. I can see now when you say you have no newspapers or radio how
the war is not so terrifying to you. We hear it all day long. They interrupt
with news bulletins all the time when you listen to programs. Your folks
were allrite until Henry [John's brother] was there. . . . After I talk to him,
I always feel, not always but sometimes, like today, I feel down, he is so
pessimistic. Or, perhaps he faces the facts and looks ahead. And we . . .
live from day to day and let tomorrow take care of itself. We will have
strength for tomorrow. Today is all we need to take care of.
    He [Henry] was talking to me over the phone, last Sat. and he men-
tioned I should tell you to write—and I explained you are so busy. I explained that some men had been sent on A.A. [anti-aircarft] guns on convoys
and so each man left had more to do. I told him I had not told your folks
for the less they had to run over in their minds that way, the better, and if
he didn't repeat it over the 'phone so they heard. As you said once before—
he always spills the beans. It rather made me angry. But that made your
mom worry more and so when I called her at Mom's and told her all the

news she was so relieved. She said if you just write a card and say you are
o.k., they can get the rest from me. . . .

I thank God you are such a fine husband I must wait for and that you
are still safe. They print no casualty lists—but you hear indirectly of those
that have gone—Oh, my Johnnie—. . . .

All my love for you, my Sweet,
Marjorie Honeybee

Mary Ida Moore was born in Chalk River, Ontario, Canada. She migrated to
the United States in the mid-1920s. In 1925, she married a widower, Herman
J. Little, and became a stepmother to his four-year-old son, Robert. The Lit-
tles operated a small restaurant in Hancock, Maryland, until the depression
forced them to sell it. Herman died in 1936.

After her husband's death, Mary Little supported herself and Robert by
working in a textile factory in Hancock. As the two had very little money and
there were few prospects for employment for him, she agreed to his enlistment in the Army in August 1940, although he was only eighteen at the time.
Robert was shipped to Greenland with the United States occupation troops in
July 1941. His stepmother fell ill during this period and died on December
8, 1941. Robert was unable to attend her funeral.

As Mary Little's stepson has recently said, "She always asked me to be a
good boy. . . . She gave her faith to me and the love of God. I thank her for
this great gift." For Mary Little, the war was a part of her life a full year
before many Americans recognized its approach.

Hancock, June 23, 1941

Dear Bob:

I have received your card and letter and was sure glad to hear from you.
I only trust you are o.k. as I presume you are many miles from home. I do
worry. It is very hot here. I guess you won't get much hot weather this
summer. . . .

I want to send you a box. I will wait for about fifteen more days then I
will send it. Possibly I may hear from you. I must close. I hope and pray
you are o.k.

Love,   Mother

Hancock, Aug. 5, 1941

Dear Bob:

Your two letters reached me today and I can't tell how glad I was to hear
from you. I was terribly worried and have had another sick fit. I did not
write to you as I thought you would not get my letters. . . .

How many days were you at sea? Near a month, anyhow. I have often
read how beautiful sun rise and sun set were at sea. . . . . Bob, I will write
again on Sunday. I only hope and trust you are a good boy. . . .

Be sure and write often,
Love,   Mother

Hancock, Oct. 23, 1941

Dear Bob:

Don't worry so about me, I am o.k. I came to Mrs. Longley's October 13th. I can soon go to work. Of course, I have to be careful as I have a tumor on both kidneys. It is a very rare thing. I was born with them and inherited from some generations, I do not know where.

I don't want you to get your discharge on my account, or do anything you don't want to do. I'll be o.k. I am going home about Monday. I can eat and sleep good. Of course, I always have to take a medical treatment, 15 pills a day. I may be able to go about my work as usual. Nothing is going to happen to me.

I had a little saved. Isabel sent me some and your thirty put me on my feet. As you know you pay my rent anyhow. Now don't you worry about a thing, I'll be here and have a home for you when ever you come. Now don't do any thing foolish and ruin your young life. I'll write you again soon.

Love, Mother

Hancock, Nov. 21, 1941

Dear Bob:

I sure felt sorry you did not get my letters. I received your two letters and $40.00 for which I can't thank you enough. I am still at Mrs. Longley's. I am gaining. I got low blood so it takes a long time to get back as my tumors are at all times giving me poison. My pills alone costs $12.50 a month. I take fifteen a day. I get blood in my veins every second day. If I keep up it won't be long till I can go to work. I go all over town and cook the meals. So, don't worry about me, child, I'll be o.k. I sort of wish you would not come home, till your company comes. The waters are so dangerous, sinking ships all the time. I don't know what you would find to do here. The strikes are so bad and work is so hard to get. Of course, I would be ever so glad to have you home. But you would only be drafted again as you are in the age. Then lose your rating and all. Possibly get dissatisfied. I sent you a box. We were notified to have our Xmas boxes in by Nov. 27th for you boys. It is not the kind of a box I would like to send you but I was not able to make cookies.

It's cold today. I am going up to Tablers and mail this letter. I also go to Dr. Johnston a few times. He sure is a good Dr. I must close. Now, don't you worry about me or risk your own life to come home.

Be a good boy, Bob.

Love, Mother

Chapter 2

Courtship by Mail

THE ENTRANCE OF THE UNITED STATES INTO THE WAR ACCEL-
erated many aspects of day-to-day life. This was especially true of courtship.
Long leisurely nights on the back porch were far fewer in number, and sometimes never occurred, as young people in love often found themselves separated by the exigencies of war.

For servicemen who were stationed stateside, the telephone occasionally
helped to close the distances that often separated sweethearts. But for many
courting couples, letter writing became the chief means of getting acquainted
and nurturing their love. In the midst of the wartime emergency, young people took time out to write "miles of sentences" as they courted by mail.

Many courtships by mail developed quite rapidly on their road to marriage.
Others were very slow in their progression. Still others followed a very rocky
route, occasionally leading to long gaps in the correspondence. Couples fell
in and out of love, debated, and even argued as the mail continued to flow
back and forth. In some cases, the relationship was broken off by the sending
of the legendary "Dear John" or "Dear Jane" letter. Yet even rocky courtships
survived traumatic events and were followed by successful, longstanding marriages.

Frances "Frankie" McGiboney and Robert "Zuke" Zulauf met while students at Park College in Parkville, Missouri, in the fall of 1942. He was a German-Swiss American from North Kansas City, Missouri, and she was of Scots-Irish, Welsh, and French descent from Nevada, Missouri.

Robert enlisted in the Air Corps at the end of the fall 1942 semester and was briefly stationed at Jefferson Barracks, Missouri, when the couple began a prototypical courtship by mail. He was twenty-two and she was nineteen.

Parkville, Feb. 25, 1943

Private Zulauf:

Oooo—am I nervous! In exactly thirty-one minutes I am to make my debut (?) in voice class.—Gulp—I'm scared stiff. All the new students have to sing a solo today. I'm going to sing "The Lass with the Delicate Air." It's the craziest song I've ever heard. Oh, well.

After you left me Sunday morning [in Kansas City], I stumbled into the apartment and I do mean *stumbled.* It was so dark I couldn't see a thing and I didn't want to turn on a light. . . .

About three and one-half hours later (ahem), Sammy [Frankie's college roommate] and I got up. We were very surprised to find a fourth party bunking in with us. One of my girl friends had dropped off here instead of going home after her date. She had beaten me by about an hour.

When Sammy and I went downtown to take the 9:00 bus, we found that the first one out for Parkville (at both stations) left that *afternoon* at one o'clock. At 8:40 we hopped a cab and arrived at the Union Station just in time to take the train. Whew!! We were exhausted, but anything was better than facing Pippy's [Mrs. Pipkin was her housemother] wrath. . . .

In 15 more minutes I go to my doom. . . .

So, you've learned to make a bed, hmmm? You'll probably have to peel potatoes, too. Goodness, you'll make someone a good wife some day.

I have Dean Baxter as my adviser and—oops, there's the bell. I'll have to trot.

Wish me luck.

7:30 P.M.

Well, here I am—back at the library, simply stuffed and not quite as nervous. I sang—and that's all I'll tell you. We had *corned beef and cabbage* tonight, and I thought of you. . . .

The paper comes out tomorrow. Curses—ever since that small sentence about "Zuke and his baby" appeared in last week's issue, I can't hold my head up. It's "baby this" and "baby that." I'm typed. How could you ha./ *ha.* . . .

Our freshman dance is going to be swell. The social committee met tonight and we have decided on a theme. I'll tell you later when we have it all worked out.

Just like any *woman,* I could ramble on quite some time, but I'm sure you're weary. I'd better close.

Escribe usted pronto, senor. . . .

I'll write more news next time. I had even more to tell you but some of it has slipped my mind. I'll be on the look out for news, now—perhaps, I ought to keep a diary.

Au revoir. A demain, monsieur (I wish.)

Love Frankie . . .

11:30 P.M. Chestnut Dorm.

P.S. No. 2. The most exciting thing is happening. About six third-floor girls went out serenading tonight without permission. Mrs. Pipkin found out about it and she is now sitting on the front steps, wrapped in her coat, waiting for them. They have been gone at least forty-five minutes.

Things will really start popping when they come in—and me with my door open—gulp. Oh-boy! . . .

P.S. No. 3. . . .

I must close now. I still have my French to go and I'm so sleepy.

Bye,   Me

Parkville, March 29, 1943

Dear Bob:

We're all out for defense.

And we really are, too! Friday night is the opening of "Mr. Pim" (the play) and admission is 35 cents in defense stamps. I hear the play is going to be super. . . .

It is now 9:35 p.m. Spring may have sprung—outside—but it's like a refrigerator in this room. . . .

I received your card this a.m. I must say I was terribly disappointed to learn that you were headed for Wisconsin. I might as well give up the idea of seeing you again—for ages. I was hoping that you'd train up at M[issouri] U.—selfish, aren't I, when I know you want to see the U.S. Have a good time, I hope you like it. . . .

Zuke, I'm getting writer's cramp. I'm in bed again, writing to you. I should be doing my Chemistry, but I'm just not in the mood.

I'm going to sleep. I'll write more later.

Bye!

Love   Gibbey

Parkville, May 10, 1943

Dear Zuke:

I'm so anxious to hear about the "Jive Bombers" [a dance band organized by the men at Robert's training station in Oshkosh, Wisconsin]. Did you all knock your audience off their feet? Who thought up the name? It's darling! And, Zuke, for the last time, are you the leader? Just think, some day when you're heading a big time band, I can drag out my little record and play it for all the neighborhood kiddies on my broken down phonograph in my little shack. I'll be a wash woman, probably, but I can dream of the good old days.

It's about 11:00 again. I still have quite a lot of work waiting for me to do. Already, though, I have cleaned out my closet and packed a few of my winter clothes that I'll be needing no longer!

Incidentally, I'd almost given up hope of ever hearing from you again. I kept trying to remember what I had said in my last letter that would anger you and cause you not to write. . . .

I realize that this is another poor letter from me. I have so much to say to you but it's all inside me and I can't seem to write it down. (News, etc.). . . .

I'd better close, Write soon.

Love,   Frankie

Nevada, June 21, 1943

Dear Bob:

I've put off writing what I call "bad" news with the hopes that Dad would change his mind. So far he hasn't and it's been almost a week since I asked if I could come to Wisconsin. Yes, Zuke, he actually said "no." I was so sure I could come that I had already planned on what I'd wear . . . etc. etc. Of course, it's not because he doesn't think it will be all right, because he'd let me go—he says. The main and it is an important reason for his saying, "no" is the fact that I'm not working this summer and Dad says putting me through school this next year will be no picnic. Thirty or forty dollars doesn't sound like much to me, but I guess it counts up. I wish we could see each other, Zuke. You were swell to plan for me coming and for asking me. Hope you do get a furlough before you go to California. Are you sure you won't? Maybe it's better that I don't come up there anyway. . . .

For a while, I thought seriously of getting a job in Kansas City and not going back to school next year. I changed my mind, though, and it's a good thing. My major is still undecided. That part worries me a little. I don't have the slightest idea what I want to be now. . . .

This letter is quite long already and I can't think of any more news. I'd better close. Please write soon. Again, I want to tell you how sorry I can't come. I'd looked forward to going sailboating on the lake. Maybe we'll run in to each other in *New York City* or Paris sometime later. Doesn't look like we'll get to laugh together for quite a while. That's war, I guess.

Adios,

Love,   Frankie

Early in July 1943, while en route from Oshkosh, Wisconsin, to Santa Ana, California, Zuke made a brief visit home. Frankie, however, was away on a trip, and they were not able to see each other.

Nevada, July 10, 1943

Dear Bob:

. . . I can't explain it, but you'd find me in a very understanding mood, if you were here tonight.

Well, we didn't get to see each other after all, did we? I was so sorry and I could just imagine how you must've felt with your home so near and your chances of getting there so slim as if you were still in Oshkosh.

Write soon as you can. I'll follow this one with another soon.

Love, Frankie

Nevada, Aug. 5, 1943

Dear Bob:

Being engaged to me might make *you* work harder to get your wings, but think how hard *I'll* work this year in school with that before me. Yes, after two whole days to think about it—as if I needed time—my answer is *"Yes, of course!"*

As you said, lots *can* happen before April to make us change our minds, but that's a chance to take. Bob, I really don't think anything *will* happen if we don't let it, do you?

I've never written a note like this before. It seems a little strange. I do wish you could get a furlough long enough to come down here so we could talk everything over. It's hard to write, isn't it? Naturally, that's impossible, but it's a nice thought.

This is all I'll write at present and you'll be receiving a long letter from me soon.

All my love, Frankie

P.S. Confidentially—I think you're "wonderful"!

Nevada, Sept. 3, 1943

Dear Bob:

. . . I agree with you—religion is another topic hard to discuss in a letter. However, I want you to know that that was uppermost in my thoughts after I told you I'd become engaged. All by myself and after much pondering, I have decided that when we marry it is really my desire to become a Catholic. This is not a sacrifice at all because when I was very young I used to think I'd be one some day. Most of my relatives on my Mother's side are Catholics, including my favorite cousin who is studying to be a priest. Naturally, Mother was a bit disappointed when I told her, just as yours would be if you changed. Now she thinks it's fine if that's what I want. My father feels the same way. It's wonderful to have parents like them—they feel it's my own life and, with a few suggestions, they let me make up my own mind about things. How do you feel about it, Bob? Do you want me to? It would save complications if we ever have children and besides, you couldn't remain a member of your church if I wasn't a member—After I wrote that I realized that it is wrong—you could.

Perhaps your religion doesn't make a lot of difference to you—I don't know—but you know that it does to me. Maybe that's being old fashioned, and from the looks of things, now—it is. I don't care, though, and I'm glad that's the way I feel. Here I go again on those "I's."

Please write and tell me how you feel. Do you think my attitude is "silly"?

Heavens, here I am on the fifth page and when I started it wasn't with the intention to write so much. You're probably bored stiff. Write soon and be good.

All my love,   Frankie

Nevada, Oct. 25, 1943

Dear Bob:

. . . I'm so thrilled about your soloing. That's just swell. Maybe it's a good thing you had to work a little harder on your landings. Now you know you have them down pat and that's one thing I can mark off my list of worries. You should be a good flyer, Bob, you're tops in everything else. I haven't worried one bit about your not being able to fly—I've been worried for fear you'd be so good you'd be sent out before anyone else. Be careful. That sounds very womanlike—doesn't it? . . .

Bye for now

Yours forever,   Frances

Nevada, Nov. 30, 1943

Dear Bob:

Howdy, grad*uate!* Your announcement came day before yesterday, but I've been so terribly busy with *more* exams that I haven't had time to acknowledge receipt of same.

It's a pretty announcement and I wish I could've used the dance ticket. It's been ages since we danced together, hasn't it?

. . . If I do go up and if it's convenient with your "papa" and "mama," I'm going to pay them a visit. I do so want to meet them and I'd better take advantage of my being in the city, then. No telling when I'll get to go back. . . .

Have any of my recent letters made you a trifle angry with me? They are quite moody, I'm afraid—forgive me.

Good night for now,

Love,   Frankie

Nevada, Jan. 3, 1944

Dear W.M. [Wonderful Man]:

. . . you might just as well settle down in the easiest chair, or bunk, you can find. With all I have to tell you, this letter will be a book and a half.

I'm feeling quite glamorous at present—Here I sit in my new robe. Mother let me sleep until eleven this morning. Then we had lunch. I washed the dishes, unpacked my clothes, and straightened up my room. Then I combed my hair, put lipstick on, just so I could look nice while writing to you.

Yes, I must admit I was a *little* jittery about meeting your folks—but, honey, the minute I stepped out of that taxi cab at 1033 E. 21st Street and saw your mother standing at the door, I was all right. She's *just* darling and she made me feel at home immediately! Now I know why you're such a swell fellow. You couldn't be otherwise with a mother like that. . . .

Your father came home a few minutes after three and I think he's just *swell*. Do you know that you both walk exactly alike? He told me about the time you all bought a blanket here in Nevada on one of your trips to the Ozarks. . . .

You were certainly a beautiful baby, Zuke. Yep, I even saw that picture of you and Jack, you know, the one where you two are sitting on the bench. You were about three, I think. You were wearing black cotton stockings, then. (For the same reason you want me to wear them? Surely not.) You had such an expression of wonderment to coin a phrase—that I had to ask your mother what was wrong with you. She said you were trying to find the "birdie" and couldn't see it. . . .

I can't wait until April when you come down here to meet my parents. Mother already likes you from what I've told her and from the parts of letters I read to her. . . .

Your father didn't tell a *single* corny joke—you said he would, you know. . . .

Love,   Frankie

Nevada, Jan. 28, 1944

Dear Uncle Bob:

When I got your letter yesterday containing the terrific news—I felt as though I were going to be an Aunt in August, too! Darling, it's wonderful. I hope it's a girl—somehow it seems to me that it ought to be. . . .

Now for a very serious paragraph. Zuke, have you ever thought of becoming a Protestant? You've said quite often that you weren't so well informed about your religion and I began to wonder if you'd ever thought about changing. It's not that I wouldn't want to become a Catholic, but I've been learning all along the beliefs of your church—and, naturally there are some I'm afraid I couldn't be educated to believe in. It's very hard to write this—don't take me wrong—but, if I did become a member of your church—I'm afraid I'd be rather an independent member. But, you said we should worry about this when we come to it—and five years might make a lot of differences in the way we feel about such things. I told you once that I was *very* religious. Well, I am, of course, but my views have changed considerably since I last saw you (I've begun to think for myself—and some of the things I think now would have surprised me last year about this time.).

I put the above very crudely, but it's extremely hard to set down what I want to say in writing. Perhaps you understand what I mean—Perhaps you don't. . . .

Write soon, I'll need some cheerful mail to give me a boost next week. Goodnight. I wish I knew some curse words. I can't seem to write tonight.

Love,   Frankie

Nevada, May 26, 1944

Dear Bob:

. . . I'm glad we're going to be married on the 7th—on Wednesday, because I was born on Wednesday, fortune tellers have told me it is my lucky day, and—although I'm not the least bit superstitious—it seems just the perfect day for the biggest step we've ever taken.

Funny, but I believe you're right—I really do believe I'm in love with you. If I'm not the kind of a wife you expect me to be—just bop me on the head—it'll help.

This letter was continued on May 28, 1944

. . . Are you disappointed that I'm not being married in white? That's what Mother and I had planned on, but I could find nothing in white that pleased me. You asked about my flowers and I told you last night when you called that pink would be best. My dress is pastel blue-green (I don't know what color it is) and accessories are a pale dusty rose. . . .

Later . . . my ring is especially bright tonight—it's sparkling "loudly." Hm, that's one reason I wanted a double ring ceremony. You should have a ring on you to show people you're tagged—it will be obvious—as for me. (That's a crazy sentence not at all the way I meant to state it.). . . .

Seriously, though, I do have all the faith in the world in you, Bob, and I've never felt that way about any other fellow I've dated—no matter how infatuated I knew them to be with me. I've never trusted men much and I've never felt much respect for them or their "activities." That's why I'm so glad I found you—before I gave up the human race as lost. . . .

I'm so mad! I've misplaced those books you sent me on the *Etiquette of the Engagement and Wedding* and now I don't know what to do. Mom knows quite a bit about everything—but since I've never been married before—and never paid much attention to the formality etc. (planning to be an old maid, you know) it's a trifle hard for me. All will have to be as proper as necessary, though.

Be good and write to me,
Love,   Gib

One more page was added to this letter, and it was finally mailed on May 30, 1944.

. . . Our announcements will be finished by Wednesday. I think they're going to be very nice. I couldn't have the paper I wanted—but everything else is fine. We'll have a lot of fun addressing them, won't we? I'm writing my "thank you notes" rather then have them printed because they'll be more personal. . . .

Love,   Frankie
P.S. Will you like me thin?

In early June, Frankie traveled to Columbia, South Carolina, where Zuke was awaiting shipment overseas. They were married on June 7, 1944. Robert had recently received his commission and his wings as a pilot in the Army Air

Force. Seven weeks after their wedding, he was suddenly transferred to a bombing squadron based on the island of Corsica in the Mediterranean. Lt. Zulauf flew seventy B-25 bombing missions. His last mission was on April 15, 1945. He was decorated with the Distinguished Flying Cross for his combat efforts. Frankie worked at the Pratt and Whitney Aircraft Co. in Kansas City for the duration of the war. During the months that Robert was in Europe, the couple wrote to each other almost every day.

Zuke returned to the United States in June 1945. After his discharge from the service, he and Frankie finished their college years together and were graduated from the University of Missouri in June 1947. For many years, Robert worked as an advertising copywriter, and he is now semi-retired. Frances works as a freelance market researcher. They have two daughters and five grandchildren. They live in Overland Park, Kansas. Robert has written a memoir, *Dear Frankie,* which is based on the many letters the couple wrote to each other during World War II.

Florence E. Webb, a twenty-year-old secretary who worked for the public school department of Gas City, Indiana, began a rather desultory correspondence with James M. Huston in 1942. Huston, who was pursuing a graduate degree in history at New York University at the time of Pearl Harbor, gave up his studies to enter the Army. The couple, who had grown up in neighboring towns in Indiana, knew of each other, but did not formally meet until family matchmakers brought them together.

In April 1944, James was sent to Europe, where he served as an officer with the 134th Infantry Regiment. After he was posted overseas, the couple began numbering their almost daily letters, and they continued this practice until their reunion in April 1946.

Florence continued to work for the Gas City school department. In addition, she trained as a nurse's aide in a nearby hospital and volunteered many hours to this activity. She also worked nights in a local eyeglass factory where prescriptions were made for service personnel.

During their lengthy and extended correspondence, Florence and James eventually fell in love. She wrote the following letter shortly after her first "arranged meeting" with James.

Gas City, March 24, 1942

Hello James:

Aunt Ruth was at our house to-day and happened to mention about it being your birthday.

I guess today is supposed to be the happiest day of your life. Or so the superstition runs. When you are 24 on the 24th day of the month that is the happiest day. I send you all blessings and I hope that it is the happiest yet, but that every year will bring more and more.

I feel I owe you a million apologies for the way, you think, I acted.

I am not a person who is in the habit of passing the blame to someone else, but I do believe that Martel and Aunt Ruth did wrong in tricking a meeting with us, the last time you were home.

. . . I didn't know that you were supposed to arrive in Anderson that night until a few minutes before I saw you.

I can't remember a time when I have felt so cheap as when I walked into the lobby and there you were.

I am very sorry if I have caused any embarrassment on your part. You were a perfect gentleman and probably if I had been in your position, I dare say that I would not have been so courteous. You were really put on the spot. . . .

I have been wanting to correspond with someone and I thought maybe you would like to do so. If you do not, it is perfectly all right, but I thought maybe a letter or some candy might clear things up.

I would rather you did not mention to Martel or Aunt Ruth about my writing you. They do not know that I have your address. I copied it down the last time I was down.

Hope you understand,   Florence
201 West North "A"
Gas City, Indiana

P.S. I would rather Aunt Ruth and Martel did not hear of this letter, and if you would care to correspond I think they should be unaware of the fact.

Gas City, Aug. 3, 1942

Dear Jim:

Surprised to find me writing to you again? I'll wager you thought that when you didn't answer my last letter, I would let well enough alone. I thought there might be a possibility you didn't mean it. I guess there is no harm in trying again. . . .

If you are going to be at this address long, Mother would like to bake a cake and send it to you. I could promise that it would be better than the one I sent.

I am not so extra good at cake baking but I'm fairly good with candy. So, if you want to, you keep us informed of your address and we will do the rest. . . .

There is no harm in a friendly correspondence, is there?

Let me know about the cake.

Yours,   Florence Webb

Gas City, Oct. 2, 1942

Dear Jim:

I was very pleasantly surprised to find your letter upon my arrival at home to-day. I had given up any idea that I would hear from you. At first, I thought that perhaps you didn't receive my letter, but later on I was given to understand that you were engaged. So when I received your letter I was not any wiser. You did not mention receiving my letters, nor the fact as to your being engaged. So I am acting on the hunch that maybe you might not mind. . . .

So if you can find any extra time and do not have anything special, I would like to hear from you. I would enjoy it, even if it was a brief letter. If you don't care to write, just say so, it is quite all right. But, unless you say you don't I will take it. . . .

I hope you do not think me precocious, in this or that I am pushing my friendship on you. But personally, I can see no harm in it. No one will be the wiser. Certain people will never learn of this from me.

Well, I had better sign off this epistle, with the hope that I will hear from you within the next six months. Try to answer sooner this time. (If you care to answer at all.)

Love, Florence

Gas City, Oct. 2, 1943

Dear Jim:

What a delightful surprise to receive your letter. Since I did not know your address, I couldn't write until I heard from you. . . .

It had been a long time since I had seen you, however, the only noticeable change was the uniform. You make a grand looking Lt. I find myself looking forward to "next time" when I hope we may be able to plan something in advance.

Affectionately yours, Florence

The "next time" came in two weeks, when the couple spent a weekend together in Alabama where James was stationed. The following letter was written a few hours after Florence had returned to her home in Gas City.

Gas City, Oct. 26, 1943

Dearest Jim:

Just a few lines to let you know that I have arrived home safely. . . .

Maybe it is a good thing you decided to tell your mother about my coming down, because it was in last night's paper. She will find it out sooner or later anyway.

Jim, I don't know of any way to show my thanks and appreciation for my wonderful trip. However, I think you know how I feel and I feel that if I say thanks, that will do for now. Maybe sometime I will be able to repay you. . . .

It really is a let down to know that I have to work all day and won't be seeing you in the evening. It is funny how much I miss you, since that is the first time we have said more than a short word to one another. . . .

Again, I want to say thanks a million. I wouldn't take any amount of money for even one minute of my trip.

Lovingly, Florence

Gas City, Feb. 17, 1944

My Dearest Jim:

. . . I suppose you dreaded going back into routine this morning. That is always the bad thing about a furlough, but I hope you won't be in the routine long before you get another furlough.

Jim, I am lost without you. I jump every time the phone rings, although it isn't for me. I can't quite understand what is wrong, or can I? . . .

The newness still hasn't worn off my pin. I think I must look at it 60 times in an hour. I certainly am proud to be wearing your pin. I hope you are just as glad to have me wearing it?

Well, my darling, I must get to work or I won't have a job to worry about.

All my love,   Florence

Gas City, March 17, 1944

My Dearest Jim:

. . . Do you think the war will last two years more? That seems like an awfully long time to wait. Don't you think that? . . .

Jim, when do you want it? I think high noon is a nice time, but for once I will submit to the judge. Do you want it to be large or small? Just what have you in mind? I guess before we decide on a time it is going to be we should decide when it is to be! . . . .

All my love,   Florence

The couple was able to be together for one other weekend, this time in Durham, North Carolina, before James was sent overseas.

Gas City, April 3, 1944

My Dearest Jim:

Back in old G.C., what a let down! I feel as though I left part of me in N.C., maybe it was my heart? I wish you would have talked me into staying, but you didn't try it so I guess you didn't want me? . . .

Jim, please accept my apologies for not thanking you for the weekend. How stupid of me to forget to thank you! Every time I see you I enjoy the time more and more. I had a wonderful weekend, darling, thanks to you. . . .

When you see the Lieutenant, thank him again for the wonderful tour he took us on. I enjoyed it ever so much. . . .

Always your loving,   Florence

They are playing the "Rosary" now. The Lt. would make a very good best man!

Gas City, June 20, 1944

My Dearest Jim:

. . .Jim, I received letter #16 today. It was written June 6, 1944. So far I have received letters # 1, 2, 4, 9, and 16. I wonder where the rest of them are. Maybe I should start numbering my letters so you may be able to keep them straight. . . .

Jim, I guess we have won over your mother to our side. She calls me by my name instead of speaking of "that girl." Mr. Caskey was telling Aunt Ruth about the change. I can't understand how it changed all at once. . . .

Always yours,   Florence

Gas City, September 24, 1944 #62

My Dearest Jim:

. . . While writing, I have been listening to Walter Winchell [a popular radio commentator of the time], but he did not have any news. It looks as though we will not be having a V-celebration as soon as we thought.

I am hoping and praying you will not be in the Asiatic War after the European war is over. . . .

"I'll Be Seeing You" until then "I'll Walk Alone," because to tell you the truth, I'll be lonely.

All my Love,   Florence

Gas City, April 1, 1945 #163

My Dearest Jim:

Easter Sunday with you, perhaps next year. It was a very lonely Easter for all of us. . . .

The war news seems to get more encouraging each day. So many people seem to think the war in Germany is over and they are for disarming the Germans, but I hardly believe that.

I heard over the radio this morning that they had started on another invasion in the Pacific, largest of them all.

Oh, I hope it isn't long before you will be home again. It can't be too soon for me.

"For I've Fallen in Love with Some One," right now "I'm a Little on the Lonely Side."

All my love,   Florence

Gas City, April 30, 1945 #175

My Dearest Jim:

I'm learning to bake. Tonight I made some Toll House Cookies, and since they turned out good, I shall send you some next time. Since the war with Germany is just about over, I thought I should learn to bake. Very soon I will try some rolls and then a cake again.

Jim, do you think you will get a furlough after the war with Germany? That would be the most wonderful thing in the world. I am afraid to count on it though. Most articles say the boys will be sent directly to the Pacific. Maybe you will be one of the fortunate ones. . . .

I am praying you will get home soon.

Love,   Florence

Gas City, May 7, 1945 #178

My Dearest Jim:

This is the most wonderful day of my life so far. Here in Gas City there hasn't been any celebrating, but I guess in New York City they really went wild.

They first announced it at 8:40 this morning, but it wasn't official. They didn't give the o.k. on it until about 5:30 this evening. I can't remember when I have been so happy.

My only fear now is that you will be sent to the Pacific. I am counting so much on your getting home, but I hope I am not disappointed.

If you do get a furlough, what have you planned? I am anxious to know if your plans are similar to mine, but I take too much for granted. . . .

Aunt Ruth called me today. She saw your mother Saturday. I guess your Mother was worried about me, thought I was ill since I haven't been to see her. I never gave it a thought. . . . I didn't want to cause her trouble. . . .

They say that they will start returning the boys home in the next thirty days. In about a month I will be on needles. I so hope you will be one of the first to get home.

All my love,   Florence

Gas City, May 17, 1945 #181

My Dearest Jim:

Two letters from you this week. I do believe that my luck is taking a turn for the better.

You asked if I have any regrets for remaining single. I can truthfully say I am sorry we did decide to wait. It hasn't done either of us any harm, but I feel we would have felt we were so much closer to each other even though we were separated by several thousand miles. But have you any regrets? Maybe you are glad?

You know how you always discuss the future when you are kids. . . . I especially didn't want a long engagement. Why waste all your life being engaged? Here I have been wearing your pin for a year, and heavens knows how much longer I will just have a pin. . . .

Love,   Florence

Gas City, May 19, 1945 # 182

My Dearest Jim:

Don't forget our agreement to meet in New York. I am looking any minute for you to walk in on us.

They announced today that five thousand soldiers have landed in New York who had been in Germany. I would give anything if you were one of them, but I doubt it. I am holding my breath for a June wedding. Remember last year you asked if June, 1945 would be too soon. Little did we dream that it might be that close. . . .

I'll be loving you, always. With a love that's true, always.

Florence

Gas City, July 15, 1945 #214

My Dearest Jim:

. . . Jim, you said that you wanted to have one foot on the ground before inviting me upon a path of uncertainty. Then, in the next line you said
I would be the one who would be running the risks if I have no objections.
I can't understand why you should have any hesitation in asking me. Don't
you think we have been waiting long enough? I don't want to let my youth
slip through my fingers, either. . . .

All my love,   Florence

Gas City, Aug. 4, 1945 #224

My Dearest Jim:

. . . This is my main answer: Jim, I am quite willing to be married even
if we only had six weeks together. On your other questions, whatever you
desire and decide to do will be agreeable with me. You are the only one
who can make the decision as to what you should do, but whatever you do,
I want to be with you. . . . I want so badly to see you as soon as possible,
but if waiting means I will get to be with you for good then I am in for
it. . . .

All my love,   Florence

James was discharged from the Army in the fall of 1945. Following a semester
at Oxford University in England, he resumed his studies at NYU in 1946,
where he completed his Ph.D. in history the following year. He and Florence
were married in December 1946. They had two children. After she and James
were married, Florence devoted most of her time to her home and family.
James taught history at Purdue University until the early 1970s. Among his
published works is *Biography of a Battalion* (1950), a history of his World
War II unit. In 1972, he became a dean at Lynchburg College in Virginia,
where he remained until his retirement in the early 1980s. Florence died in
1983. James lives in Lynchburg and writes historical fiction.

Emma Calp and James Cheshier met on a blind date in June 1943. She was
a nineteen-year-old secretary working for the War Department in Washington, D.C., and he was a twenty-two-year-old enlisted man in the Navy who
was visiting the nation's capital on a weekend pass.

Their blind date was followed by a whirlwind, three-month courtship during which they exchanged many letters. In addition, James, whose home port
was New York City, visited Emma whenever he could arrange a pass. They
were married on September 11, 1943. Following a two-day honeymoon, James

left for sea duty in the Pacific. In their first two and a half years of marriage, they were together for just under two months.

Washington, D.C., Aug. 24, 1943

My Darling Jimmie:

I am at the office now, honey, and I thought I might start my daily letter to you because there *is* going to be a daily letter. I just put a 10 page letter in the mail box this morning so there isn't really much news, but I just want to remind you that I still love you and am waiting for your return to me. They say that absence makes the heart grow fonder but not so in my case because, Jimmie, I couldn't possibly think any more of you than I do now. I never realized it was possible to love any one person so very much, but I know now. I do miss you more and more all of the time, but every day away from you just makes the day closer when we'll be able to be together again. That's what I keep telling myself. It is a little consolation but that still doesn't keep me from missing you. I read your letters over, eventually I think I'll know them by heart. . . .

This morning I took some dictation and typed it up and went to lunch at 11:15. Honey, are you eating now? You better had or you'll get sick. I got my notice of my appointment for Monday to donate blood. I'll be rested up pretty well by that time so it won't hurt me.

My flowers are still very lovely, my sweet, and I am taking good care of them to make them last as long as possible. I don't know how I'll ever be able to thank you for everything you've done for me. . . . I've gone with a good many boys on dates, but I've never felt about anyone the way I feel about you. If you ever get tired of me, honey, I couldn't go out with any boy and have a really good time again. Honey, if this letter sounds crazy don't blame me, you made me crazy about you. I just miss you so much that I want to let you know how I feel. . . .

For now, my sweet, I must say good-bye. Get a good night of sleep, honey, and I'll be with you always in thought. Remember that.

Yours forever,   Emma

Washington, D.C., Sept. 13, 1943

My Dearest:

How did my husband get home this morning? I bet you were tired, weren't you, after standing on the bus so long. Who did you get for a sitting partner on the train. Well, darling, that's enough questions for this time.

I got home in fine shape about 1:30, ate a tomato, and went to bed. . . .

None of the kids . . . said anything about my ring yet, but you should have heard the girls at the office. They really gave me the "ribbing." When Ginny (the girl in the office with me) came in she asked me if I got married over the weekend, and I told her, yes. Honey, she was just kidding, but we weren't were we? They found out like wild fire spreading after a couple of them found out. Some of them still don't know it. They were congratulating me, wishing me luck, shaking my hand and everything. I am very proud to be married to you, Darling. Several of them agree with you. They like the wedding band best. I love them both and I suppose they mean more to me than anything else. . . .

Honey, when I left you last night I just hurried as fast as I could so people wouldn't see the tears. I guess you noticed that I didn't even look back. I didn't get a chance to put our money in the bank today but am going to do so tomorrow at lunch time. I didn't get any of my War Dept. records changed either because the girl who takes care of that wasn't there. I did change my name on the mail box and the door bell thing. . . .

Darling, I miss you dreadfully but I don't feel as badly as I did the other time that you left. Because now, honey, I'm yours altogether. I'll be waiting for you always and am going to try to find a nice room so that when you get in for awhile you can be comfortable. I'd like to get a place where I could cook for you but I hardly believe it would be worthwhile, do you?

I got a letter from a boy in North Africa today. He is a cousin of a girl in the office and I don't even know him. He is engaged to a girl from his home town. His cousin asked me to write to him because he was lonely.

Well, darling, I must close for now. Write real often, honey, and may God bless you and keep you for me.

All of my love,   Emma

Following James's discharge from the Navy in 1946, the couple settled in Manchester, Maryland. He worked as a metal fabricator in nearby York, Pennsylvania, for forty years, and Emma became a full-time homemaker. They had four children. After their youngest child entered school, Emma began working at a local nursing home. James died in 1987. Emma continues to live in Manchester where she works part-time in the local nursing home. She has six grandchildren and one great-granddaughter.

———————————⋦⋗———————————

Mary Louisa Hernandez and Nicholas "Nick" Ortiz began dating and fell in love while she was still in high school. Mary's parents were migrant workers from Mexico who eventually settled in Garden City, Kansas. Nick's parents, also from Mexico, immigrated to Kingman, Kansas, at the end of World War I to work on the railroad.

Mary graduated from high school in 1944, when she was in her early twenties, as her work as a migrant laborer prohibited her from attending school on a full-time basis. Nick attended three years of high school and then went to an arc welding school, run by the National Youth Administration, in Wichita, Kansas.

In 1942, Nick was inducted into the service. Later that year, he was sent overseas where he experienced intense combat in North Africa and Italy. He spent thirty-two months in combat and earned five Bronze Star decorations for his work. While Nick was overseas, he and Mary regularly wrote to each other. Mary's first letter to Nick was written from Scott City, Kansas, where she was working as a migrant laborer.

Scott City, Oct. 12, 1942

Dearest Private:

You are always surprising me with something. I received the letter you wrote to Scott [City] and did I get a surprise. My mother gave it to me. The worst thing about it is that she didn't say a thing. After all you are right, I do not receive the letters as fast as I should so I guess it is best that you write to me in Scott [City]. Maybe my folks will object to my writing to you. I do not know but I do not care, because it is the only thing I can think of. I doubt if we go to Garden [City] very often now that we are going to start topping—almost every body in Garden [City] started today.

About not seeing each other for a long time, I really don't know what to say or think. I had hopes of seeing you again soon, but I guess I will have to wait. Sometimes I wish that I could be with you but I guess it can't be done and that is all that there is to it. Maybe some day we will be together and at least I won't have anything to worry about, but I'm afraid you will. . . . After all it is a privilege for a girl to have someone fighting for her. Darling, I do realize that it is a serious problem we've got and that is why I'm backing you.

Darling, maybe you really know how much I love you. I remember on the last ride we had that you asked me if I had somebody else in mind and I said no. I guess the answer will always be no as long as I'm sure that you love me and expect me to wait for you.

Yes, there are times when I feel blue and discouraged but with your letters, darling, and your picture and I don't mean the one I got lately, I feel all right. Maybe, if I hadn't met you things would be different but since I did meet you and although Lolo Gonzalez had to do the talking, everything came out fine. I didn't think you were such a Romeo as you turned out to be. Anyway, *I love you* very much.

I am sending you a little gift just to show you that I still love and remember you. Darling, please read the directions that go with it and you will have better results. (I hope.)

About the picture, I haven't forgotten that either, but I will not tell you when I'll send it because I want it to be a surprise. And you better not say anything about it either. But, since you think you're the boss, I guess I'll have to do what you say. Even though my temper is rather hot sometimes, I guess everything will be all right.

I can't promise you to do what you asked me too. But, I'll try. Now, don't get angry, I promised. Write and let me know if you received your gift.

Miss Maria Louisa Hernandez

Garden City, Jan. 1, 1943

My Dearest:

. . . Connie Robles was one of the happiest girls last night. She is going with a certain soldier from Texas and he was here, but they moved him some place else but he got a furlough and came to see her. She got a tele-gram from him telling her that he was on his way to see her.

I wonder when my day will come? But, I'm not losing hope and know that as much as I care for my soldier and as much as he cares for me, we'll see each other when the time comes. I am very glad to know that you received the Christmas Card.

My mother keeps asking me about you, if you are fine and I keep telling them, darling, so the only thing that we need is you and I am sure we'll have you with us. But you'll only belong to one person and that's me. Well, my darling I must close and I made a New Year's resolution. Did you make any? I will not tell you mine but I will keep it. Never forget that I love you.

Yours,   Mary Lou Hernandez

Garden City, Jan. 7, 1943

My Dearest:

I received two letters from you today. They were dated Dec. 17th and 21st. I am very happy to know that you did receive the air mail that I wrote November 23. We have got quite a bit of snow lately and it is still snowing. Say, it seems to me that Leap Year is sure coming handy. I heard that we're going to have a couple more weddings. Three of the boys are in the Ma-rines. One of them in some other. They're David Aribe, Rudy Ramirez and Jesus. . . . So, most all the boys are gone except the ones that did not pass. I did receive the letter when you asked me to send you David's address. I always forget to ask Ginny for it, but I'll send it. Darling, I have not got any news to tell you just that I love you and I'm sure you know that.

I hope that the weather tomorrow will be warmer because it is very cold. If I could only hold your hand and you could get my hands warm. I must close but don't forget. I'll write regularly.

Yours,   Mary Louisa Hernandez

Garden City, Aug. 18, 1943

My Dearest:

It has really been a long time since I have written a long letter as this one. But from now on I'll try and write one at least once a week. Well, I finally did receive the letter you wrote me August 4th so you want me to answer you all the questions that you ask me. It's a long story but I do remember every bit of it.

Ginny, Louisa and I went to town that nite and you were standing with Lolo and some other boys in front of Graves Studio by the Duckwells store. You said Hello and I answered right back. We passed again but you didn't say a thing. I noticed that Lolo was following us, but I did not have any idea that he wanted to talk to me until at last he called me and I stopped. He asked me that you wanted to talk to me and I said he's a fine guy wanting to talk to me and sending someone else in his place. After that we met inside of Graves Studio at nite and at first, my dear friend, you just looked at me and I did too till at last you asked me if I cared to go riding the next day which was Sunday. After you spoke to me for a little while I told you I had to leave because the girls were waiting, for it was then that you got closer and kissed me for the first time. We made a date for Sunday. The next day Betty went with Lolo and I went with you. Of course, you told me that you were going at that time with someone other than Cruz Gonzalez. I do remember you told me that you and her quarrelled too much over every little thing. And I told you that I had been going with Ralph but that we had called it quits. From then on it was nothing but dates and more dates until the last day you were here. I remember the day when I ditched school to go with you and we didn't get back till late and your brother James was very angry because he wanted the car and you had it. And another time, it was your brother's turn to get the car, I mean Marcos, and you persuaded him to let you have the keys, so he did.

Well, have I got a good memory or not? It seems to me that I do remember everything so real that I can recall from the first day we met to where we left off. So you remember everything especially if someone reminds you. Well, don't worry I'll keep on reminding you. Is there anything else you would like to know?

It's very cloudy today, but I don't mind as we've been having such warm weather.

Mom was here today and she brought me my birthday present. A very lovely black velvet dress. The only thing I regret is that the right person that should be here to see me with it on isn't here but he'll be here. I remember you told me that the color black really suits me fine. So you want me to have my hair just as I have it in the picture. I also remember that you never did like for me to have my hair short. You told me once when I had my hair set that I looked like somebody working in an office and that you'd prefer if I just fixed it myself. . . .

Katherine Ayala was here right now and she came to get an envelope. I forgot what I was talking about. I haven't received the shoes yet. Do not think that I have forgotten when your Birthday is, if I recall it's the 10th of September. Last year you really did get a small present. I mean because you had to leave for the Army that day. Darling, you probably know that we can not send any presents unless you ask for something that you may want. All except the Christmas gift. What could I send my Beloved Soldier? I'd be glad to send him anything, all except myself. You'll have to come for me. And I'm sure that you will. Until then I'll be waiting, hoping and praying. You got your wish for an air mail letter.

Love To My Soldier,

Yours, Mary Lou Hernandez

Garden City, Sept. 4, 1943

My Dearest:

Today Anita and Freddie are getting married. Jess and my Sis just left for the church. I stayed home as usual. I can't figure it out why I do not feel like going to any weddings. But, do not worry, I'll be there for mine. That's one wedding I won't miss.

. . . The dance will be in Holcomb and I'm very sure that I am going but not to dance because I told you before that in the first place I never could dance and I haven't danced since you left. Now I can't even move my feet. But, I'm sure that both of us will learn when you return. I've got your Christmas Gift picked out but I am not going to tell you what it is. So don't even ask me. I have not received the letter wrote the 24th, that's the only one I lack for the month of August. I'll let you know tomorrow how the dance turned out to be. I'm waiting for my sister. They're coming to the dance. Well, darling, I love you very much and always will.

    Yours, Mary Lou Hernandez

Garden City, Nov. 1, 1943

My Dearest:

    I've been very lucky these past weeks. I got quite a few letters from you. I received the one you wrote the 29th of September, Saturday, which was the 30th of October. But Darling, that was a swell letter. You say that why do we speak about the children we're planning on having. That before we have them you must have me. Yes, my darling, I realize that but I do know that I will have nobody else but you. But, just as you say, we'll have a little girl first but I do want a boy. You're the boss. Yesterday I received an air mail you wrote Oct. 15. Darling, I do have the silver dollar and all the rest of the things that you send me. I'll always save them until we're together. Today we had our first snow. By the time you receive this letter, we'll probably have had more snow. I also received three letters today October 17, 18, and 20. So you went to a dance, darling. I know I can trust my soldier about drinking beer, but be careful, don't go too far about it.

    I went to the show Sunday, as usual, and saw the picture, "So Proudly We Hail." I think that picture was really good. Why is it that every time I see a show that I like it reminds me of us. Darling, I'm very sure that God will grant us the one wish that both of us desire, to be together. And, my darling, let's not lose a bit of hope. . . .

    Yours, Mary Lou Hernandez

Garden City, Jan. 24, 1944

My Dearest:

    Received your letter that you wrote Jan. 7th in which you answer my questions. I guess it must have been my fault. I don't recall. It seems to me that everything you did was my fault. But, I promise that I'll never ask any more questions. You also ask why some of the boys and girls went over to Mexico. The reason is that they got tired of staying here so they went for a visit. Some of them are back and they say that they really liked it. You tell me that you wish for me to say in Garden [City] till you get back. I wish I knew that you'd be back some time this year but I'm hoping you will be. I'll let you know if anything happens to prevent me from staying here. As far as I know I'm planning to get a job if possible sometime during the middle of the year. I'll let you know later on what happens. I did promise to wait here but sometimes it is impossible to keep promises. . . .

    Yours, Mary Lou Hernandez

Garden City, April 10, 1944

My Dearest:

Yesterday which was Easter was a very lucky day, for me. I didn't receive one single letter during the whole week but I received four V-Mails,
an air mail, and pictures yesterday. Darling, you look fine in all the pictures,
just the way I want you to look. I showed the pictures to a friend of mine
who is from Wyoming and she said that we'd really make a good looking
pair, so, Darling we mustn't disappoint her. . . .

Your,   Mary Lou

Garden City, May 16, 1944

My Dear Soldier:

I'm fine and hope you are the same. I tried to write yesterday but it was
impossible. But today while Mom is putting my presents away, I'll take time
out and write. Darling, I received my diploma last night, so now, hon, wish
me lots of luck, because I need it. I wish you could have been here to see,
but when some thing is impossible, it just can't be done. . . .

Tomorrow, my folks are making me a picnic so I can invite all my friends.
If you were here I'd invite you and only you. We'd have the picnic by
ourselves. Wouldn't that be fun? . . .

Darling, I didn't think I had so many friends but I do and I received
some very lovely gifts. . . .

Most of all take care of yourself. I love you so never forget.

Yours,   Mary Lou

Garden City, July 7, 1944

My Dearest:

Today I received the air mail you wrote June 29th. Darling, I'm very
sorry if I didn't make myself clear. About the sentence I wrote saying that
I'd understand if you didn't write sooner. I meant to say if you were busy
and didn't have time.

I recall the day I wrote that letter very well. I was very nervous all that
week. I'm sure I wrote and told you of my having those bad dreams. I had
three of them one after the other and in the same week, Ginny had to wake
me up three times. I haven't had any for some time.

About my job at Denver, I made up my mind, and not even you or any
body else can change my mind. If my staying at Garden [City] makes my
soldier happy then that can be made come true. Nothing else counts but
my soldier's happiness. If you can forget about having the dreams and not
finding me, I'll be here at the same place you left me. Darling, so far, I've
been receiving your air mails a lot sooner than the V-Mails. . . .

Darling, don't get any ideas that I don't enjoy your letters because I do.
Every day I go to a certain place and that happens to be the post office. It's
the only thing that keeps me from stepping out and that's my love for you
and your letters. Remember, I love you and am thinking about you.

Yours,   Mary Lou

Nick remained overseas until the fall of 1945. However, the letters which Mary wrote to him during his last year in the service were lost or destroyed. In February 1946, Mary and Nick were married. They had fourteen children, seven girls and seven boys. While Mary maintained their home, Nick worked in a processing plant. In 1979, the family opened a restaurant, El Conquistador, in Garden City. They have twenty-three grandchildren.

Barbara Sanz was a twenty-four-year-old divorced mother with two young children living in Valparaiso, Indiana, when, during the spring of 1944, her brother, Roger Salisbury, persuaded her to write to his buddy, Lester "Mac" McClannen, a cryptographer in the Army Air Corps stationed in England. At the time, Barbara and Mac were two lonely people hungry for love. Both had experienced the deaths of their parents while they were children. As an orphaned teenager growing up during the Depression, Barbara was forced to drop out of high school and go to work. When she was only sixteen, she opened her first beauty shop. Mac was raised by an older sister who had died shortly before he was sent overseas.

Barbara and Mac corresponded for about a year. By the summer of 1945, when Mac returned to the United States, their letters had become very warm and affectionate.

Valparaiso, June 6, 1944

Dear Mac,

Now I understand why I have not heard from you. The "Day" has come. I can't explain the feeling I had when I first heard of the Invasion. I heard it when I walked in the [beauty] shop this morning, I was stunned. We all knew it was coming and were happy that it is started, so it can all end soon. When it actually happens it's a shock. It was such a gloomy day, rained all day. That didn't help much. We had the radio going all day. The President gave a prayer tonite that the nation was to join. Believe me, when I say I put my whole heart and soul in that prayer and will continue to pray knowing that you and the other boys have help and come out on top. And as for you especially, Mac, do take care of yourself. I am still anxiously waiting to meet you and will keep on waiting. You must promise me your "first date." Or am I being selfish? Then you can see your "other girls."

Everyone was so quiet today. It's a day that I'll never forget. It was like the day War was declared. That was also a gloomy day. I hope you will still receive my letters. I will write as often as I can. I know letters mean so much to you boys. Wish I had to time to write everyone of them. . . .

It's so cold here again I had to build a fire tonite. It was so comfy in the house tonite and I was wondering how "comfy" you are. It almost makes you feel guilty when you're enjoying the comforts of home and thinking of the hardships you boys have.

There isn't must more I can say to you tonite, Mac, I just don't feel real cheery tonite, although I hope I've cheered you up a little by letting you know I'm thinking of you and praying for you.

God Bless You,   Barbara

Valparaiso, Oct. 3, 1944

Dearest Mac,

. . . Another day gone by and all's well. Had good luck with all my permanents today. Two cold waves and one machine wave. Had an awful evening for a little while. Nine salesman came in, a customer for a comb-out, besides my permanent. Beverly from next door came in and the two kids started acting up. Thought I'd go batty for a while. Then the salesman left and Beverly, my comb-out, and I put the kids to bed and went ahead and finished my permanent. But we get thru these moments. The salesman said he can't see how I handle all I do, and I said I *definitely* have my hands full. He said he never comes at nite but what I'm working. . . .

You know I have a little flag I wear at the point of my V neckline on my uniform and, honey, that's for you. It's a little pin. I should wear a service pin with one star on it. After all, my honey is at war.

I sure miss your letters when I don't receive any. I feel so empty when I look in the box and there's nothing from you. But then I keep busy and that helps. I'm glad I am kept busy. It doesn't give you time to think too much. Although I can't get you off my mind completely.

I read tonite where they smashed thru the Siegfried Line. Maybe that will mean a lot for us. Things have looked a little discouraging before but I'm going to be optimistic about the whole thing. They *must* give up soon. There's not a nite that I go to bed that I don't say my prayer for all the boys. Whether it helps or not I just can't help it. It's all so heartbreaking. I feel for everyone of them. I know when it's *all over* we should forget about celebrating and thank God it's over. . . .

Goodnite Sweetheart,   Barbara

Valparaiso, April 8, 1945

Dear Mac,

Together again Sunday evening. Snuggle up close honey. Gosh darn it, honey, I would sure do with a little loving from you tonite. Or any time.

Let's always make it a rule, when we are married, to never work on Sunday. Just loaf around. I've had a little too much working on Sunday. The shop is all papered and I'm proud as a peacock. Just scrubbed and waxed the floor and am waiting for the wax to dry and then will move all the equipment in. Don't tell anyone I said so but, I think it's the cutest little shop in town. Just wait til I get my new pull drapes up—Oh boy!! I'm proud, honey, because it looks so nice and has taken so much hard work. The men came at 10:30 in the morning and didn't finish until 8:30 at nite. Imagine two men, and they took that long. Then I finally went ahead and papered the back of my screen and shelves. They are not professional paper hangers and even though they took a long time, they did a fine job. . . .

Gosh, honey, I'm so dirty. I'm been in a lot of dirty work today. Will have to soak about an hour in the tub. How about scrubbing my back for me?

I'll bet I'll get some mail tomorrow morning. Honey, that's the only "thrill" I get out of life right now, although I'm not complaining. I'm very thankful for everything and having you, the sweetest man in all the world and I love him so.

Must start shoving equipment now and then my tub and—bed.

See you in my dreams.

Love,   Barbara

On August 31, 1945, one month after Mac's homecoming, he and Barbara were married. They had two children. Mac died at the age of seventy-six in October 1986.

Barbara McClannen lives in Lafayette, Indiana, where she operates a beauty salon, "The Mad Hatter," out of her home. She has traveled to Europe, India, and China. About five years ago, she began tap dancing with the "Cherry Lane Dudes," a local group composed largely of retired university professors. She has fifteen grandchildren and ten great-grandchildren.

Katherine "Kay" McReynolds grew up in the small town of Trenton, Missouri, where her father was employed by the Rock Island Railroad. After spending a year at Central College in Fayette, Missouri, she transferred, in the fall of 1943, to the University of Missouri in Columbia. She knew James "Jim" McKemy from childhood as he was also from Trenton. Jim graduated from the University of Missouri in June 1943. The summer after his graduation, he and Kay began dating.

In August 1943, Jim was selected for Naval Officer School and underwent training at the University of Notre Dame in South Bend, Indiana. Early in 1944, he was sent to the South Pacific as a supply officer, stationed in the Admiralty Islands. Shortly before he was shipped overseas, he and Kay became engaged. Kay continued her studies at the University of Missouri where she was an active member of Delta Gamma sorority. Her letters contain a detailed account of campus life during the wartime period as well as enthusiastic declarations of her love for Jim.

Trenton, Aug. 20, 1943

Dear Jim:

. . . Every time the postman comes, I think, "Now there's no point in looking for a letter. I just got one, and besides, he's too busy to write," and then I dash madly to the porch to look. There are always just scores of insurance statements or telephone bills or something. There should be two mail boxes at each house, one for business and one for personal letters. Anyway, when I do get a letter from you, I tear it open and read it so fast that it's all gone in just a minute. I think I'll start rationing myself to one paragraph an hour or something. You can depend on each letter you write getting itself read "a million or more times," because I do read all of them over and over. . . .

Last Tuesday night as I was driving . . . home from Kansas City, I kept thinking how positively beautiful the moon was, and if it were that beautiful at Notre Dame, and if you were seeing it. I must have been receiving a telepathic message from you, because that was the night you were on roving watch. At least, I like to think it was mental telepathy, because that's almost like talking to each other. . . .

If you are home from September 26 to October 1, I just won't pledge [a sorority] until later. If school is going on it won't matter, because classes never interfere with my personal life. Cuts don't bother me a bit. If I don't finish in eight semesters, I'll make it in nine—or ten. Last year I had, roughly 35 cuts, and I'm transferring 31½ hours. It's all a matter of smiling at the professors and speaking to the registrar every morning.

I am going to change my major from language to nautical terms, so that I can more thoroughly appreciate your letters. You know, nautical but nice. . . . Next winter, when I get brushed up on my German, I shall write to you in that language just to get even with you for making me look up half the words you use. Secretly, I rather enjoy it. . . .

Love,   Kay

Columbia, Nov. 26, 1943

Dear Jim:

Shirley [Kay's roommate] says that whenever I'm writing to you that goodness just radiates from me. First I get her a glass of ice for a coke, and then I actually condescended to use the desk light so that she can sleep.

Darling, you don't know how much it means to me for you to like me because I'm wholesome and nice. That's the nicest compliment I've ever had paid to me. Virtue is its own reward, they say. Sometimes we girls get to wondering if it's really worth it to live up to the best standards, but it's fellows like you who settle the question. Knowing that you, who are the best, want *us* to be the best is what keeps us being good girls. *Especially* in war time. . . .

Love,   Kay

Columbia, Jan. 26, 1944

Dearest Jim again,

It is *extremely* late. Shirley and I have been having a big old bull session. She still thinks Justin is sweeter than you. I just can't convince her that she is wrong. . . .

If you or any of your friends want some war stamps or bonds in addition to those taken out of your pay, *please* have them buy them through the Delta Gamma house. We're having a contest, and we want our candidate to be queen. No kidding, I'm serious. Have the checks made out to Kappa Epsilon Alpha, and they'll send the stamps and/or bonds back to you. But be sure and have the checks sent to the Delta Gamma house first. Of course, no one probably wants any—The contest ends the 11th of February. . . .

I love you, I love you, I love you, and I guess that really settles that.

Goodnight morning,   Kay

Columbia, June 6, 1944

Dearest Jim:

Such a day! Last night before we went to bed, the German invasion announcement came over the radio. Shirley said, "Oh, please, don't let the invasion be tonight. I'm so sleepy." But, the phone rang about three this morning and the Delta Gamma house really began to hum. There are quite a few J-School [journalism] students in the house and they all went over to put out the extra. *The Missourian* scooped *The Tribune,* so we were all happy about that. Shirley left at three-thirty with her dress in her hand. She had it on when she got to J-School, but it was all over school. She developed pictures. I listened to the radio until I went to sleep at about 4. Then, I woke up again at 6:30, and all the radios in the house were going full blast. Of course, we talked invasion all morning in classes, except psychology, where we took a final. The question we are all asking is "Where is the German Luftwaffe?" . . . Life is full of little perplexities. . . .

I think I shall study and go to bed.

I'm just dead tired.

I love you,   Kay

Columbia, Sept. 19, 1944

Dear Jim,

The last three days have just been a madhouse. You can't imagine how awful rush week is. Every morning we had meetings from nine to twelve, back and dressed and downstairs at 1:15. Then those horrible rushees to entertain until 4:45. Then meetings until 6:30, dressed and ready at 7:15. More rushees—until 10:45. Meeting until one, and the same schedule the next day. No kidding, it's awful. Yesterday morning I woke up feeling horrible. I suffered for about two hours until it dawned on me that hunger was my main trouble. So I ate and feel much better. We hadn't eaten for a whole day, or that is, a real meal. We survived on ritz crackers and peanut butter.

Now for the actual rush news. We have a wonderful pledge class, which moves in at noon tomorrow. . . . Our social chairman is frantically trying to find blind dates for our pledges. Of course, they will all be in love in two weeks. . . .

Lippitt [a sorority sister] just passed by the room and said to tell you she loves you because naval officers are so good looking. Poor thing. She is merely practically engaged to an Army air corps lieutenant. I'm sorry she can't be lucky like me. Army uniforms are grim. . . .

I've got to get to bed. It's 0100 and 0830 will roll around mighty fast.

I love you,   Kay

Trenton, Dec. 31, 1944

Dearest Jim:

I sure feel sorry for the unengaged and unmarried girls tonight. Only 1½ hours in which to catch a man! What do you suppose my status will be come next leap year. For whom will I vote? Roosevelt or the other guy? Gee, I'll be 24 during that year. Old age is practically upon me. . . .

We came home [from visiting friends] and I ironed, in the living room. The fire is so pretty that I hate to leave it. However, I *did* pull down the shades so the neighbors couldn't see my sinful ways. Reminds me of the good old days when I used to have dates.

The radio has been playing tunes from "Oklahoma!" Don't forget that you asked me for a date to go see it sometimes. I hope that doesn't go by the wayside like some other dates I've been asked for. . . . Everyone has either gotten married or else disappeared. I don't care because they are all very dull, but I'll be *most* unhappy if you stand me up. However, I love you so much that I'd be very contented just to see a movie with you. On second thought, there are much more exciting things to do than movies. For instance, watching trains come is a very pleasant pastime, I've found. Perhaps I've just inherited a love for railroads. . . .

I wish you were here. The fire is simply beautiful. Maybe next year?

I saw the *prettiest* picture of a house tonight. It was yellow with white shutters and sort of a gray shingled roof. The door was set back in, and there were two bay windows in front. . . .

I love you,   Kay

P.S. Happy New Year!!

Columbia, Feb. 3, 1945

Dearest Jim,

. . . What a day! Every registration day the red tape gets redder. This time it was terrible. . . . Anyway, I finally got registered and paid my fees. . . .

Abey and I really worked today. The War Board is trying to get at least 90% of the students to buy a 10 cent war stamp each month so we can fly the Army Navy E flag for schools at war. The stamps will be contributed to the University then to be used for building a war memorial. But our memorial isn't going to be a depressing statue of something. Nope, we are building a new student union. We have $1600 already in a fund, and we hope that if we show enough interest, the state legislature will break down and appropriate a couple of million for it. We really need a union here, as you know. Of course, Abey and I won't ever get to use it much, but we want to get it for future years.

Incidentally, I'm not meaning to imply that the Misses Abey and Mc-

Reynolds are carrying on a personal campaign. We were just on the committee to contact all the men (wow) as they left registration today. We organized teams from all the houses and dorms, and those poor fellows couldn't possibly get by without contributing. However, we still have just about 65% of the students. The women are being contacted through house presidents' council. Life is so full of a number of problems. One immediate one is a little matter of the sorority sing. I *have* to get some arrangements worked up not later than tomorrow so we can start practicing. Of course, no matter what Duffy and I work up, at least half the chapter will dissent. But I've gotten to the place where I just say tough and go right on and do as I please. They forget about it in two days time, and I have much less trouble. . . .

Don't say I'm not ambitious. Tonight I washed my hair, clothes, me, and cleaned my room. Cleanliness, thy name is Kay.

It's midnight, so I think I will go to bed.

I love you real much,

Buehla Pennysnatcher

Trenton, Aug. 8, 1945

Dearest Jim:

My next to the favorite country is Russia. Of course we didn't get the original flash today. We always turn the radio off just before some momentous news. Aunt Jessie called and told us about it, and then we listened and started calling other people. I called your mom, and she hadn't heard it yet. Isn't it wonderful? It will bring the end of the war sooner, but I'm not one of these optimistic souls who are saying that it may be over in two or three weeks. But, with the atomic bomb, maybe we won't have to lose so many lives in an invasion. Yes, Darling, I know you really did some fast talking to get Stalin to declare war. I don't see how on earth you ever managed along with all your work on the atomic bomb and the Potsdam conference. What did you tell Truman to say in his speech tomorrow night? I can't wait to hear it. . . .

I love you,   Kay

Trenton, Aug. 14, 1945

Dearest Jim:

. . . It's going to be quite an adjustment, this peace stuff. I can't even remember a time that we weren't in a war or preparing for one, or at least talking about it. But I must add that it's an adjustment I'll make with relish.

The announcer is saying that it is expected that President Truman will make an announcement any time. The message arrived at the White House less than an hour ago. We heard a broadcast not long ago from Bern, Switzerland. Honestly, the suspense is almost unbearable. No doubt you are the same way. We are hearing about the reactions of the men in the Pacific. . . .

This is the most wonderful day of my life! I know you and the others have this same feeling, only multiplied. I feel awfully proud right now, and rather humbled. So many men, including some of our friends, have given their lives just for this day. . . . The fire siren and egg plant whistle have been blowing and a train whistle, too. We're all crying, even Daddy. Mama just said that she has felt that way only once before, when I was born. Just think, you'll be coming home to stay! And, maybe our children will never have to know what war is. . . .

Good *does* triumph over evil! How can we civilians ever repay the armed services? Yes, I feel most humble. . . .

I love you,   Kay

Columbia, Nov. 8, 1945

Dearest Jim:

Sometimes I get to feeling that if I can't see you *right now* I'll go stark raving crazy. . . .

I feel so funny about us. I have never stopped loving you for an instant, but it's just like straining desperately to hang on to something. In the last month, for the first time, it has seemed that the Pacific Ocean is actually separating us. Darling, I've tried so hard to keep our love what it first was, and it's worked out pretty well. But, I keep feeling that if something doesn't happen pretty soon, I'm just going to break. . . .

Mrs. Black [the housemother] thinks we all seem so mature. Why shouldn't we? Franny's Richard and June Digby's twin brother were killed. Meyer's fiance spent six months in a German prison camp. The rest of us have been worried sick and hopelessly lonesome for years. It's a wonder we aren't old women. As I said, I'm a heel to complain, because it's *really* been tough on the fellows. But, there are *two* sides to it. So what happens? . . . What point is there in being in love, anyway? You're just that much worse off.

This letter is a big mess. It's all your fault too. If I didn't love you so much, I wouldn't be so bitter about our separation. I want to cry and there isn't any shoulder handy.

Jim, I love you with all my heart, and please remember that. But I'm a terrible failure, and so weak. The fact that you love me does more for my morale than anything else.

I love you,   Kay

Jim arrived home on December 26. Three weeks later, on January 18, 1946, he and Kay were married. Kay graduated from the University of Missouri, Phi Beta Kappa, in 1946. The couple then moved to Beaumont, Texas, where Jim took a job in public relations. They had two children. In the late 1950s, Jim was transferred to New York. Kay began graduate work at Columbia University, receiving her M.A. degree in 1960. She taught English at Westchester Community College for twenty-five years. She has written several articles about her wartime college experiences and one juvenile novel. Jim died in 1981. Kay now lives in Sedona, Arizona, where she teaches literature in an adult education program. She has two grandchildren.

Anne Gudis of Newark, New Jersey, began a correspondence with Samuel Kramer from Ithaca, New York, early in 1942, after a friend gave his name and address to her. At the time, Samuel was undergoing basic training at Ft. McClellan in Anniston, Alabama. Anne was nineteen and had recently taken a war job, working as a stenographer for an Army Signal Corps Inspection Station in Newark. As time went on, she was promoted to a supervisory position. The primary purpose of the office was to oversee local manufacturing and insure that the quality of the work remained high. Another responsibility of the office was safety in the workplace. Toward the end of the war, Anne was occasionally employed as a government health and safety inspector of plants and materials.

The couple managed only a few meetings before Samuel was shipped overseas. Although the relationship began to bloom, it intensified more rapidly for Sam than it did for Anne. This situation was complicated when the couple missed connections at two different planned meetings at Pennsylvania Railway Station in New York City. In the summer of 1942, Samuel was posted to Army Special Services in England. The couple now began a three-year, albeit sometimes unsteady, correspondence.

Samuel did not save any of Anne's letters. Her letters are available only because she saved the drafts which she wrote before typing the letters in final form for mailing. Very few salutations, closings, and dates appear in the drafts.*

Newark, May [?], 1942

Hi, Sammy:

How are you? I bet you think I am awfully bold calling you by your first name when we don't even know each other. Well, that's where you are mistaken. I do know you. Of course, I have never met you personally, but I've heard so much about you I feel that I know you anyway. Where did I hear about you, in this remote New Jersey town? Ah, that's a secret. Of course you will find out soon, that is, if you answer this letter.

I know you aren't in the Army long, so how is Uncle Sam treating you. Are you used to the heat? I bet it's terrific compared with that little town from upstate N.Y. that you come from. I know I shouldn't belittle Ithaca, because, after all, it is your home town.

I'll bet you are anxious to know all about me, aren't you? Looks, shape, brains, etc. Well I'm an awful tease, so I'll wait until I hear from you before I divulge my information.

Hoping to hear from you soon. I remain.   Anne Gudis

The following letter may not have been sent, although it exists in typed form.

---

*Ann Kramer's World War II letters are located in the Kramer Family Archives, Cornell University Libraries. Printed by permission of Anne Kramer and the Cornell University Libraries.

Newark, Dec. [?], 1942

Your unexpected V letter arrived yesterday. . . . Can't make out what message you are trying to convey to me . . . [about] the incident in Penn Station. As far as I am concerned, it is just a closed chapter, which if the future persists, may be opened for further explanation.

I am glad to hear that you are happy in your new surroundings. I always listen to the broadcasts from the American Eagle Club in London. Perhaps some day I will hear you speak from there. . . .

Sammy, all your letters to me were like a rainbow leading up to the pot of gold and when I reached the climax and came to the end of the rainbow, the pot was empty. I was disappointed both physically and mentally. I then and there said to myself, "The hell with it all especially men," and may take your advice too chalk you down as another male. But don't think that I give up so easily. I'm still hoping for a chance after you return home.

Newark, Dec. [?], 1942

Mr. Kramer,

This letter is going to be brutally frank and I'm not going to spare any words. It is not my nature to use them, but if I do it's entirely your fault. I only hope this letter leaves you feeling the way I did after reading your last two letters.

After reading the one I received last month, I decided to hell with him, he isn't worth the time, or effort it takes to write to him.

You're so damn conceited you think that if a girl so much as looks at you she wants to marry you, and the same with my letter writing. I thought that something could come of it, but after these few incidents at Penn Station, I lost all romantic interest in you. How could I hold on or be in love with you, when you take into consideration the circumstances of the whole incident. Please understand I have no marital interests in you whatsoever.

I wrote to you as a friend and thought my letters would be appreciated but since they annoy you so, I shall stop my so called folly.

Don't tell me what to do either. You nor anyone else will dictate my life for me. Taking that course in psychoanalysis has helped me understand why you are so very heartless. Of course it's not your fault that you should forgive and forget, but because you don't you deserve whatever you get. I have to laugh, you once wrote and told me to have compassion, well why don't you practice what you preach, you inebriate and don't tell me to get married either.

When I get married, it's not just to sleep with a man, because I can find plenty of bed mates, without being married, and remember for the past 10 months, I haven't even had a date or kissed a fellow. Perhaps I am not normal, that's why. And I don't want to marry the type of man you represent. But, damn it, you men are all alike.

It was most thoughtful of you to thank me for the cards. Didn't think it was in you.

Pauline [a co-worker] is highly flattered when you send your love. Flattered to such an extent that she has asked for your address and like a dope I gave it to her.

Upon rereading this letter, I find that it doesn't contain half of what I wanted to say. However, I shall let it go as is.

Of course, I don't expect any reply to this outburst of anger, but if one comes I certainly shall be anxious to read it and see what affect this letter had on you.

I was relieved to learn that you had burned my letters. As for yours, they are still collecting dust in the top of my closet. But, don't worry, they will never be used against you. I don't want anyone who doesn't want me.

My boss, who you are so anxious for me to marry, gave me $75 as an Xmas gift. P.S. He is already on his second wife, so leave the poor man alone.

What New Year's Eve or the N.Y. holds in store for me only time will tell. At this point, I'd like to wish you a very Happy New Year. I hope that with the coming of the N.Y. you will get a more pleasant disposition. Stop being so bitter, forget whatever happened, don't carry grudges and start life anew. You will find that you will be much happier.

In case I don't hear from you again, I shall look forward to the end of the war when perhaps we can really get together and laugh over the whole matter.

Anne

Newark, April 20, 1943

Sam:

I would have answered your nasty V-Mail sooner, but Mom had pneumonia and had to be rushed to the hospital for oxygen. Another thing, I've been going out a great deal lately, and haven't had time to give you a thought.

Your letters don't bother me in the least. I used to feel bad when you wrote nasty things but now I take from who it comes. You can't help it if you don't know better. . . .

I hope in your next letter I won't have to read about what an awful person I am. So far you are the only one who has had the nerve to tell me. I'll certainly hate to disillusion you when you come home.

Anne

Over the next several months, Samuel's letters to Anne continued to upset her. She finally reacted with a "Dear John" V-Mail in early September. It is available today because Samuel sent the letter to *Yank*, a weekly magazine published for enlisted men, where a photograph of it appeared in the September 27, 1943, issue.* The headline read, "The importance of Being Terse." In

*We have heard from several World War II veterans who received "Dear John" letters. However, the letters were not saved. The letter by Anne Gudis is the only "Dear John" letter in our collection.

his cover letter to *Yank*, Samuel wrote, "Dear Yank: I desire to lay claim to having received the shortest V-Mail ever received in the E.T.O. Cpl. S.J. Kramer."

Newark, Sept. 7, 1943

Mr. Kramer:
    Go To Hell!
    With love,
    Anne Gudis

Anne found herself the object of a great deal of unsolicited attention after the publication of this letter. Indeed, her letter created a furor, both in Samuel's unit and back at home, as it was also discussed in the New Jersey newspapers. Approximately one hundred GIs, sailors, men in the Royal Marines, women in the United States, and others wrote to her. Some sought dates and others wanted a pen-pal. Worse for Anne were those who chastised her for damaging morale, for possibly putting Samuel in danger, or for otherwise not living up to the "unwritten law" of how women should behave in wartime.

Samuel's commanding officer wrote to her, as he felt that morale was suffering. He was answered by a friend of Anne's, Mrs. Irene Linden, who knew the story fairly well.

Newark, Oct. [?], 1943

My Dear Lt.,
    I am taking the liberty of writing you as a close friend of Anne Gudis, who has been acquainted with the association of Anne and Cpl. Sam Kramer. Although I am an outsider, I have been living at Anne's house for the past months and was not aware of the strain between these two until today. . . .
    In all of S.'s letters he spoke of the types of women or entertainment he enjoyed. He also gave her a picture of the nature of the woman that he could fall in love with and foolishly enough, Anne patterned herself in her letters only, after his likes and dislikes. Knowing her personally, I can say that she is not as tawdry nor as garish as S. has come to believe. . . .
    . . . After his return [from the missed meeting], he wrote her a brief letter which was not very complimentary. Anne . . . chose to explain that their not meeting was an error on his part.
    Instead of dropping the issue completely . . . Sam began to write insinuating and offending letters. . . . Anne cannot explain why she took all of his insults and continued to write except that she had grown fond of him and did not wish to destroy something that had started out so splendidly. [The second missed meeting occurred] and Anne did not get a reply until Sam had reached England. By this time there was a tension in their letters and the agony continued across the ocean. . . .
    Anne would have stopped writing but she felt the matter had to be cleared and the grudge against her be erased. . . .

Finally, in desperation she pleaded with him to stop sending the type of letters he had become accustomed to mailing. . . . For awhile there they seemed to have recaptured some of the happiness they had known in the first few months of their friendship.

Although we in the states are told to be very cheerful, when corresponding, especially to some one overseas, there were times when Anne was feeling blue and could not help but put that feeling in one of her letters to Sam. Instead of being understanding, as most friends would, Sam reverted to the humiliating letters.

I have noticed your name as censor appears on the V-Mail and I believe you should have a vague idea of these letters.

After receiving the nastiest letter he could possibly have written her, she, in a fit of anger, wrote the letter that has caused all the disturbance and has remained ever since very despondent. . . .

She cannot obtain a release [from her war job] to join the WACS or any other military organization. She will receive a dishonorable discharge from the government as a civilian. To compensate for it, she devotes her spare time to aiding the war effort on the home front. She is very active in the Civilian Defense. . . . Cpl. Kramer has taken the liberty of ridiculing her willingness to do all she can, and has referred to the above as "lamebrain organizations." . . .

Anne attended a college in N.Y.C. and is by no means inferior as to intellect and comprehension. She has realized the error she has made in using such bad taste in writing a letter of that caliber in writing to a man in the service. She fully realizes the duties of a woman left behind and through this misunderstanding has gained a world of deeper understanding. I can truthfully say that she has benefited by the mistake that she has made. . . .

You must excuse this lengthy letter but I felt as you did in your letter that this matter should be straightened out. From your message, I can see that you are not only a friend of the boys but a companion as well and I thought it proper to come to you and explain in detail exactly what has occurred.

Your duties are many, yet I ask a small favor of you. Do whatever you see fit and answer me accordingly.

Anne has had enough penance.

Sincerely,   Mrs. Irene Linden

The couple renewed their correspondence soon after this letter was written. On November 30, 1943, Anne sent Sam a cablegram, with messages numbered 59, 93, and 31. In the Western Union code designed for servicemen, this meant, "Loving Birthday Greetings. Delighted hear about your promotion. [Sam had recently been promoted to the rank of sergeant.] All my Love."

In December, while thanking Sam for his consideration and the good letters he was now writing, Anne remarked, "The mailman is most pleased that all is well between us now. For one who does not know all the circumstances, he should be. I am going to buy him a box of candy for Christmas. For he has been very nice to me. He always gives me your mail when he meets me or if he is too far from the house, tells me whether or not there is mail from you."

From this time on, most of Anne's letters to Sam are available, although still in draft or carbon form.

Newark, Nov. 1, 1943

Come on brains. I've just lubricated you, so give out some new ideas to start a letter off with. Guess I'll give it a chance to penetrate—Grind to the right, rip to the left, but to no avail. They haven't been used in such a long time they are stuck together. Well, I'll have to go back to some of the old stand-bys, but what should it be? Hello, Hi, Good-morning, no, they are all so formal, so I'll use the old stand-by?

Dear Sammy:

I've seven of your letters to answer all dated October and find it most difficult to begin. . . .

Newark may be a city of 429,760 people, but when it comes to something like this, it's a smaller place than Ithaca. The people could not have had more to say if I had murdered someone.

No doubt this has also caused a good deal of gossip in your home town. . . . I am still receiving letters of comment from abroad and can overlook them no matter how nasty they are. I have thought of making a statement to the *Yank* magazine which would clear me of any doubts in its readers' minds as to why I wrote the shortest letter ever received in the E.T.O., however, I do not want to make more of an issue of this matter than has already been made. . . . Sammy, when we first started to correspond you told me that I was letting myself in for a great deal of sorrow. Little did I realize how true would be your warning.

In the past I have enjoyed your frank and open letters and am wondering whether it is foolishness on my part to expect our friendship to resume its original course. If you think this is possible to straighten out, . . . I'd like to continue writing.

In any event I would like to receive a reply.

Sincerely,   Anne

Newark, Dec. [?], 1943

If I were a man I would have accomplished all that you have, if not more. I always tell the girls that I'd feel sorry for any female that crossed my path if I were the opposite sex. There is an old Yiddish saying which translated means, "What was, Was," and that is how I feel. As far as your being faithful in the future, that all depends on how happy I can make you, and by George, I'll do my utmost.

Sammy, I've said this once before and I'll say it again. I have cast all other men aside as far as the future is concerned and am waiting only for you. . . . I have put my every last hope into you and am eagerly awaiting the day these hopes will be fulfilled.

With all my deepest love and devotion.

Your,   Anne

Dec. [?], 1943

No, you are not sticking your neck out when you write as often as you do because I enjoy hearing from you. You will have to be patient until my mail reaches you. The Christmas rush has probably delayed its reaching you. . . .

Sammy, don't care in the least what happens before we two get together. The past was yours to do with as you pleased and the future remains to be seen.

Seems that we are both reluctant about putting our utmost faith in each other, but in spite of what has been, I'll never tire of waiting for you, the thing that bothers me most is what the outcome will be.

Thus, my sweet, with this thought in mind, I close my letter, thinking of you as I always am.

As Ever

Newark, Jan. [?], 1944

Sammy:

. . . many of my friends have done a great deal of wondering, but if they had any doubts in their minds about you, you may be sure that I have done my utmost to erase them. I've defended you to the nth degree. In fact, I've done such a good job, people ask me if we are going steady or if we are engaged. . . .

Will love to tell you what I know about life but frankly I think you will have to teach me. I have no objections to men being unfaithful, if they must, but it is easier for a woman, no matter how emotional she may be, to control herself.

Newark, Feb. 2, 1944

Dear Kramer:

. . . I believe that you are so strongly set in your ways that no matter what anyone else says or does, they cannot change your mind or your convictions, not that anyone wants to, but should they, I think it would be impossible.

I'm not worried about the above, just wondered. You see I can acclimate myself very easily to anyone, and that is one of the reasons for my having so many friends. . . .

So you enjoy tormenting people. Well I'm not too much of an angel myself. Should anyone cross my path, be it male or female, and I don't like them I'll do anything to aggravate them and act very spiteful, but innocent. It's just the meanness in me but so it is. On the whole, I've only met about five people in my life that I didn't like. . . .

Well, my dear, as this page ends, so do I.

With all my love,

Forever and ever,   Anne

Newark, April 26, 1944

. . . One of the new girls in the next department became engaged yesterday and we are making her a party. I sure feel like an old maid when these young kids of 18 start coming in with diamond rings. Somehow I don't envy them. Keep thinking that when you come home I'll have all the happiness I've ever dreamed of and even more. You seem capable in more ways than one for making me happy.

Went to an Air Raid Warden's meeting last night and was awarded a ribbon and a certificate of merit which reads as follows: "This is to certify that in appreciation of the loyal, unselfish and patriotic volunteer efforts of Anne Gudis, who has rendered meritorious services in the forces of Civilian Defense, a special insignia of merit has this day been awarded on behalf of the citizens of the City of Newark," signed by Mayor Vincent J. Murphy. See Sammy, I don't have to join the WACS or the WAVES to do my bit for my country. I'm doing my share right here on the home front.

Newark, May 3, 1944

Even though you wrote to me once before about our becoming engaged, your second proposal came as a complete surprise. My being engaged to you appeals to me ever so much, but there are certain obstacles which do not permit it being publicized as you wish. I'd like to talk this matter over with you even though it may take some time through the mail. . . .

I'd like very much to meet your family and there is no reason why I shouldn't meet with their approval, but what if I shouldn't and they wrote you about me. . . .

I also realize that an engagement at present would not be as full of thrills and excitement as if you were here but that doesn't matter, just knowing we belong to and are waiting for each other will have to suffice for the present. . . .

So, my darling, stay well and sober.

Newark, June 2, 1944

. . . It's been published in the papers and announced on the radio that there is no mail from England and no one knows when it will be coming through. I try my best not to worry about you and have my fingers crossed that all is well. I hope your family knows about this situation and isn't too worried.

Have been sitting here and pondering over what to say and truthfully am at a loss. It's funny though, just when I was awaiting a reply from you to my letter about your engagement the mail stopped. Now I don't know how you feel about it and so don't know what to say. . . .

Newark, June [?], 1944

. . . Sammy, you ask that I be more definite, in regard to us. As long as in our hearts we are both engaged, I don't see why we have to make it public. I've given up all other dates, think of no one else but you, all I haven't done is make a public announcement of our engagement, and dear, that will be done when you come home. . . .

My feelings for you are getting to the point where it is difficult to explain in words just how I feel. If you were here and I could hold your head in my lap, or put my arms around your neck, then I could show you how my feelings are. As it is now all I can do is to tell you how very much you mean to me and how I long for the day when we can be together again.

> Newark, July 29, 1944
>
> . . . Would very much like to meet them [Sam's family] but as far as my going up there it is like this, I think that they should write and ask me to come up. . . . I just know I am going to like them.
>
> As far as my writing to your Dad in Yiddish, you don't have to dare me to do anything. It's either, you want me to, or you don't want me to but please don't dare me to do anything. My knowledge of Yiddish will amaze even you. . . . I'm not trying to boast about how much I know, but I am proud of the education I have had. . . .

> Newark, Sept. 3, 1944
>
> . . . Received three super super letters from you yesterday. . . . This letter is in reply to No. 7 and I shall try and be as explicit as possible in regard to the situation concerning us. I thought I had written a satisfactory answer in one of my letters but it seems that you didn't interpret it as such.
>
> The situation between us is not insignificant. As time goes on I realize more than ever that there can't be anyone else for me other than you. . . . Whether I've talked this into myself or whether I am really in love with you, which I am certain I am, I do not know. I've waiting two years now. In waiting I've grown older and not younger. I'm content to go on waiting till you come home because I believe that Kismet has meant us for each other. . . .
>
> As you asked I shall refrain from writing so much about the office and the hospital. Instead I shall write you about my dreams. How wonderful it is to have you hold me in your arms, to be able to look into your eyes and find them burning with passion and love. To walk on a deserted road at the lake in companionable silence pausing only for a kiss when we have been overcome by the beauty surrounding us, or having you row me to a secluded spot on the lake under a cluster of trees and then have me succumb to the charms which were endowed you as a man. . . .
>
> With all my love
> Yours only and always,   Anne

> Newark, Sept. 30, 1944
>
> Have so much to write about that I am lost as to where to start. I had a simply wonderful time in Ithaca. Getting acquainted with your family brought me ever so much closer to you and after hearing all the stories about your childhood and so forth, my love for you has deepened immensely. . . .
>
> Your mother stayed in the living room waiting for me and just started to cry. She kissed me and then held my hands and looked at me with tear filled eyes and I knew that I had met with her approval. . . . Your father

got a big kick out of my speaking Yiddish. I also looked through the family album. . . . I was thrilled with the place and it was like being with you. . . .

Newark, Oct. 31, 1944

I could brain you for letting ten days lapse without writing me a single letter. Confound it, I worry too, perhaps not as much as your sister Rose, but enough. You are all I have and I need you more than ever. No mail from you is definitely bad for my morale. . . . While you are gone your letters have to take your place. They are indeed a poor substitute but this is war. . . .

Lately I feel like one of those adolescent kids who swoons at the mere thought of Frank Sinatra because that's how I've been feeling over you. The first two years of waiting weren't so bad. They were bearable but lately I'm getting so impatient. When? When? When? I keep asking myself and that's so silly because I know the great event can't be too far off. Everyday I hear stories of boys returning and I know that someday soon you will be one of them. I often wonder whether you will let me know in advance or just pop unexpectedly. . . .

So my darling as in all my other letters this one too, now comes to a close.

Newark, Dec. 15, 1944

If I don't write too often during the next week or so or my letters are a bit short, it's not because anything is wrong or that I love you less. In fact, I love you more and more each day, it's just that it's the end of the year and the work is just staring us in the face. I worked so darn hard yesterday that as soon as I finished eating dinner last night I went straight to bed. Pearl [Anne's assistant] and I are working like mad and cleaning out files, making reports, planning the tuberculosis drive schedules etc. . . .

Finally got around to having my picture taken and will get the proofs tomorrow. Hope that they come out good. Am giving one to you, your family and one for the house. When your Mother was at my house I gave her a picture of me that she wanted but which I didn't think was any good and so I decided I had to take another one. . . .

Well my sweet and precious one, shall see you in my dreams. Remember that date on the 3rd cloud on the left?

Newark, March 5, 1945

Well today marked your 30th month overseas. . . . From now on I'll keep my fingers crossed every single day for your return. They can't keep you over much longer now.

Sam, I've been so mixed up these past few days that I wish you were home now more than ever. Then I could say good-bye to my job and have nothing to worry about except making you happy cause I too shall be much happier. . . .

Samuel returned to the United States in the fall of 1945 and was discharged. Anne and Samuel's engagement was formally announced, and six weeks later, in November 1945, they were married. They have been happily married for forty-five years. They lived in Ithaca until 1980 when Sam liquidated his auto parts business. Anne worked as a research aide and secretary at Cornell University while they lived there. They now live in Virginia Beach, where Sam is a parts specialist at Western Auto and Anne has a résumé service. They have three children and four grandchildren.

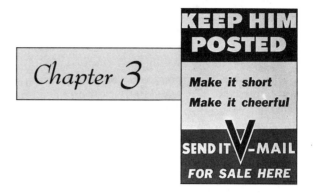

Chapter 3

KEEP HIM
POSTED

Make it short
Make it cheerful

SEND IT V-MAIL

FOR SALE HERE

War Brides

WITH THE OUTBREAK OF WAR, THE MARRIAGE RATE BEGAN TO
climb. In fact, there were approximately one million more marriages between
1940 and 1943 than would have been expected at prewar rates.

War brides often traveled thousands of miles to be with their husbands at
distant postings. A reporter for the *New York Times Magazine* described these
young women as "wandering members of a huge unorganized club" who recognized each other on sight, exchanged views on living quarters, babies, and
allotments, and helped each other in times of difficulty.

Young war brides were faced with many new and difficult challenges. One
mother, writing to her son in combat, gave a succinct description of their
situation: "These poor little war brides, they are finding life a confused and
perplexing situation, too. It's pretty tough to have to fight a battle like they
are doing. . . . But such is war."

War brides often set aside a special time each day to write to their absent
husbands. They reported on the news at home, discussed the growth of their
young children, described their war jobs, and wrote beautiful letters of longing and love.

Edna Gladstone and John Golan both grew up in the Bronx, New York. Edna's parents had immigrated to the United States from Poland, while John's

parents were from Argentina. In 1940, they began a two-year courtship which led to their marriage in June 1942. Because the Gladstones were Jewish and the Golans were Catholic, there was a good deal of parental resistance to their marriage.

Three months after they were married, John entered the Army. He served in the Medical Corps and was stationed in Europe from September 1942 until his return late in November 1945. Edna lived in an apartment in New York City and worked for the Signal Corps and for the Ordnance section of the War Department. She was a member of a group of war wives, called WIVES, which was primarily concerned with the welfare of service wives.

Edna and John were prolific wartime letter writers. Fortunately, John was able to save virtually all of the letters which his wife wrote to him. During the twenty-seven months that he was overseas, she sent him a total of 1,000 letters, 134 cards, 19 telegrams, and 86 packages. Edna often wrote seven- or eight-page V-Mail letters, numbering each letter, so that John could read them in sequence.

Edna and John were, in many ways, the quintessential New York City couple. They enjoyed music, liked going to the theatre, and were attracted to and interested in the constantly new and different life dramas which they observed everywhere in "Baghdad on the Subway." Edna and John were especially conscious of the many ways in which different racial and ethnic groups came together in the great metropolis. Edna's letters are remarkably lyrical love letters, but they also celebrate city life and describe her perceptions of the changes in New York as the war progressed. She used the diminutive "Yannie" when referring to John and referred to herself as "Yedna" in much of her correspondence.

New York, Sept. 3, 1942

Hello Darling!

I have the blue moods again, my Darling, and I know you won't blame me for your letter came today saying you are on your way. I got the pine pillows and the new pair of shoes too . . . thank you, Darling. I think I'll keep the pine under my sleeping pillow so I can make believe that I'm sleeping in a fragrant pine forest. . . .

Had a physical exam at the Y.M.C.A. in preparation for the calisthenic course I'm going to take, and the woman doctor said I had a slight heart murmur although not enough to impede any activity, whatsoever. I think she's a quack, Darling, however, because I've always been told my heart was sound!

Met up with an odd couple today, a sloppily dressed young woman and a dirty little boy. The woman was carrying two satchels, coats, newspapers, brown paper bag and trying to watch her mischievous 4 year old at the same time. When I met her, I offered to help and was soon told her story.

She had an argument with her husband, packed up and left with the kid, but before she even reached her destination she realized she was wrong and turned back to the Bronx again. How I felt like pitching into her and saying,

"My God, Woman, you in these times have your husband and son beside you. Make the most of your happiness and be thankful for it for how can you tell how soon it will be grabbed away?"

Dearest, I love you and please be assured that I'll always be awaiting your caresses.

Oh, Darling, come home soon.

Yours Forever, Edna

New York, Oct. 18, 1942

Yannie, My Dearest Love:

It's Sunday evening and I'm plopped in the soft chair at Mom's. There's music over the radio that's saying all I want to say to you for these songs of great love and passion seem to be made for us. Darling, isn't it wonderful to know that there still is music to share together.

My baby, I've spent the day . . . at the Bronx Zoo. How I wish you could have been there, too, Darling, for we fed the seals (5 cents to throw a fish), it was sunny out, we rode on a camel and went to the Children's Zoo. Today, their guest of honor was a beautiful specimen of a skunk who's name was Lord Hol Yer Noze. I also discovered something new, "The Farm of the Bronx Zoo." They presented the improved animals of today. They were all near enough to touch, *smell* and feed so we gloried in baby calves, lambs and just hatched chicks. . . .

Darling, tomorrow I'm sending you your shoes plus some other "chatskis," and I hope you have fun unpacking them. . . . Yannie, if there is anything that you or any of the boys can use please let me know. . . .

After wanting to see [my cousin's] four year old son, Michael, I finally met the lad! Darling, he's a beautiful youngster, a thick shock of blond hair that is completely in ringlets and large, deep set blue eyes. As a gift I brought him the records from Pinoccio and though I didn't mention a word, when he saw the picture on the album, he exclaimed "A Pinocchio Symphony." He speaks of his doll as being "inanimate" and is altogether a precocious youngster.

Children seem to be the only people left in the world who can find any happiness in it. That's why I've surrounded myself with them this weekend, my dearest, because I must find again this joy in being. It's so hard to believe, Darling, when you who are my one comfort and pleasure, are so far. . . .

Darling, I'm reading a very fine book now, *Moscow War Diary* by Alexander Worth. If you could contact it someway, I'm sure you would enjoy it too. It takes you through the eventful July, Aug., and Sept. of Russia's 1942, and is written by a news correspondent who spent his life in Britain and Russia.

I love you, my darling, and please keep writing steadily so that these gaps between letters can never be our doing. I kiss your lips, my darling, and your ear—no! I won't cut it out!

Your ever own, Yedna

New York, Nov. 26, 1942

Hello, My Darling!:

It's so good to be writing to you once again, sometimes the lust to write to you fills me for days until I can quench it, for early rising, persistent work, long train rides, fatigue, and social obligations insist upon keeping me from you.

It's Thanksgiving Day today, my darling, and I hope you had a merry one. There was work today, a Turkey sandwich luncheon with Doris and Helen [office friends] and then home, to finally curl myself up in the soft chair and permit myself to drift to you—what can I find to be thankful for amidst this frustration, longing and loneliness within me? Well now, let me see—.

First there is the fact that I came home and that a letter awaited me—a beautiful letter from my own love telling me again of his devotion and dreams. Then, there is home itself where Mom and Pop are still alive, and where many souvenirs of happy hours spent are about me, "The Wagner Libretto," "Shakespeare", "The Prophet", "Salome" the beautiful music we've heard so often before, the dog-house from Portland, the "Bohemian Girl," Bebe's smoking stand, the ring on my finger and a photograph of my radiant Yannie. Yes, Dearest, in spite of all this misery and chaos I am thankful to be alive for I love you, my love, and a beautiful future beckoning to us. . . .

My love goes out to you,

Your own loving,   Edna

New York, March 30, 1943

Beloved Mine:

Tonight our victrola is playing once again, at the moment it is Galli Curci singing Solweig's Song, Pop is cutting out a hat for Jean, and Mom is calling, "Who wants tea?" I think, Darling, tonight I will play the records that you used to bring me, way back in courting days. . . . Let's see, there is "The Blue Danube," "The Bartered Bride," "Carmen," and can we consider "Danse Macabre" in that category? And then I'm sure you brought me "Moonlight Sonata."

Dearest, many have tried to fix this victrola, but there are still many adjustments waiting for you. Each time, a repair man arises from tinkering with it, rises and says it is in good shape, I always find that there is still plenty left undone, and I am happy, for then something else is waiting for Yannie. . . .

"Danse Macabre" has just struck the witching hour and in this room the fingers or our clock point to 12 too. Dearest, I love you and please protect me from these goblins who are running after me! Oh, now you have me . . .

Dearest, what do you think of my letters? I sometimes wonder if you find them silly or beautiful, vital or light, provocative or boring?

Please keep well, Dear, and happy, for that is the way I like to think of you.

Your own,   Yedna

New York, Feb. 16, 1944

Yannie Beloved—

The mailbox is still bare but I do have your telegram to tell me that you are well and that letters are coming so that perhaps next week at this time I'll be reading one of those beautiful gifts from you. Yes, my Darling, you could never give me a more beautiful gift than these thoughts of yours put down on paper to bring me happiness, courage, and intimacy with you again. . . .

Yannie Darling—are you asking if it hurts when other men come home and there's been not a sight of you for so long? No, Darling—for though there is pain in loving you and having no way to get to you—for the others I can just feel gratefulness that this emptiness and helplessness we have is not theirs. However, Darling, when this is all over, our time will come, and it will be good then to find peace and happiness for ourselves when we know that blood is no longer being spilt and that insane dictatorship governments have been given back to the hands of the people. . . .

Your own adoring, Yedna

New York, June 6, 1944

My Own Angel:

This has been such an exciting morning that my insides just refuse to stop throbbing. It all started on the way home from work during the wee hours of the morning when Bella and I stopped for coffee and apple pie for it was there that the German announcement that the invasion had started came through. And then, afterwards, taking myself to bed, I switched the radio on and until at last amongst bunches of announcements and music from the "St. Louis Blues" to MacDowell's "To a Wild Rose"—came the Allied confirmation that our troops are in France!

And then sleep, to awaken to Mom holding out two V-Mails to me, for Dearest, the mail has come through and again I feel the happiness, love and peace that only your letters can bring me. They are the missing pages 1 and 4 of your May 16 letter which was the last one to come two weeks ago, and Darling, it is so very wonderful to know that the silence is ended. I was happy to hear that Freddy is so close by that you can go swimming together and that you're staying at a real home. Darling, I saw "Thank Your Lucky Stars" about ten months ago, but your description brought it back to me and Dearest, I'm glad that you enjoyed it too. . . .

Dearest, our memories are wonderful things and just a few of them that I'll never forget is the beauty of having you so very, very close to me, how sweet it was to lie beside you in the darkness or in the light talking to each other, and to wake to the new day to find you beside me fast asleep and be glad that the clock woke only me so I could kiss you awake.

Darling, I want to pray that peace and victory comes soon without too much payment and that soon you will be home with me.

Your own, Yedna

New York, June 11, 1944

Darling:

I've just returned to the newspapers and radio broadcasts, after a lovely day spent in the Palisades. And I have been mentally putting down memories to write you about all during the day. Now I can only think of how proud I am for the human race today, with major results reported in France, our armies steadily advancing and Russia on the *march* again to meet on some day in Berlin. For Darling, we're really regaining what Hitler tried to destroy, all the advancement that man has made in thinking and creating a better world for himself during all the years of living. You know, Darling, as I write, I'm just slightly afraid, knowing how you must be duped with it, that you'll read what I say, and think—"Darling, you too with propaganda?" (remember the joke about the proper gander?) But, Yannie, these are my thoughts, and I can't help but bring them to you, though I am so aware of the different worlds we are living in these days though it does seem to me that there is very little of me here when all of my thoughts, desires, and loves are with you.

May the gods be kind and have you soon back with me.

Your own,   Yedna

New York, June 21, 1944

Darling!:

. . . Darling, I took some time off from work today and went aslumming downtown. Yop! New York is as crazy, loveable, excited and gay, as ever at least on the exterior! At Times Square there is a continuous bond rally that never stops except for a few hours each night. It all centers around a huge cash register which is on top of a tall platform and is about the size of a house. Each bond that is sold, and there is a steady stream constantly buying, is recorded in the register and all the time aboard the platform volunteer entertainers are singing out through huge loud speakers. Yop, Darling, for blocks around I couldn't escape from Kate Smith and Cab Calloway!

Then, passing by the Apollo, I couldn't resist going in, for the short, "The Negro Soldier" was playing and I had long ago decided that I wanted to see it when I read (I can't remember where right now) that some usually apathetic Negro regiments had seen it at a camp theatre and that they all stood up and cheered. And, Darling I wanted to stand up and cheer too as I realized that here at last was a film which recognized the Negro people as a race capable of any art or enterprise along with any other peoples of the world. The two feature pictures were exceptionally fine too, Raines in "The Man Who Seeks the Truth" (guess I like French pictures better than any other nation's, my darling) and the English portrayal of H.G. Wells's "The Remarkable Mr. Kipps" which starred Diana Wynyard and Michael Redgrave. . . .

Keep well, my beloved, and come back as soon as you can for your, Yedna.

New York, Sept. 13, 1944

Happy Birthday Morning, My Dearest!:

. . . There was our beautiful music playing from the moment I awoke, my darling, "Afternoon of a Faun," "Peter and the Wolf," and one we have never heard together, Shostakovich's "Sixth." It would seem that even the radio realizes that this is your birthday and has silenced hysterical soap operas and has put melody in their place.

It's more than just wonderful, Darling, how everything we've ever done together has always been such fun, whether it was cooking a meal, reading a book, watching a fountain spout, writing these letters, or the crazy way we had of working in the store. Remember, Darling, how we would dance between customers and how we would turn symphonic music on to rid the store of the zany? Oh, my dearest, I love you so! . . .

Dearest, you know how it is in our family of two, and I want it to continue no matter how numerous we grow, that when a birthday comes, the celebrated one can make a wish for anything that is in the power of the family to make come true. What is your dearest wish on this birthday, my dearest, that I can do for you?

And so, Darling, with 29 kisses, 29 hugs, 29 socks, 29 blows in your ear, and 29 beautiful caresses which I doubt if I've forgotten the knack of, and a wish that you've had fun today, as is, your own forever adoring,   Yedna

New York, Dec. 1, 1944

My Own Dearest Stinky:

. . . The only real thing I want is to have you home, and the only way I can help to get you home is by working and so that is really the path I can follow. I don't know how you bear with my constant contrary ramblings of "I'm doing this," "I'm not doing this," you've brought me up, my darling, to believe that you're interested in everything about me, and so I do not spare you even the arguments that go on between me and me. It's as if you have a permanent bleacher seat within my mind, the way I must tell about every game of every team that plays within it.

I'm looking forward, hungrily, to tomorrow, Darling, for tonight's paper had an item saying that a record amount of mail from servicemen overseas has arrived, and I'm aching so for a fat, juicy letter from you. . . .

And now sleep, and so Good Night, my Darling, and please try your best to be in my mailman's sack tomorrow.

Always your own nut to crack,   Yedna

New York, March 14, 1945

Dearest Mine:

Walking to work today, I smelt a queer smell and heard strange noises— the smell was the turning of fresh earth and the sounds were the singing of birds, so that even me, the city slicker, knows that Spring is on its way. However, I guess I would never have known it if my new job didn't take me to Carnarsie, for here, at least, there are private homes. The only way I ever know, in the Bronx, that Spring is coming is when I can hear a neighbor battle with his wife and the sounds rise up to my open window; when the middle aged of every hue of political thinking congregates in the parks or, of course, when flower and vegetable gardens grow suddenly on women's heads. . . .

Always your own,   Yedna

New York, May 2, 1945

Dearest Mine:

I'm having a wonderful wish! Time you were here!

But, no kidding, Darling it's a beautiful day and not only the elements make it so either, for there's a man alive named John Golan who is going to return soon to his woman, Edna, for world events are constantly pushing him closer and closer to home. Mussolini's death this week and now the German announcement of Hitler's. . . . Queer, though, isn't it that the proclaimed day of his death should be May Day, the international workers' day? . . .

It's queer, my Darling, to know that the women in France are voting for the first time this year, and I don't quite understand why suffrage wasn't granted to them before, France always seemed one of the most forward democracies before Hitler tramped in.

My Darling, this note really seems to have more world news in it than personal news, but the older I grow, the more I realize that everybody's news is our news, in fact, our very lives are dependent on the headlines. But the way I love you doesn't, for that goes on and on and on 'till death do us part, and then it couldn't stop either.

Be seeing you, My Darling,

Always your own,   Yedna

The message on each of the pages of the following letter was written in the shape of a large V, commemorating the long-awaited end of the war in Europe.

New York, May 8, 1945

V-E Day at Last, My Darling, My Own Dearest Beloved:

At this moment, Beck and I are sitting in Central Park. There is an Army Band playing "My Hero," and the reason as you must have guessed, My Darling, is that we find ourselves at the great celebration that the little stink weed planned for months. [Fiorello La Guardia, the mayor of New York City, was nicknamed "The Little Flower." This was Edna and John's name for Mayor La Guardia.] We arrived at dusk for, of course, work has never halted while the menace of Japan is still there, to the tune of "Air on a G String," which Adolph Busch and Rudolph Serkin were playing. The park looks beautiful with all the trees and grass in their most beautiful shade of green, and especially with wafts of lilacs coming forth into your nostrils occasionally. Now, my Darling, there's a thrilling young voice singing "Rodger Young" [a World War II folk ballad about a hero] and now a Presbyterian minister saying a prayer (ministers of many different religions spoke before he came and there are still many to follow) and following him, a WAVE choir. During the singing, my Darling, there were birds twitting in the trees just above and I'll be darned if I didn't feel the warmth of your hands within mine.

And now, my Darling, you are very close, for Mischa Elman is playing Schubert's "Ave Maria," and so the birds are singing again! Yop, my Dearest, this is the day of celebration you helped to bring about. Now, my Darling, the beautiful voice of Dorothy Kirstin singing a prayer, and now Frank Kingdon talking.

In the darkened sky above there have appeared enormously long flood light rays, my darling, which were used in former days for practicing to find enemy planes, and now they are joined into a huge V.

Now, Darling, "Marche Militaire," . . . Darling, a WAVE chorus is singing "Bless This House!" and I know as I listen that the house they sing of is our house too.

Now, Dearest, the Russians are here! for there is a piano duet of the Coronation Scene from Boris Godounoff. But, now make way for the little stink weed, himself. Now, my Darling, sit very close to me for Nathan Milstein is playing "Polonaise." (Darling, he can fiddle around me anytime!) Vladimir Horowitz is here too, and he is playing his own interpretation of "Stars and Stripes Forever."

My Own Beloved. It's the day after the night before now, still another day to reassure me that the German surrender has really happened, and oh, my Darling, if you were only here to accept this passionate kiss upon your lips which has been reaching out for you for so long.

Soon after I stopped writing yesterday, My Darling, we left the park and it has been a thrilling sight to see New York ablaze with lights once again, especially the lights in the huge apartment houses which shone through the trees like precious stones while the strains of "United Nations on the March" reached us. . . .

My Darling, I love you with all my being and whether these celebrated days mean that I'll see you in a few weeks, months, or years, you will find when you do come home, that this is the woman who will love you all her life.

Your own,   Yedna

New York, June 28, 1945

Love of My Heart—

'Tis a beautiful day and all the aches and pains of yesterday are gone except for this yearning for you within me. . . .

Last night, Dearest, was another meeting of WIVES and I'm gladder than ever that I am one of them. It was mainly an educational meeting with discussion and quiz about minority groups. I didn't make out any too well on this quiz, but thusly had a chance to learn many facts I didn't know before. I'll try, my Darling, to get a copy of it for you. . . .

Mr. Unger has just come in Dearest, to tell me that the missing lumber has just appeared—which means we'll make our quota of production for this month. Yippee! I love you very, very much.

Your own alone,   Yedna

New York, Aug. 9, 1945

Me Love:

Can you feel the brilliant sunshine on this page? And the peace? And hear the splashings of the summer? And the laughter of the children? And the hardness of this seat in this anchored row boat? And see the trees and the clouds reflected in this lake of fresh water? And see the goldenrods, and the lovely bushes and trees all along the edge of the water? . . .

For the events of these last four days give great reason for . . . optimism what with the atomic bombs and the announcement of Russia's declaration of war on Japan. As far as the atomic bomb is concerned, my Darling, I can see where the end of fighting for us might be sooner, but it's a great sacrifice, my Darling, for this really seems to be, the beginning of the end of all civilization. My darling, I need you much more to tune me in than I need for any radio, and I always will. . . .

Yannie, I love thee, and always will.

Your Bee,   Edna

John returned to the United States in late November 1945. Following his discharge from the Army, the couple settled in the Bronx. Edna worked as a school aide and John returned to his prewar position with the Muzak Corporation. They had three children. They retired in the 1980s, still live in the Bronx, and enjoy traveling and visiting with their six grandchildren.

Vernon Lange, a Minnesota farm boy, was drafted in November 1940. In March 1941, while he was stationed at Jefferson Barracks, Missouri, he met Catherine Cole of St. Louis. They fell in love and became engaged. In May 1942, Catherine and Vernon were married. The following March, Vernon was sent to Panama and then to the Galapagos Islands, where he served as a pilot of B-24 and B-25 bombers. While Vernon was overseas, Catherine lived with her parents in St. Louis.

The couple wrote to each other every day that he was overseas. Her letters, usually six to eight pages in length, were written at about the same time every night. Vernon has since described his wife's letters as "glorious messages of love and caring. . . . They made it possible for me to retain my sanity in an insane world."

The following letter was written shortly before Vernon went overseas. Catherine had just returned from a visit with Vernon in Tucson, Arizona. She was pregnant with their first child.

St. Louis, March 14, 1943

Sweetheart:

I couldn't leave on that early train Friday, so had to wait several hours and saw a bit of the city. . . .

I'm thankful a thousand times over that we had a chance to see each other again for now, I too, feel so much better about your leaving. . . .

On the train coming home I met a young girl with a baby just six months old and she was going up to Washington. The baby was darling and I held her while her mother was busy fixing her clothes. As I held her, I thought— it won't be long now, and we'll be having one of our own or maybe two. . . .

All my love,   Kay

St. Louis, March 28, 1943

Hello, Darling,

. . . Honey, how I wish that you have reached your destination but I suppose those convoys move so slowly. I pray too, that you haven't spent much time "leaning over the rail," as they say.

Since I've been home I haven't been a bit nauseated and Mom says that I'm really lucky for some girls are miserable for quite some time. Today I wore a two-way-stretch [girdle] to church and thought I'd expire before getting home so suppose I'll have to buy a larger one. . . .

Goodnight my darling. I'll never stop loving you.   Kay

St. Louis, April 17, 1943

Dearest Vernon:

. . . St. Louis was the first major city in the U.S. to go over the top in the bond drive. It's quite an honor but everyone has been working hard to keep that record from the First World War.

Baseball has started again—another sign of spring. I don't imagine they'll have the crowds they did for most everyone is doing something in the War effort. . . .

Mom says she has been thinking about you but until the housecleaning is over she can't think of hardly anything else.

Bye now,

Love,   Kay

St. Louis, June 14, 1943

Dearest Vernon:

. . . I asked the doctor enough questions today. He weighed me and I've gained eight pounds since leaving Tucson so that's about what it should be, measured me and was trying to listen to the heart beat and find how the baby was placed. He said it was a little early to hear the heart beat, but it moved around for him.

Surely, I know you could feel it honey. You'd probably feel just about as amazed as I do each time it happens and sometimes it makes me smile thinking about it. I know you'd be gentle and careful but my tummy is so firm I don't think anything would hurt it very much. . . .

You just come home and try taking me in your arms and kissing me. No matter where it was I surely wouldn't mind but I'd probably just about hug and kiss you until you were weak—Would it be too undignified, Lt.? When we really did some loving *you* were the one who always got tired faster. That's what I like about writing. I can say something and you can't answer me on it—and besides you did get tired first—you sissy! . . .

I feel so perky. I could give you at least a dozen of those naughty but nice kisses—but that's for later this evening, dearest hubby. Bye now.

I love you,   Kay

St. Louis, Aug. 18, 1943

Honey, honey:

. . . Vernon, I'll try not to grow up the way you mean but somehow everything seems so much more serious than it used to. We did have fun acting like kids at times and we will again, too!

You know, I was just thinking that when a boy baby is born in a hospital now it is circumcised. I'll have to ask the doctor about it. Honey, I think it would be a good idea anyway, there wouldn't be any harm done, and it's a lot less painful if done at birth than some time later. None of the boys in our family had it done, however. Is it okay, then, to do it?

Night, honey and pleasant dreams!

Catherine

St. Louis, Aug. 19, 1943

Hello, Darling!

We've been canning tomatoes almost all day and it's a long job. Alice was down and Mom was showing how to do it. All I did was skin tomatoes— and more tomatoes! It's a good thing to can though for if you get them in the stores by the can you have to use so many ration points. . . .

Bye now and I'll talk to you again tomorrow, Sweetheart.

Love to the dearest husband in the world.   Kay

St. Louis, Sept. 11, 1943

Dearest Vernon:

. . . Honey, I spent most of the afternoon in the basement looking thru some things and finally finished. I was reading some of your letters from two years ago. . . . In a way that seems so long ago, doesn't it? In one letter you said your folks thought us foolish to marry then. I've often wondered what they did think when we married anyway. My folks didn't think it such a good idea, either, but Vernon, not one time have I regretted marrying when we did and often think how lucky we were to have had as much time together as we did. . . .

Night, Vernon

Love, Kay

The couple's first child, Patricia Ann Lange, was born on September 19, 1943.

St. Louis, Sept. 20, 1943

Sweetheart:

This is rather hard to do—writing while flat on my back and I still feel rather weak so don't know how far I'll get.

I saw Patricia for the first time a few hours ago and honey, she's the sweetest, dearest, most precious, little baby you ever saw. She's not very big for us—do you think but she's formed so nicely and her head and face is as round as can be. Her hair now is as black as anything and her eyes are deep blue like yours. Let's see—her hair isn't curly but might be later and she has so much of it for a new baby. Gosh, dearest, I wish you could see her. . . .

I started labor at nine Sat. night and Patricia wasn't born 'till Sunday at 5:20 in the evening. By that time I was so worn out, I didn't care what happened. The lady in the room with me said when they brought me in, I was crying and kept saying, "Vernon, it's a girl," and sounded so unhappy, but I don't remember it and I am so thrilled with her. . . . Well, now I know it's a very, very, different experience from anything I've ever had but honey, when I saw her this morning, I could hardly believe she was here and was yours and mine. It's hard to think that in nine months such a perfect thing could be formed. . . .

Love from Kay and your dear little daughter, Patricia.

Vernon was able to come on home on leave in December 1943 and see his infant daughter for the first time.

St. Louis, June 6, 1944

Darling:

Since we've heard that the Allies have started invading the continent, I can't think of anything but those poor fellows. All day long there have been prayers, dispatches and interviews—some even of fellows on the boats waiting to land. Honey, it's a sad, sad thing and we can only hope that it will end soon. One commentator said, "You can't tell the families of the men not to worry, but you can tell them their boys have the best of equipment in the world" and then went on to say or rather name the weapons. There's really nothing to say that counts now for it's much, much too big for mere words. . . .

Sweetheart, I just can't seem to think straight enough to write tonight. If you were here I could really cry on your shoulder tonight—would you mind? I remember one night in Tucson after we had gone to bed, I felt that way and you thought you had done something to hurt me! Was that years ago? It must be! . . .

I'd like to fall asleep and dream of you, my sweetheart—Will you be there tonight? I'll be waiting—always. I love you, Vernon—so much.   Kay
Night Daddy! Here's a great big hug and a kiss from your little girl.   Patricia

                                                    St. Louis, April 25, 1945
Dearest:
    . . . Vernon, I so hope you're wrong about the War ending in 1947. I feel differently about it and build up hope—even though it might prove false hope. They tell us that the Japanese Air Force is nothing comparable to ours and the places of building planes are surely being put out of production by many bombings.

The Frisco conference opening was broadcast at 6:30 p.m. and it was very unimpressive. I believe if Stalin gets what he wants he'll help in the Jap[anese] War and if he doesn't—well, he'll just forget to remember there is one. . . .

    'night and pleasant dreams to our Daddy.
    Our love Always,   Kay and Patricia

                                                    St. Louis, May 7, 1945
Honey:
    . . . The A.P. "scooped" the big three with their early report on the unconditional surrender of Germany. We are told an official announcement will be made at eight tomorrow morning (Our Anniversary too!).

I heard an early broadcast from Times Square and Vernon, people sounded like they were mad. While I think we should thank God that the European war is over, I can't see any excuse for these wild demonstrations—but then I can't go for that sort of thing for any cause.

We hear of the German atrocities and yet people condemn the treatment of Mussolini. True, the Partisans hated him but so did the Germans hate some of their victims. . . .

    I Love You,   Kay

After the war, Vernon remained in the Air Force, retiring in 1960. Following his retirement, he worked for the federal government for thirteen years. He was next employed as a charter bus driver. He retired from this position in 1986. Catherine is very active in church work and has been employed as a receptionist in an insurance firm. The couple has six children and eight grandchildren. Vernon has written a three-volume memoir in which some of his and his wife's World War II letters are excerpted. They have lived in Tacoma, Washington, for the last thirty years.

——————————— ✒ ———————————

Ethel Gardiner and Herbert "Buddy" Wiggins were sweethearts while students at Auburn University. They graduated in 1941. While a student at Auburn, Herbert received military training in ROTC. On July 25, 1941, he entered the service. Three days later, he and Ethel were married in Florence, Alabama. The newlyweds had a one-night honeymoon before Herbert reported to duty at Camp Forrest, Tennessee. For the next year, Ethel followed her husband to his various postings. Late in 1942, he was sent to England. By that time, a son, "Herbie," had been born. Ethel returned to her home town of Florence to live with her parents while her husband was overseas. During the war, she taught in a local elementary school while her mother cared for Herbie. Lieutenant Wiggins participated in the landings in North Africa in December 1942 and in Sicily in August 1943. He was promoted to captain after the Sicily landing. Herbert went ashore on D-Day with the 1st Signal Company of the 1st Infantry Division.

Ethel's letters are filled with her pride in her husband's accomplishments, but underlying this pride is her fear that he might not survive. The letters included here are ones that were written while Herbert was in the midst of heavy combat. Ethel often noted, when writing to "Buddy," that their young son was a source of comfort to her during these agonizing months.

Florence, July 14, 1944

Buddy Darling:

. . . I was really awfully pleased over it [the purchase of a new dress] until I came home and read that the Germans were using robot bombs against the Americans in Normandy. That makes clothes seem unimportant. Daddy said that they were not as dangerous as a lot of other things you've had to face, but I just can't help from being worried about it. Sweet, do everything you can to protect yourself, and pray that you will be all right.

Mother just bathed Herbie so we can go mail this. I bathed him after four o'clock, but fifteen minutes later he was filthy. You've never seen anything like it. Anyway, he came in and told me that he was real clean (Mother told him to come tell me). I told him he was mighty sweet and he repeated it in such a satisfied way. . . .

Darling, you must be either thinking about or dreaming about me. Suddenly I felt so close to you that it is almost as though you were talking to me.

I love you, Ethel

Florence, July 19, 1944

Buddy Darling:

I got my flag today, sweet. I'm so glad you sent it to me. I wouldn't take anything for it. If you can, please tell me how you got it, sweet. And please tell me more about the Silver Star if you can. I want to know, precious.

. . . Buddy, I'm so proud of you, precious, and I love you so terribly much. You are the most wonderful husband in the world, and I'm so thankful for you.

I love you.

Ethel

Florence, Aug. 16, 1944

Buddy Darling:

. . . Herbie is just begging to "Write Daddy, Momma"; so I guess I'll let him scribble a little.

He has learned to say "Daddy's in France." He's talking so much. Today he pointed to the places that the lightning burnt the bark off our big tree and said, "Lightning struck the tree up there." We weren't even talking about it. He really is a smart little angel. . . .

I love you, darling.   Ethel

Florence, Aug. 16, 1944
[second letter of the day]

Buddy Darling:

I do hope that I will get a letter from you in the morning. I know that if I don't I'll be so cross all day that nobody can get along with me. I'm supposed to start menstruating Monday or Tuesday, and you know how I feel for several days before that. Mother says I am so mean that nobody can live with me when I don't hear anyway. It's not quite that bad, though. But, of course, I worry more when I don't hear.

Buddy, I don't see how they are going to close that trap without shooting each other. The Allies, I mean. Somehow, I feel almost as tense over this as I did over the first days of the invasion. I guess one reason is that for about the first time since you've been gone, it looks as though the war might end in a few months, and, of course, the closer it is to the end, the greater the suspense. Darling, pray that you will be all right all the way through and that you can come home to Herbie and me soon. I love you so terribly much.

Herbert is sitting up playing with a war map I got. He won't go to sleep. I don't care if he tears the map up, though, because it isn't any good. He just reached over and said, "Hold My Hand." He is the sweetest little angel in the world.

Buddy, I'm so lonesome for you tonight, darling. It would be the most wonderful thing in the world if I had you here by me. I'd be so happy. Darling, they've just got to let you come home to me soon. Pray that you will be all right all through it, precious, and that you can come home soon. You are the sweetest, most wonderful husband in the world, and I'm so proud of you.

I love you, darling.   Ethel

Florence, Aug. 19, 1944

Darling:

This is my third letter to you today, though it will be tomorrow before it is finished (it's almost twelve o'clock.). But I'll sleep better if I write you tonight—I was so worried about not hearing from you that I didn't go to sleep until after three o'clock. And then I had nightmares all night. But one reason for that is that I'm suppose to start menstruating in a day or two, and it has made me so jittery this time. You know how it has always affected me. And then it's just this strain of waiting. Precious, we are both so tense now that we could fly off the handle over nothing, so let's be careful. I love you so awfully much. Sweet, I hope that you'll get the second little note that I mailed at the same time as the long letter. That long letter was just "letting go," and, if it doesn't upset you when you get it, I'll feel better for having gotten it said and over with.

. . . Buddy, if you get back to England, please try to stay away from the areas those robot bombs hit, though I guess that if you come home, the war will be over or at least, they will have captured the place they launch the bombs from. Buddy, take better care of yourself than ever, precious. You just must. I guess the suspense and strain are worse for both of us now than they have been at all, but if you just can get through it safely, we'll be so happy. I love you. . . .

I love you.   Ethel

Florence, Aug. 28, 1944

Buddy Darling:

. . . Buddy, if you get a chance to come home, don't you volunteer to stay over and don't volunteer to do a lot of dangerous stuff you don't have to do. A boy in the Air Corps who married a Florence girl had finished his missions and had told his wife to go to New York to meet him, and she left for N.Y. He volunteered an extra mission and was killed.

Really, Buddy, please don't do anything that you don't have to do. You've done more than your share as it is, darling. That may sound unpatriotic, but I don't have so much patriotism left anyway. Precious, I'm just sitting holding my breath until you get home, so *please* take better care of yourself than ever and pray that you can come home to me. . . .

I love you, Darling,   Ethel

Florence, Oct. 28, 1944

Darling:

. . . you know I have faith in you. I always have and always will. And, as I wrote you in the other letter, if you want to dig ditches when you come home, that's what I want you to do. I hope you will keep studying and working with electricity, too. You are so smart in that. But, I want you to do what you want to do. . . . All I'm worried about is you back here. . . .

Buddy, you don't have to worry about my not letting you kiss me when you come home. I don't believe you can ever kiss me enough to make up for all the time we've been apart. I love you so terribly much, precious, and I'm so proud of you. . . .

I love you, darling,   Ethel

Florence, Oct. 30, 1944

Darling:

. . . Buddy, from two or three things your mother said, I know she is expecting us to stay with her all of your leave when you do get it. In fact, she told somebody the other day that we would. I didn't say anything then, but she can consider herself lucky if she has you for even a week. And she said if she heard you were on the way home, she'd fly up here to be with you when you get leave. She needn't, darling, because I've had to get along without you so long that when I do get to be with you, I'm going to be completely selfish and Herbie and I are going to have you to ourselves for at least two weeks. I know she doesn't think I'm such a good daughter-in-law, but she doesn't like Edith [another daughter-in-law] either. But we are just going to be with ourselves and Herbie and do just what we want to when you do come home, aren't we precious? I know I'll act lots sillier over you than I did when we were first married, but I love you even more now. You are so sweet and precious and I miss you so much, Buddy. . . .

I love you,   Darling

Herbert returned home in the autumn of 1945 and was discharged in January 1946. After the war, he went to work for the Tennessee Valley Authority as an engineer. When the Korean War broke out, he was called back into service. Ethel gave up teaching to become a full-time homemaker. The couple had two more children. Since the early 1960s, Herbert has worked in the Huntsville, Alabama, area in the aerospace industry. Ethel died in 1987. Recently, Herbert completed a personal memoir of his military career, *Signal Memories.* He lives in Decatur, Alabama.

———————————— ✿ ————————————

Catherine "Renee" Young was born in Scotland in 1922. When she was four years old, she and her parents immigrated to the United States and settled in the small town of Esmond, Rhode Island. Catherine and her future husband, George Pike, were childhood friends and high school sweethearts. They were married on November 15, 1941, three weeks before Pearl Harbor.

The following August, George was drafted and ordered to Camp Wheeler, Georgia, for basic training. In December 1942, he was sent to Officer Candidate School in Ft. Benning, Georgia. Catherine, who was pregnant and expecting a baby in March, lived with her parents and younger brother and sister during the seven months that her husband was stationed in Georgia.

The young couple wrote to each other almost every day. Occasionally, they supplemented their letters with telephone calls. In her first letters to her husband, Catherine often commented on her work at the Worcester Textile Co. in North Providence, Rhode Island, where she inspected olive drab material that was used to make Army shirts. After she gave up her job in October, she devoted considerable attention to telling George about the progress of her pregnancy.

Esmond, Sept. 11, 1942

My darling Husband,

. . . They asked me to work till 3:30 today but I said "no." What the heck we have to work all day tomorrow (that's Saturday). I guess the whole mill will work to make up for Labor Day. Boy are they wise. They don't fool me one bit. They would have had to pay us time and a half for Labor Day but instead we work all day Saturday and that will just make up our 40 hours with no time and a half. . . .

I was figuring that if I get some more bonds from the mill I won't have to worry about income tax. I'll just cash in all my bonds. Although I'd rather be buying more. . . .

Well, it's all round the room that I'm going to have a baby. . . . I'm going to keep mum and try to keep them guessing. . . .

I love you—I love you—I love you.

Your wife,   Renee

Esmond, Oct. 28, 1942

My Darling,

. . . We were going to take pictures last Sunday but it was a dull day so I hope it is nice this weekend then we can take some. But listen, George— I'm sending these pictures so *you* can see how much fatter I've gotten and if I've changed, etc. Now, don't go showing the ones with me on them around your barracks cause they'll think I'm naturally fat. Promise? . . .

Well, I went to Dr. Allen for another check-up yesterday. When I was first pregnant I weighed 138 pounds on his scale. Now I weigh 142 pounds. I said to him, "Gee, I've only gained 4 pounds," and he said he was glad. So I guess it's good to just gain a little. . . .

Boy, if you were home now we'd have lots of fun. I wouldn't be working and I could do *all* the housework myself. And I'd feel more like cooking nice things for you cause I wouldn't be tired from working. Everything would be so cozy. . . .

I love you, George, with all my heart and soul and every bit of me. Boy, wait till I see you again!

Your loving wife,   Renee

Esmond, Jan. 13, 1943

My Darling,

. . . Your mother came up yesterday but I had gone out to the doctor's with my mother. She brought me up her cotton robe with the flowers on it because I haven't one to fit me now and she also brought me up a dress that she used to wear when she was stocky. I called her up to thank her last night and she told me when I write to you today to tell you that we'd call you this coming Sunday. I only hope that this letter reaches you in time. We'll call you at the U.S.O. We'll put the call thru as soon as I get to your mother's. I figure I'll get there just after 12 noon. So you won't have to be at the U.S.O. until noontime. As I sit here writing to you, I just thought to myself, "Who the heck will we ask for? I guess we'd better ask for Officer Candidate George Pike." I know that once before you told me in a letter that when your call went thru they call out "Corporal Pike." Gee, I wish now that I had asked you what we should call you. I want to call you the right name cause I know that they'll yell it out and I wouldn't want you to feel embarrassed or anything. . . .

I told your mother that you wanted some more woolen socks and she's going to start right away knitting some more. I was going to knit you some but now that it's getting nearer March I'm quite busy. You see, I've got quite a drawer full of baby stuff and I've got to wash every bit of it before I can put it on the baby. I also have to use all my spare money now and go downtown and buy a lot more baby stuff. Then I've got to wash and fix the bassinet and carriage. The back legs on the bassinet keep collapsing and I'd hate to put the baby in it and have it collapse. My father said he'd fix everything for me but I don't like to have people doing things for me so I'm going to do that myself. The hood on the carriage is pretty well all shot. I wish I could buy one in a second-hand store someplace. Well, we'll see.—About the socks again—I figure the way you talk that you need some right away. Well, I've noticed in passing the Victory Knitting Mills on Union St. that they have hand-knit woolen socks for soldiers. So I'll go in the next time I'm downtown and look them over and get you one or two pair (It all depends on the price, whether you get one or two.) . . .

You were saying in your letter that you'll have a lot of stuff to talk about when you get home. I'll bet you will and I guess there's a lot of stuff about being pregnant, etc. that I'll be able to tell you that I can't explain in letters. Gee, I like to think about things like that—about you coming home and talking to you and loving you, and kissing you, and just the wonderful thrill of looking into your eyes.

Yours forever,   Renee

Esmond, Feb. 3, 1943

My darling Husband,

Last night I had a whole mix-up of dreams. But one thing I dreamed was that I was eating banana splits one right after the other and were they good! When I awakened I thought to myself, "Boy, what I wouldn't give for a nice banana." But that is just wishful thinking. I don't think anyone in America has seen a banana for over six months.

Well, George, the civilian population is certainly feeling the shortage of food-stuffs now. Last week we didn't have a scratch of butter in the house from Monday until Friday—and how I hate dry bread! It's a lot worse on we people in the country than it is on the city folks. They can go out and get some kind of meat every day while we have plenty of meatless days up here. They can also stand in line for 2 or 3 hours for a pound of butter, but up here there are no lines as there is no butter and when there is a little butter everyone gets a ¼ of a pound. So you can imagine how far a ¼ of a pound goes in this family of five adults. And that's supposed to last us for a week.

Yesterday I didn't take any meat not because we didn't have any but because I'm sick of the same thing. You see, the thing that they have the most of is sausages but people can't keep eating the same thing every day.

Everyone wonders why there is so much sickness and colds this winter. Well, they might not know but I certainly do—it's because they can't get the proper foods and we hardly ever see good steak anymore. And steak is the main meat that gives us strength. My Dad just came back from the store and all he could get was blood pudding and how I hate that. . . .

I received a swell letter from you yesterday. Gee, it seems that all the letters I've got from you recently have been the nicest letters. . . . I love you, George, more than anything in the whole, wide world.

Yours forever, Renee

Esmond, March 4, 1943

My Darling.

I've just been thinking that you'll miss getting my letters when I go the hospital, won't you? . . .

I'm beginning to get weary now and nervous. I want to go and get it over with. You see, Darling, I've gained 25 pounds since I first started and at the end like this you get sort of miserable. Last night after I got to bed I had what is known as "false labor." I had quite bad pains in my stomach but I didn't tell anyone and I dropped off to sleep after awhile. But it makes you think that your time has come, believe me. . . .

Honey, whether I've had the baby or whether I haven't why don't you ask for a furlough when you're through with your schooling. Of course you know better than me if you should but let me know what you think about it. O.K.?

I want to see you so much, Honey, and I miss you something awful, especially lately. I love you with all my heart and soul and body.

Yours forever, Renee

After receiving his commission as a second lieutenant in March 1943, George returned to Rhode Island on a short furlough. He arrived on March 25, the day before his son, "Georgie," was born.

Lt. Pike's next assignment was Camp Blanding, Florida. Catherine and Georgie remained in Rhode Island. Almost immediately, the new parents began to discuss the possibility of Catherine and Georgie moving to Florida. Catherine's letters to George describe the joys and frustrations of being a new mother, her concerns about traveling with a baby, and her desire to be with her husband.

Esmond, April 21, 1943

My Darling,

Just as I start to write this short letter to you your son lets out a squawk. He wants to be fed. Well, I'll write as much as I can until he really becomes violent and then I'll have to attend to him for an hour or so before I'll be able to finish this. . . .

Both your mother and my mother think it's what I should do—go to you. The thing is though, they were discussing just what was on my mind—how hard it would be to travel with a baby and I certainly couldn't go alone with him. . . . Another thing, I'll have to find a good reliable baby doctor in Florida. Because babies have to have injections about every month for different diseases, you know. Gee, I sure wish I were there and settled with you. . . .

I miss you an awful lot today, George. Even though Georgie keeps me busy and takes my mind off you sometimes, still I miss you just as much if not more than ever. I love you, sweetheart and I'm longing and needing and wanting you so much.

Eternally yours,   Renee

Esmond, May 3, 1943

Dearest George,

. . . Here's something that I was going to tell you over the phone if you called but in case you don't call I'd better tell you now. I know that it is going to be awfully hard for you to find a place for me and that you might have to take a place that isn't exactly what you want. Well, Honey, that's O.K. but here's something to remember. There are two conveniences I've got to have—1. I've got to make a formula every day which requires some place to heat it. 2. I've got to wash at least every other day for the baby which will require hot water and a place to hang it. It isn't so easy with a baby, you know. . . .

I lay awake for quite awhile last night thinking about our first kiss and all the other events that led up to our marriage, baby, etc. I sure like to reminisce like that. I love you my Darling.

Your loving, adoring wife,   Renee

Esmond, May 11, 1943

My Darling,

I'll start this letter now and I guess I'll finish it later this afternoon.

The first thing I want to tell you is that I just called for plane reservations. However, I have to wait until she calls me back to find out if New York will verify my reservation. I made it so that I leave New York at 8:25 and arrive in Jacksonville at 3:55 on Saturday, May 29th. So I hope you'll be able to meet me. I won't mail this letter until tonight and then I'll know if New York verified it. I asked if the plane ride would affect the baby and she said no. Also, I'm allowed 40 pounds of luggage so I guess I'll be able to take some of my own clothes all right. You had me scared when you said to take just one little suitcase.—I just got my call now; the reservation went through. O.K. So now everything is up to you. I'm depending on you to have a place for us to live and gee, if something turns up that you can't meet us I don't know what I'll do cause I won't know where to go. . . .

I love you Sweetheart and oh boy, I'm all excited about seeing you again.

Yours forever, Renee

Catherine and Georgie flew to Florida in late May as planned. It was Catherine's first plane ride. The Pikes lived in Florida until August 1943 when George was transferred to Camp Joseph T. Robinson near Little Rock, Arkansas. Catherine and the baby went with him. In March 1944, Lt. Pike received his orders for combat and was sent to Ft. Meade, Maryland. Catherine and Georgie returned to Rhode Island to live with her parents.

In April 1944, shortly before George was shipped overseas, Catherine, along with two other war wives, made an impromptu trip to Ft. Meade. The three war wives sneaked into the fort one evening and spent six precious, but unauthorized, hours with their husbands.

George was first sent to England where he received final preparations for the D-Day Invasion of June 6, 1944. He went ashore in Normandy only a few days after D-Day. In August, while fighting in the hedgerows of France, he was wounded and sent to a military hospital in England to recuperate. He returned to the battlefront in the late fall of 1944—just in time for the Battle of the Bulge. As a member of the 2nd Infantry Division, the spearhead for the First Army, he was involved in some of the fiercest fighting in the European Theatre of Operations.

During the fourteen months that George was in Europe, he managed to save many of the letters which his wife wrote to him by filling up empty K-ration boxes with her letters and then shipping them back to her. The hundreds of letters which Catherine wrote provide an important chronicle of the stresses and strains faced by many young war brides throughout the United States during the Second World War.

Esmond, June 6, 1944

My Darling,

. . . 6:45 a.m. The phone just rang about ten minutes ago. It was your mother. She told me that the Invasion had started. I just put on the radio and this time it's real. I don't quite know what to say, Sweetheart. It goes without saying that I feel very nervous and very afraid. I do feel though, that you weren't in this first wave. I hope and pray, Darling, that if I am right you will never have to go in. I suppose I want too much. The reason that I hope and pray and feel that you might not have been in the actual invasion is because I don't think that you've had any command training. Of course, not knowing what you've been doing over there, I may be wrong.

As I listen to the radio here I can't understand why the Germans haven't given more opposition. Either they're pretty weak or they have something up their sleeve.

Well, Darling, for all I know you may be in combat when you receive this. I pray not. But if you are, please be careful and try and take care of yourself as well as is possible in battle.

Georgie just woke up so I'll have to go get him.

I love you, Sweetheart, and I'll always love you. I miss you terribly and I'll pray for you night and day. Georgie is saying, "Da-da" as loud as he can. Come back to us, Darling.

Yours now and forever,   Renee

Esmond, June 9, 1944

My Dearest,

It is a beautiful day here today. It's not too warm and not too cool. I just got through hanging out the baby's washing and as I stand in the yard looking up at the sky in the distant horizon I wondered where my Darling was and if he was all right. Three big four-motored bombers roared over about then. But you'd never know to look at this quiet calm little village that there was a terrible bloody conflict going on over there. You'd never know to look at this little village that there was a sad, heavy-hearted girl living in it, namely me.

I received two letters from you last night, Honey. They were written on Friday and Saturday, the 19th and 20th of May. I'd be very happy about it if the invasion hadn't started. I'm happy about it anyway, of course, but I wish the letter written on or before June 6th would hurry and come through. . . .

I want to keep on loving you forever as I do now, with all my heart, my soul, my mind, my body, and my strength. You're so very, very close to me today, Darling, I wonder why?

Yours now and always,   Renee

P.S. Kisses and love from Georgie and me.

Esmond, Aug. 24, 1944

My Dearest,

. . . I guess when I received the letter from you last night I nearly went hysterical for a minute. I felt so terrible to think that you had been hurt and even as I read your letter I was thanking God that that was all that was the matter, bad as it is.

After I had read your letter over about three times, I called your folks and told them to come up. George, I hate to cry in front of anyone so through will-power I kept myself composed while they were here. But I didn't go to bed until 2:30 and I didn't sleep until about 4:30. I wanted to write to you but I didn't know what to say. My thoughts were all jumbled. . . .

Well Sweetheart, I'll write again this afternoon or tonight as the mail from Esmond goes out in half an hour and I want this to go as soon as possible.

I hope your leg takes long enough to heal so that Germany will be finished. Don't be like you always are and pretend you can walk on it and sit on it before you really can. Please don't Darling. . . .

So until this afternoon God bless you and keep you and speed your safe return to me.

Yours forever and always,   Renee

Esmond, Nov. 25, 1944

My Darling,

It is very cold here today and a thin blanket of snow covers the ground.

As I hung out Georgie's wash this a.m. my hands became so cold that I could hardly move them. It made me think about you. Gosh, Honey, how can you shoot when your hands are stiff? I wonder if you'd like me to send you a couple of pairs of gloves? You could wear them when you're not shooting maybe. I don't want to send anything that's foolish, you understand. . . .

Well, Darling, no mail, no lovin', no kissin', no nothin'—so I guess I'll close for today. . . .

Yours for always,   Renee

Esmond, Jan. 10 [?], 1945

My Dearest,

My thoughts tonight are far-reaching. I know my thoughts of you are very tender ones. Perhaps it is the classical music on the radio, or perhaps it's just because it is Saturday night—our night that has prompted me to write tonight (my second letter to you today). Whatever the reason, I know I love you and miss you so terribly tonight. . . .

[My thoughts take] me back to a cold, windy night in Maryland. We were standing together in the darkness beside a building at Ft. Meade. It was almost time to say our last good-bye—almost time. You ran your fingers through my hair and said, "Whenever I feel cold, Honey, I'll think of you and I'll feel warm." I thought of how you hated to be cold, and I thought that soon you'd be leaving me, and I tried so hard not to cry and I said, "Oh no, don't ever be cold George; don't be cold, Honey." You ran your fingers through my hair again, "I'll be cold lots of times, Renee, but I'll just think of you."

I watched you until you were out of sight in the heavy fog that lay over Ft. Meade that night. There were terrible emotions fighting within me. I wanted to run after you; I wanted to call out your name, and I wanted to cry and cry and cry until I couldn't cry anymore.

Later, the cab driver must have sensed my feelings as he drove me to the train station. He said to me, "Is your husband going overseas?" I looked out into that deep, dense fog where you had gone, and I said, "Tonight may be the last time I will see him for a long, long time."

I hope this letter doesn't make you feel "blue," but just once I had to put my true feelings on paper. There will be more "cheery" letters tomorrow.

All my love, all my life—until that day when God brings you home safely to me.   Renee

Esmond, Jan. 31, 1945

My Darling,

I really feel terrible to think that I'm sitting here in a nice warm, cozy house and you're out in that terrible cold fighting. Yes, I know you're fighting, Darling. I figure that you must have gone into action on January 30th before dawn. Your division has been mentioned in the paper as one of them. Your division has also been mentioned on the radio as one of the "crack" divisions. . . . They also told about your unit receiving the Presidential Citation. . . . I know you've asked me time and again to live with you as your letters come and not think where you'll be two weeks hence but I just can't. Frankly, I think the radio tells us too much for our own good. In the last war they didn't know half as much and it's better that way. Why I even know where you are exactly by following the news closely. . . .

This lonesomeness for you just gnaws at my heart continually. Oceans of love, Darling, and a kiss on every wave.

God bless you and keep you and speed your safe return to me.

All my love, all my life,   Cathie

Esmond, March 22, 1945

My Dearest,

Here I am once more and still no mail. It is the start of the fourth week now since your last letter was written. Gosh, I'm so worried. . . . Gee, if I'd only get some mail, Darling, I'd be so relieved. Also I'd stop biting my lips and I could go to a show and enjoy it. I was going to go tonight but I'm afraid to go. I'm afraid to leave the house for even an hour in case a telegram should come. Oh, if only this war would finish! I'm afraid I'm war-weary or have war nerves or something. If I were a soldier they'd say that I had battle fatigue, I guess. . . .

George, you'd be surprised if you knew how much I know about the war, how much reading I do about it, and how well I can talk about it. . . .

Well, I guess my letters won't be so hot until I get some mail, Dear. I find it very hard to write when I'm so worried about you. I pray that you're all right, Darling, and remember that I love you and am waiting for you—God bless you and keep you and speed your safe return to me.

All my love, all my life,   Cathie

Esmond, May 7, 1945

My Darling,

. . . What news greeted us the first thing this morning? That's right—the end of the war. Well, my dearest, my feelings can only be described as mixed emotions. It looks as though you'll get home at least for 30 days. I still hope that you don't have to go to the Pacific. The whistles ought to start to blow soon. . . .

As I sit and write here I'm looking at your "combat picture" taken in Brussels. It's the full length view of you. I'm wondering if maybe soon I'll be able to put my arms around that same you, Darling. I'm even afraid to hope. Gosh, even though this is V-E Day there are so many "ifs" and "buts." This is wonderful *if* he's all right (meaning you, of course). This is wonderful *but* there is still the Pacific *and* will my Darling have to go *and* if so will I see him for 30 days? . . .

God bless you and keep you and speed your safe return to me.

All my love, all my life,   Cathie

George returned to the United States in mid-July on a thirty-day furlough, en route to the Pacific. During this furlough, the atomic bombs were dropped on Hiroshima and Nagasaki and the war was brought to a dramatic conclusion. Lt. Pike was sent to Camp Swift, Texas, where he was discharged from the Army in the fall of 1945.

After the war, Catherine and George Pike settled in Greenville, Rhode Island, where they bought their first house with the help of the G.I. Bill. George became a master baker, and the couple owned and operated a bakery shop for twenty years. They had two more children. They are now retired and spend the winter months in Tarpon Springs, Florida, and the remainder of the year in Johnston, Rhode Island.

Chapter 4

War Wives

HUSBANDS AND FATHERS WERE INITIALLY EXEMPTED FROM MIL-
itary service, but by the end of 1942 even fathers were being drafted. For
couples who had married before 1941, wartime separations could be excru-
ciatingly difficult.

With their husbands away in the service, war wives almost always experienced a reduction in family income. In order to help make ends meet, they
moved in with other war wives, took in boarders, returned to their childhood
homes to live, and sometimes sought war work.

Through their letters, war wives attempted to bring their husbands back
into the family circle by describing the minutiae of daily life on the home
front and reminiscing about the times they had spent together. Of course,
their letters also contained profound declarations of love.

***

Isabel Alden and Maurice A. Kidder met in the early 1930s while students at
the University of New Hampshire in Durham. They fell in love and were
married in 1935, the same year that Maurice graduated from the university.
The couple then moved to Boston where Maurice attended a theological seminary. Their first child, Joel, was born in 1936. After Maurice completed his
seminary training, the family moved to Hanford, California. He served two

rural parishes, and Isabel played the piano for the services. A second child, Phyllis, was born in 1940.

When the war broke out, Maurice entered the Army in the Chaplain's Corps. After he was shipped to England in the fall of 1942, Isabel returned to Durham with the children. While Maurice was overseas, Isabel resumed her studies at the University of New Hampshire. During this period, various friends and relatives also roomed in their rented New Hampshire home.

Isabel's letters were written in serial fashion, almost in diary form. At the top right-hand corner of the letters, she often indicated the number of days that her husband had been absent from the United States. Her letters include an intimate look at the stresses and anxieties brought on by their three-year separation and the devices which she used to weather the wartime years.

Durham, Eighth day—Oct. 12[?], 1942

Darling:

I knew all along that the shocks would come from the little things. I did my errands today, and was just walking home when the game was over, the bell tolling, and New Hampshire had beaten Maine 20-7 and the gay crowds began coming down the streets, flooding the town with that particular quality belonging only to a football afternoon when the leaves are golden underfoot. . . . [I] met a navy man and his girl. They were so happy, and they kept squeezing one another's hands. And a lump as big as a cannon ball came up in my throat, remembering homecoming games last year and how happy we were, and just wishing we were back in school again, anyway, and all was safe. . . .

Isabel

Durham, Twenty-fifth and Twenty-sixth days—Late October 1942

Darling:

When I got on my bicycle this morning and was riding down the Wadbury road, I thought, "Suppose I am riding toward a letter," and the conviction grew on me that I was. And, I was. I couldn't quite believe it, and just stood there with the letter in my hand and the silly tears standing around my eyes. I wasn't then in any hurry to read it. It was an overwhelming enoughness merely to look at your handwriting and realize you *were*, actually somewhere, and once more in communication with me. I'm glad I didn't open it then and there, for that time was the best of all. After I read it, longings and fears and inadequacies returned to me and it was not the same as that preciousness of holding the letter in my hand.

I'm glad it came also because yesterday was such a dull day, and I despaired of having anything worth writing to you about. The hopelessness of sending letter after letter out as I have been doing with no knowledge of its reaching you was beginning to get me down. I still don't know that you are receiving letters, but I feel better that at least you have reached out and touched me. . . .

Loving you always,   Isabel

Durham, Seventy-sixth day—Dec. 18 [?], 1942

Darling:

I've sort of fed up with dragging out the typewriter and I thought I'd treat you to my handwriting again. I went over and over the heading hoping it would go through the carbon but no luck. It looks like a faint scratch.

We are in for another windy night. I'd rather freeze in a still cold than in a howling wind. I really believe the wind is the only thing I mind. I'm really almost afraid of it. It makes you think of how temporary man is, and of all his cowerings in the waste places of earth. . . .

I read a long letter from an interned Japanese girl today. Barbara [a friend] had it. Conditions are not much better than a concentration camp except there is no brutality. But think of the fine and sensitive people that must be suffering mental agony of the deepest kind. There is *no privacy*, the children want to go home, they play games and none of the little boys want to be the "Japs" in the war games. It is pitiful. This girl got a personal letter which some friends brought in to her. It made her radiantly happy and she was walking along reading it when a member of the internal police appeared at her side and read over her shoulder, questioning her about everything in it. . . .

Goodnight, dear.

Durham, 230th day—April 29, 1943

Darling:

Well, back in harness again, after a seven-day lapse except for one V-Mail. But my term paper was due and I worked twenty hours on that, and cleaned the cellar as a start on my spring housecleaning, and got the back yard raked and cleaned up and the garden ready for plowing. . . .

I hardly know where to begin. I guess I will begin with Jane. You know, the girl I had living with me. She was very moody and unhappy all the time, but was buoyed up by the fact that she was to be married as soon as Sonny got his wings. Well, he got them and an instructorship down in Alabama, and she went home perfectly delirious with joy. But his folks felt they were too young . . . and the folks wouldn't hear of it. She kept putting pressure on, and having got her wedding dress made, etc., and finally, last week, three months after he got his job, she left alone on the train for Alabama and the wedding. She hadn't even seen him since last summer. She was due in on Friday or Sat. and at a little after ten o'clock Friday morning he was killed in a plane crash. Of course, they couldn't reach her until she arrived. I am simply sick over it. The poor child. Imagine her arriving all pepped up to actually see him and all. The irony of it is that they didn't get in a smile or a kiss. I think the burdens of this war in terms like that are going to wear down a lot of people. Me for one. How many things like that can people keep locked up in their hearts and not have it change them? . . .

I love you so much and miss you so increasingly that I can hardly bear it. The thought that I might actually see you again sometime seems almost a dream. And I am tired. What women are like who have gone through three years of being apart, I don't know. . . . I don't know but that I dread the summer worse than winter.

You Sweet Thing,   Isabel

Durham, 337th day—Aug. 16, 1943

Sweetheart:

Joel was talking to me before he went to sleep last night and he said, "Do you know I'd like it better if Daddy went to work in the morning and came home every night." And I said I would too, only that thousands of little boys' "Daddies had to be gone at the war," and he said, "And thousands of them will get killed too." That old bugbear never leaves him. I always wish I could reassure him somehow, and whatever I do say seems so inadequate, like, "Well, all we can do is hope for the best," etc. . . .

I don't have much to write about since I didn't hear from you last week. . . . Phyllis keeps asking for another little note. You could tuck one in for each of them every time with small extra trouble. She was thrilled with that tiny one, probably an afterthought on your part, but there you have the heart of a child, happy, anyway, in ignorance. I didn't find it until several days later when you asked in another letter if I had found it. I then went back to the envelope and sure enough, there it was, in the corner. . . .

Isabel

Durham, 403rd day—Oct. 21, 1943

My Own Darling:

Here comes an air mail, my first for a week or so. But I have more to say than I can say on a V-Mail, and here goes. First, I am enclosing the type of article which appears in the papers regarding the chaplain situation. Thought you might like to see it. I am wondering if your division is fully staffed at last. It seems as if it must be if it has gone somewhere. . . . Joel hopes that you are in Africa and that you will write thrilling tales of what you find there. I am afraid, however, that his mind rather turns to lions and tigers than French and Arabs. When we were going downstreet this evening, he said to me out of the darkness, "What do you suppose you would see in a boa constrictor's stomach just before you died?" Answer that, my fine friend. . . .

Maurice, I feel pretty low at times when I consider just how my life is spent. There is no real test of courage or anything else in it, such as you will know, maybe have already known. And how am I going to stack up against the women you will meet who are really doing things is what bothers me. I feel so hopeless, so left out of it. I feel as if maybe I would never know what I could do. And you will never be able to talk to me about so many things. . . . You and I have never had anything big like this which we did not share before. What will it do to us? . . . I think of it almost constantly these days. I am still going on, wearing sweaters and skirts, and going to the hairdresser, and cooking three meals a day and nagging at the children, when most of the women you meet have either been through things or will do so. . . . I wish, if it doesn't ask too much, that you would put what you think and feel as you go along, down on paper for me. Try, even though it is hard for you. Hold me close.

Isabel

Durham, 538th day—March 5, 1944

Darling:

. . . Oh, darling, I've had such a bad time. Imagine what turned up! Your mother sent me a long long clipping from a North Carolina paper, which was an account of a wedding, and I looked it over and thought, what on earth, and then saw it was an English wedding and read it through, to find that you had given the toast. It hit me like a ton of bricks. I feel exactly as they say Mrs. Eisenhower feels on going to the movies and seeing her husband in the news reels. They say she can't go to movies at all hardly, for that is the thing that cuts her up the most. It is the impersonal publicity touch, showing how completely how vast a gulf exists between our lives. And what a full life you lead in which I have no part, and of which I know nothing. . . . Oh, honey, I wish you'd come home—it's only the time of the month I guess. I used to want you quite sharply twice a month, out of habit, I suppose, but now it's only once that it bothers me in an aching way. I couldn't settle to anything yesterday. I wouldn't describe to you in this letter just how it affects me, but you know. I knew exactly how I wanted you, and it hasn't dulled at all, not one physical symptom of it. . . .

Isabel

Durham, 631st day—June 6, 1944

My own Beloved:

So it has come. I can't stop to write much, but I feel released, I can write to you now I feel sure. I haven't written for a week, felt too choked up, too stifled, too tense. But I have thousands of things I could say right now. I am about to take the train for Boston . . . for I simply feel I have to go someplace where I can worship . . . I have planned on doing this for weeks.

We shall be closer than ever, I feel sure. Do not lose courage, and do everything the best possible that you can. I know you will be a tower of strength to your men. I know too that God will be with you, not in the sense of miraculously taking care of your physical body, but taking care of your spirit so that it can withstand whatever comes upon it. If you are not in this initial invasion you will be in one by the time you receive this, I know. And look when you get it I shall be with you, standing upon a mountain top. This, whatever its darknesses, whatever its terrors and hideousnesses, is your mountain top. Nothing can pull you down. This snapshot was taken up on the tipty-top of Prospect Mountain, in back of New Durham, in a high wind, with the world spread out on all sides of us. . . .

I am not alarmed. I am excited. I am relieved with a terrible relief. I am afraid, but I know your fear is infinitely worse than mine. I love you to the

utmost that I am capable of, and our love is of God. Be with God, and you
are with me, as I am with you.

Your own,   Isabel

Isabel wrote the following essay, "Wartime Wife—Another's D-Day," and included it in her June 6, 1944, letter to Maurice.

Dear W.W. "This is it" meant many things to many people. Let me give
you one version of what it means. David has been in England for nearly two
years, preparing, with his men, for the day when the world, including me,
his wife, would say, "This is it" and just as he couldn't have known how he
would act, neither did I. We both depended on the long months of training,
not to let us down, and now I know, they didn't. . . .

Living alone and managing my house with two children, voicing my star-
kest anxieties and cowering fears to no one, coming to the slow conclusion
that no matter what happens it is all right, has taught me poise.

D-Day, no matter what its darkness, or hideousness, is David's mountain-
top, and I sat right down and mailed a snapshot of myself standing on top
of a mountain which I had been saving, for on that day, I reached a peak in
my training also, and wherever he is, we are together.

New Hampshire Captain's Wife

Durham, Oct. 10, 1944

Sweetheart:

The clock is striking nine, and I must up and go to bed as soon as I finish
this. I have had a long day in Boston, and have to be in Chaucer class with
Dr. Richards at nine tomorrow morning. When it came right down to it,
there weren't any courses that came at a time I could take them. I am not
free yet you see, so I am only to take that one, unless by some miracle I
could get a student on Friday afternoons and they would let me take pho-
tography. . . . The life of a housewife is not her own, and there will undoubtedly be some sickness, and I'll have to miss classes etc. With my Sunday School class, and all my chairmanships *(three)* I just don't think I could
swing it. But I could easily finish in one summer school after this one course,
and that might be fun sometime (providing I can ever get to the point where
there isn't a pre-school child in the house). There is no sense in breaking
my neck to finish this year. . . .

Isabel

Durham, Dec. 10, 1944

My Own Darling:

My heart aches for you constantly, and I suppose for myself also. For
you, because you have to be where you are and cannot be with us. And
because things are going on so very badly, and your Christmas will be such
a terrible one. Oh, how I pray that just one of your packages will turn up,

the one that has all the old snapshots of us in it. If you miss all the rest, I do want you to have that. Maurice, I feel increasingly bitter. I know I shouldn't say it, but it is the truth. If you should be killed now, it would be uselessly. I have felt that more and more for a long time now, since the Germans knew the game was up in fact, but now it is especially so. Oh, honey, Monday morning in Chaucer class I got to picturing your back, just after you had taken your shorts off, and I could see those two little dimpled places you have, clear as crystal, and I wanted to sneak up behind you and put both arms around you and press my face against them, and I couldn't pay any attention to Chaucer. . . . Every time my mind slipped away from the subject at hand it went right to your back, and a lump came to my throat, and I had to blink all the time. There have been tears crowding up in me for nearly a week now. . . . I got through the other two Christmases, but I am too tired this time. I am not going to do it up brown this year. I think, what's the use, even the tree isn't much good, but I don't seem to care. . . . I'd lots rather they'd pulled you men out and let you spend a couple of months back somewhere, which in my estimation is what some of your veteran divisions need. The rotation business to me seems a sop to keep you satisfied rather than the rest which they must know you need. There, all that is off my chest. I feel better already. No, I don't, that's a lie. I feel worse every breath I draw. I want to hear your voice, see your eyes looking deeply into mine, feel your hands searching my body, and to be at peace. If you ever get that hour's notice, you come. . . .

   Your dispirited Dimity.

                                                Durham, Dec. 28, 1944
Hello there:
   . . . I find that I am thrilled at some of the visions I have of our life when you get back, but I am in the grip of my old fear of telling you what I would like to for fear I wouldn't live up to it. And then, too, they seem like such trivial things. But some of the things I think about sweep me like a fresh breeze, and seem to cleanse me of a lot of wrong thinking. . . . There is really nothing I need for your return. It is only a question of what I need to *become* inside. I feel like a stranger beholding a great sweeping land of promise. The vision fades, I realize, and I don't stick to it, but I play with it again and again. . . . It seems to me at times that I cannot wait until I have the chance to try myself before myself and before you. . . .

   Your Dimity,   Isabel

The remainder of Isabel's letters have been lost. Maurice and Isabel were reunited in the late summer of 1945. She graduated from the University of New Hampshire in 1946, and Maurice received a master's degree from Yale Divinity School the same year. They had a third child, Alden, in 1947. During the late 1940s and early 1950s, Maurice taught at Ohio Wesleyan University and at the University of North Carolina. Isabel worked at library jobs and operated a typing service. In 1956, the Kidders moved to South Hadley, Massachusetts, where Maurice was called to a small parish. Isabel began graduate work at the University of Massachusetts and received an M.A. degree in poetry in the mid-1960s. Maurice died in 1975. Isabel taught English at Holyoke Community College, retiring in 1986 at the age of 73. She died in 1989. At the time of her death, Isabel had begun work on a memoir, *Days of Absence,* which was to be based on her World War II letters.

Marjorie Reid and Elliott R. Killpack met in the late 1930s while they were students at Utah State University. He entered college after military service and received a degree in Range Management in June 1940. She had returned to college after three years of elementary school teaching in Utah. The couple was married in August 1940.

Elliott enlisted in the Marines in 1942 and attended Officers Candidate School, receiving his commission in April 1943. During her husband's first year in the Marines, Marjorie taught school in Utah. After he received his commission, she joined him in Quantico, Virginia, and, like thousands of other war wives, she began to follow her husband to his various postings, including assignments in North Carolina and California. While they were in Quantico, she worked as a seamstress for a military uniform tailor in Washington, D.C.

After Elliott was shipped to the Pacific theatre of war in January 1944, Marjorie returned to Utah where she secured a job in Ogden with the American Red Cross as a Home Service Worker. She was assigned to act as a liaison for families on the home front and servicemen stationed abroad when problems and emergencies arose. A challenging job, it helped to diminish the anxiety she felt about her husband's dangerous combat situation.

Price, Utah, Jan. 15, 1943

My Dearest:

In a sense this is an eventful day, it was just a month ago today that . . . I had my last night in your arms. This not being able to see you at night and have you cuddle me to sleep is the hardest part of our separation. I love you always and devotedly, dear husband, and will never forget the richness of our life together. . . .

I did not receive a letter from you today, dear, but I've kept my promise to you—and reread your one really lovely letter and find more gleaning bits of love and encouragement to buoy me through the night—so you see, dear, I'm not complaining but loving you always. . . .

I had to work quite late tonite to finish marking [report] cards and it was a pleasure to finish this week. . . .

Goodnite, my dearest. Keep well, work hard and remember I'm proud and love you so very very much each moment of my life.

Yours Always,   Marjorie

Ogden, March 8, 1944

Dearest Husband:

You're famous, not so much in worldly ways, but in a manner most important: famous for your kindness, your love, your wisdom, character and manliness. A thought similar to that was expressed in "Mme Curie" tonite—and stayed with me because it so fit you dear. If you have a chance to see that show, it is really worthwhile—and their life together was so sweet. . . .

Elliott, I've had something happen today, I hope will meet your approval. Margaret Keller told me to call this Mrs. Greenwell of the American Red Cross. They were in need of case workers. I did and am beginning in the morning for a trial period for the balance of this month. It is something that will be completely absorbingly new and that which I've wanted to try for a long time.

She said they were not supposed to take individuals without this training course that is given at Salt Lake but took the matter in her own hand and told me to come tomorrow.

There is a girl getting married on the first of next month and I'll work into her job. They wanted to send a 21 year old girl up from Salt Lake, but Mrs. Greenwell said she couldn't see a young girl inspiring very much confidence.

I have to stand by for night telegrams every other week and have duty every other week end, but both girls who are working there say there's constantly something interesting happening—and it's absorbing.

Elliott, I have tried my best to make good decisions. This is not certain I'll stay with the Red Cross but at any time it would be a good recommendation for other work. Hope you'll think it's okay—if you don't want me to, let me know as soon as possible. Your approval is necessary to my happiness and peace of mind. She said my personality was the kind that would take—and well—I'd like to try it. . . .

My greatest wish now is to hear you've received word from home. It just breaks my heart to think my letters haven't been getting through to you.

Goodnite dear one, heaven's blessings on you.

Yours Devotedly,   Marjorie

Ogden, April 7, 1944

Dearest Elliott:

One year ago today I was so desperately proud of a very grand marine, the one and only of my life, my husband. He received his commission and of all the fellows that walked across the stage a year ago, none could possess any finer qualities of character and manhood than mine.

Remember how you had to rush to change barracks and get into those new uniforms. Gee, Elliott, we've had some grand times together. . . . Last year was a really happy one and I was as contented as a kitten just to be by you, or meeting you some place for a snack. Remember, last Easter Sunday when all the eating places closed there in Quantico and we had to go in that dive to get something. That was fun, tho' 'course you were with me. . . .

I've put the deposit on the phone today and it will be installed tomorrow morning and I'll be on [Red Cross] call, Monday, Saturday and Sunday. . . .

Goodnite, dearest husband, and happy Easter. Did you get the card I sent you for Easter? I pray God will see fit to help end this strife and unhappiness before another Easter week rolls around. Keep happy and remember I love you so very much, always.

Yours devotedly, Marjorie

Ogden, Nov. 1, 1944

My Dear Husband:

One year ago now we were settled neatly in Carlsbad, were we not? Gee, that was such a wonderful three months. We've really been lucky to have had them, dear, for those swell memories make the separation easier to take.

Gosh, Elliott, I must be really possessive but as I recall, after we just first settled in [San] Diego, I just revelled in having you to myself, and was jealous of every minute you had to spend away from me.

Do you remember the broken bed at Mrs. Royens and how damn squeaky it was. Also the bed we broke down at Mrs. Kelly's in Quantico. Gee, we've sure left a "trail of broken beds" behind us. Ha! What made me think of it was this one—It's very good inasmuch as it's soft. But is very shaky, and wouldn't stand much working on. . . .

Well, dear, my life goes on, busily but certainly my days are not complete, for you are gone. It's good I can't think too much as I'd spend my time in trying to heal a very lonely and empty heart. I'm only half here without you, my dear, and love you more than life itself. Goodnight, sweetness.

Yours, Marjorie

Because of his difficult combat situation, which included four major invasions in the Pacific, Elliott was unable to save the letters which his wife wrote to him during his last year in the service.

Following Elliott's discharge from the Marines in January 1946, both he and Marjorie resumed their studies. She completed her undergraduate degree from Utah State University in 1947, and he received his doctorate in veterinary science from Colorado A & M in 1953. For twenty years, Elliott practiced veterinary medicine in Rancho Palo Verdes, California, and she taught school in Los Angeles. They had two children and also raised two nieces. Marjorie retired from thirty-four years of elementary school teaching in 1976, and her husband retired from his veterinary practice three years later. In 1979, they returned to Ogden to live. Elliott died in 1982. Marjorie lives in Ogden and does volunteer work for the YWCA and a local Crisis Center. She has five grandsons.

Marjorie Kenney and Richard S. Haselton were married in Reading, Massachusetts, on July 5, 1939. Their first child, Meredith Jane, was born in Worcester on December 24, 1941. In August 1942, the family moved to Athol, Massachusetts, where Richard found employment at a toy factory which had been retooled as an essential industry. He was inducted into the Navy on May 3, 1944, one of four brothers to serve in the Navy during World War II. After boot camp, he graduated from the Naval Amphibious School and from the special duty "Scouts and Raiders" School in Fort Pierce, Florida.

On September 6, 1944, while Richard was going to school, Marjorie gave birth to their second child, Stephen Scott. Her husband was given one week of leave, when Stephen was five weeks old, in order to assist his wife's move to a new apartment. The couple did not see each other again until his discharge in March 1946. In the meantime, she coped with caring for her young family on her very meager allotment check.

Athol, May 16, 1944

My doll, my pet, my pretty white dove! (I hope no one reads that over your shoulder!):

I received your lovely, eight page (!) letter today, and as a result I feel very serene, safe and much loved, which is a wonderful way to feel. I don't expect nor want you to fill every letter with laments over missing me, but I *did* want to hear it once, anyway. As you know, things were still a bit up in the air when you left. No need now to repeat all the things which were said and done that hurt me so much. I remember bringing the painful subject up on your last Sunday home, and you neither denied nor defended your position, so I felt and have been feeling a bit lost as regarded your attitude toward me. Probably my condition made me more sensitive (You'll never know how unlovely and unwanted pregnancy can make you feel!), but I kept wondering if you *really* felt toward me as you had in the past. After all, people do tire of one another, and though I still felt the same, I thought perhaps you were changing. I realize I am not, nor never have been the glamorous type, and I was beginning to think it made a difference to you. But now your letter has cleared the air and made me feel like a new woman! I feel sure of myself again, and believe me, it's grand—I love you too, do you know it? . . .

Well, baby another letter comes to a close. . . . Be good, honey and don't worry 'bout us. . . .

All my love, Me

Athol, May 25, 1944

Dearest Dick:

I probably won't get far with this, as it's an awkward time, and Meri [Meridith, their first child] is in a misty mood. But I'll try and get it done early so I can be in bed in decent season. You're not alone in your restless nights. I don't think I've slept well one single night since you've been gone. Probably I'm more acute to every move Meri makes because I'm in sole charge of her now. She's been terribly jumpy nights—crying out sharply though she doesn't always wake. But her cries always seem to come just as I'm droping off, and I nearly jump out of my skin. . . .

Sometimes I get so nervous being with her night and day with no relief. Most girls have a devoted mother, sister or aunt they can park their charge with, just for a breather once in a while—but there's no one I can ask. Seems funny for me to be complaining about a job you'd probably give your eye teeth to have! . . .

What a "tripey" old letter! I've been sitting here [listening to the radio] from Baby Snooks to Bing Crosby, and what have you got? Three pages of griping. Let's hope for a sunny day tomorrow and a more cheerful outlook.

There's one thing that doesn't change with the weather though, and that's how much I love you and miss you, darling. And Meri does, too, small as she is.

Love and Stuff, M—

Athol, July 19, 1944

Darling—

. . . While I wait for the water to heat, I'll get started on my daily letter. As you said, it is a moment to be looked forward to; when we can sit down and talk to each other, even if it is one-sided.

That blue letter I wrote last night—well, I am afraid this one won't be much better. I've been about as low in spirit the last few days as I have been at any time during our separation. My financial worries keep my mind in a torment, and added to the strain of missing you, it seems pretty hard. . . . I don't imagine you and I are the only ones who are having it tough sledding. Probably plenty of your barracks mates are worrying too, and I don't see how you all can be efficient sailors with so much on your minds. . . .

Well, I got rather frantic thinking it all today, so I called up the Red Cross. I wanted to know what I could do to get you home until after the baby comes. I didn't come right out and say it, but that's what I had in back of my mind. The person I talked to was very kind and sympathetic, but my chances of getting you home to see me through this are as remote as the North Pole. . . . You can't imagine how humiliated I felt, having to go to a stranger with my troubles, but I thought she might possibly know of some way out for me. She was nice as could be, but all she can do for me is to have me come in and she'll go over my budget with me and see what she can suggest. All very well, but I can see for myself, just how far $80.00 won't go, and I don't see how she can help the situation any. . . .

A beautiful picture, isn't it? As I see it, *I*, am no one's responsibility but my own, and whether Meri and I live, die or starve to death, nobody really gives a damn. That excludes *you*, of course, but you are powerless to do anything for us while you are in that legalized concentration camp. Now I don't mean that I want you to go over the hill, or anything drastic like that, because I agree with you that the resulting disgrace wouldn't help the situation any. . . .

Again, I'll say I'm sorry to unload this lousy letter on you. Please try to forgive me, honey. I hate to make you any more miserable than that lousy place makes you any way.

Oh, honey, how I love you!

Your first, last and, I hope, only, M—

Athol, Aug. 8, 1944

Darling:

. . . Monthly Expenditures

Rent	$20.00
Elect.	3.75
Tel.	2.00
Milk	6.50
Laundry	4.00
groceries	30.00
insur.	2.95
Range oil	2.80 (25 gal in summer)
	72.00

Monthly Allowance $80.00

That leaves a balance of $8.00 for clothing, medicine, heat in winter months, newspapers, periodicals, amusement, etc. (Also, there are bills, mostly contracted since your entry into the service, amounting to $45.00). . . .

I'll give up for tonight, and sign off with love to the best husband in the world, barring none.

Mummy

Heywood Memorial Hospital
Gardner, Mass., Sept. 6, 1944
(Stephen *Scott's* Birthday)

My Own Darling:

At last I am writing from the vantage point I've been dying to write from, lo these many months.

We have a lovely little son, dearest. I've only had one glimpse of him, but he's got the things he needs to make a perfect baby. He's not as pretty and pink and white as his big sister was though. He's a little redder, and has a slight *thatch* of *dark hair* (thank goodness). I'll have a better chance to get acquainted with him at the ten o'clock feeding, which will be the first time I'll have had a real good look at him. From first glimpse, I'd say he was a bit on the homely side! He weighs 7 lbs. 12 ozs.

I might as well tell you the whole tale. At about 5 p.m. Tuesday I had some pretty sharp pains, except there was not any regularity to them. Around 5:30 p.m. who should blow in but Clarence Christian. He has a new job and a pretty good one as a salesman for Brown and Williamson Tobacco Co. I was tickled to see him and invited him to supper. Ruth came over, too, as she had planned to anyway. All during supper I had pains off and on. Ruth invited us over to play cards as she was expecting a call from Tony. He is to be shipped out within 3 or 4 days and *thinks* it's South Pacific!

Well, I didn't really care to go, but I didn't want to spoil the fun, so I went along. We played until about 10 p.m., then I got up to go to the Johnny, and my water broke! In the bathroom, thank goodness, but I didn't need to guess, it was genuine and no doubt about it. . . . So Chris, Ruth, and I piled into the "Raleigh" truck, and went to Gardner. Ruth was tickled pink to be in on it, and tried to run the show, as usual. I got here shortly after 10:30, was "prepped" (shaved to you) and had an enema—grrr. Then I began the long business at hand. The pains were hard enough, but it wasn't until the last couple of hours that I was in agony. I really felt worse than with Meri somehow. I'm afraid I did my share of tossing and whimpering because it was really the worst pain I've suffered so far in life. I kept pleading with the nurse to put me under but she just sat there and read. They get so used to seeing this sort of thing. They gave me five sodium amytol capusles which didn't even knock me out. They only made me sick and throw up three times. You know how I love that.

But one *very* good feature. They wheeled me into the delivery room about 6:15 a.m., put me right under ether, so I didn't know a thing after that until I came to, in my bed in the ward. He was born at 7 a.m. Then they told me it was a boy. I hope you don't mind my changing the name to Stephen Scott instead of Stephen Richard. First of all, I think it fits better, then too, I know how thrilled Scotty and Evvie would be. It'll make a nice nickname, too, if we find there are too many Steves around. . . .

Please excuse the scrawl, and the pencil, but I forgot my fountain pen, and, too, a prone position in bed is hardly conducive to perfect penmanship! . . . .

Good night my sweet darling, and Thank God the whole thing is over.
Me

Athol, Sept. 24, 1944

My Darling:

. . . If you come home, will you take me out at least one night? Somewhere we can dance? I listen to the music on the radio and just long to be dancing in your arms. It would be heavenly. When I hear, "Goodnight, Wherever You Are" it's all I can do to keep still. It's just the right tempo for a nice dreamy, foxtrot—grapevine and all. Mmmm . . .

Gee, Thelma has me sleeping on the loveliest mattress! I'll be spoiled for my own bed. It's one of these sponge rubber ones—me for one of those when the war's over. It's like sleeping on a cloud. It gives me ideas, too. Last night I took a shower, put on a fresh nightie, and went to bed between clean sheets. *More* ideas! Only I'm still off the list as far as that goes. But I can dream, can't I? . . . .

Reading between the lines, you might get the idea that I'm lonesome. Strange, isn't it? Well, I *am* lonesome—so lonesome for you and Meri I could cry until I died! But I haven't cried and *won't*. It only makes me feel worse. I love you so much I *ache*.

Nighty-night Mummy

Athol, Nov. 27, 1944

My Sweet Honey:

    I'm listening to those programs that always make me feel closest to you on Sunday nights—9 to 10. Did you happen to hear Charlie McCarthy tonight? Some girl on that program sang a new song, "I'm a Little on the Lonely Side." I've heard it several times now, and it hits me right where it hurts. Me and a couple of million other lonely gals in this country. You know, it's no wonder swing is on the decline and ballads are in again. It's the mood of the whole country with most of its lovers separated. . . .

    I feel very strongly that you *will come back to us* when this is over, no matter what dangers you may be exposed to. We have too great a bond between us to have any outside force separate us from each other. I have strong faith in our good life to come, and if you have courage and faith to match it, then *nothing* can happen to spoil it. When the going gets tough, darling, don't *ever* give in. Just grit your teeth and say to yourself, "I *will* get back! I won't let *anything* stop me." And you'll do it. I'll be doing the same thing at home. Then, no matter how many, many miles you are away from me, there'll be a cord of steel reaching from you to me. Invisible though it is, it'll be there just the same, and no matter where you are, that bond of love will keep you safe. Maybe that all sounds far-fetched and a bit melodramatic, but I believe, firmly, and so must you. . . .

    Goodnight, my own darling.   Mummy

Richard was shipped overseas late in 1944 and was engaged in difficult and dangerous work which involved flying to India and then over "The Hump" into China. He spent the last months of the war behind Japanese lines engaged in espionage, weather observation, and other "hazardous" duty. He was once forced to parachute from an aircraft and was rescued by Chinese troops. Marjorie knew nothing of this work until he returned home. The letters which Marjorie wrote to her husband while he was in combat were lost.

    After the war, the couple settled in North Reading, Massachusetts, where they raised their two children. In 1949, they bought a second home in Sanbornton, New Hampshire. They moved, temporarily, to Sanbornton in 1974, where Richard died the following year. Marjorie then returned to Massachusetts and worked for three years as a bookmobile librarian, retiring in 1978. She now lives in New Hampshire.

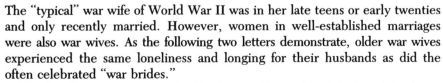

The "typical" war wife of World War II was in her late teens or early twenties and only recently married. However, women in well-established marriages were also war wives. As the following two letters demonstrate, older war wives experienced the same loneliness and longing for their husbands as did the often celebrated "war brides."

    The first letter was written by Evelyn R. Alvey of Carlsbad, California, to her husband, Robert, stationed with the 83rd Infantry Division in Europe. The Alveys had been married for eleven years at the time this letter was written. Robert cherished this letter, carried it with him throughout the war, and brought it home as a special keepsake.

Carlsbad, Dec. 2, 1944

Dearest Honey,

This will be your Christmas letter. If you get it before Christmas (as you should, if the mail isn't held up) save it, and read it again on Christmas Day.

First of all, I looked all over town for a card to send with this ring. But none of them were good enough—some said "Merry Christmas," and that isn't what I want to say; some said "I love you," and while I want to say that, there are lots of others things I want to say, too. I decided I could write it better than any store-bought card could tell you. At least I can try.

I hope you like the ring and that it fits you, honey. Oh, God, how I wish I could put it on your finger! If it doesn't fit, send it back and try to send me your correct size somehow, and I'll have it fixed. . . .

Christmas, 1944, won't be a merry one, honey; but it will be a loving one. It won't be a happy one, either. I can't be happy without you. But I shan't be too unhappy if I have some recent mail from you, and you are all right.

As for you, dear, I hope all of your packages get there before Christmas; I hope you have a decent place to sleep, and decent food to eat; and don't be too lonely dear.

Remember that this is positively our first and last Christmas that we aren't going to be together. Think of all we have had, and just think of all we have to look forward to—years of happiness, and each year better than the last.

With this ring, honey, I want to renew the promises I made September 15, 1933—to love you and to cherish you forever.

Your devoted wife,   Evelyn

After the war, Evelyn and Jack settled in San Diego, California. She worked as a secretary and he worked for a dairy. They had no children. Evelyn and Jack both retired in 1970. They recently celebrated their fifty-seventh wedding anniversary. They live in a retirement community in Carlsbad, California.

Hilda Rice of Waterbury, Connecticut, had been married twenty-five years when she wrote the following letter to her husband, Reuben, a Sea Bee who was stationed in New Caledeonia in the Southwest Pacific. At the time he received this letter, he was hospitalized, suffering from battle fatigue. The Rices had three children, and the letter mentions their two sons, Ken and Bob, who were also in the service. Their daughter, Alice, lived at home. Two weeks after writing this letter, Hilda Rice suffered a stroke and died.

Waterbury, March 1, 1945

My Dear Husband:

Received two letters from you, glad to hear you are feeling better.

Wish you were coming home but if that is impossible, hope you will be able to rejoin your bat[talion], and be back with your old friends again.

I was hoping you would be home for our twenty-fifth anniversary, but it looks as though I will have to observe it alone. Oh, well, there's better days coming and we can make up for it then.

The President is speaking on the Radio telling about his 14,000 mile trip to the Crimea. It is very interesting.

Just had a V-Mail letter from Bob. He said it was very hot and he bet about three layers of skin peeled off his face. Maybe some day he and you will meet. I hope so. He is only a kid, but he can take care of himself, I guess.

Had a letter from Ken yesterday. He is probably at sea again. He sent Alice a pretty pillow top for her birthday, with a very nice verse on it and said he meant every word of it. He said he was doing a lot of studying and was kept pretty busy. It seemed good to hear from him again as I hadn't received a letter for so long. I have to go down early and pay my personal tax as this is the last day. I also have to see about my income tax.

Good bye for now.

Lots of Love,   Your Loving Wife

Evelyn and Jack Alloy, both from Philadelphia, Pennsylvania, were married in the summer of 1940. She was twenty-four and he was twenty-seven. Jack practiced dentistry in Philadelphia prior to entering the service in the spring of 1943. After his basic training in Fort Dix, New Jersey, he was transferred to Fort Knox, Kentucky. Evelyn followed him there where she worked as a clerk-typist.

Jack left for overseas in the spring of 1944 and was stationed at the 140th General Hospital, near Bournemouth, England. Evelyn returned to Philadelphia to work for an engineering firm. She organized a Surgical Dressings Group which met weekly in her home church and also wrote many columns about the war for the local community paper, *The Chat*. Very few of Evelyn's wartime letters have survived, although several of her letter/poems, written on V-Mail stationery, were saved by her husband.

Philadelphia, March 27, 1945

For April 18, 1945, 32nd Birthday

TO MY HUSBAND:

> The Ocean lies between us,
> Ceaselessly pounding, fierce and loud—
> But above it can be heard, dear,
> my love, beating strong and proud.
>
> It beats across the ocean,
> And then into your heart,
> And, on this day—as on all days,
> It says, "We're not really apart."
>
> . . .
>
> Soon this evil we'll uproot together,
> With this struggle we will be done,
> Onward we'll go to bright new horizons
> Love blazing the way like the sun.
>
> Together from then on we'll be, dear,
> life moving like a well ordered stream,
> Together we'll strive for fulfillment
> Of all our wishes, our hopes, our dreams.

All my love always,   Evelyn

Philadelphia, June [?], 1945

FOR FATHER'S DAY

> . . .
>
> It wasn't our fault
> the war changed our plans,
> the simple dreams
> of a girl and her man.
>
> Dreams built of love,
> Thoughts of children, a home—
> Of security and quiet
> When the day's work was done.
>
> But how could this be
> With fascism alive in the world?
> Gaining strength and power,
> Banner of black death unfurled?
>
> So fight we had to,
> And fight it we WILL—

With all our wisdom
Our guts and our skill.

Then we'll have the right
To return to our dreams,
To fashion a world
Free of all fascist schemes.

. . .

Love, Evelyn

Jack returned to the United States in July 1945. Their only child, a son, was born in 1947. After Jack was discharged from the service, he re-opened his dental practice in Philadelphia, retiring in 1980. At the age of fifty-nine, Evelyn received her B.A., summa cum laude, from Temple University. She has written a book entitled *Working Women's Music*. Evelyn and Jack live in Philadelphia.

Flora Gaitree of Marietta, Ohio, was working as a reporter for the *Marietta Times* when, in 1938, she met Erman D. Southwick, another reporter. They fell in love and were married on July 30, 1939.

Erman was inducted into the Army in the fall of 1943 and received training at Fort Riley, Kansas; Fort Ord, California; and Fort Campbell, Kentucky. In June 1944, he was sent to Europe where he was assigned to Supreme Headquarters Allied Expeditionary Force (SHAEF). As he was thirty-three by this time, he was not chosen for combat duty and spent the war in SHAEF headquarters.

Flora continued with her work as a reporter for the *Marietta Times* until a bout with influenza, early in 1944, forced her to resign her position. In addition, she devoted considerable time to caring for her semi-invalid mother.

Flora's letters are available because Erman often responded to his wife's queries by writing directly on her letters. He then returned the original letters to her, along with new letters which he had written. Not only are Flora's letters moving love letters, but her reporter's eye also vividly captured many of the important events of the wartime era.

Marietta, Oct. 17, 1943

Dearest Darling:

How wonderful it was to have the opportunity to talk to you last night. I had been wondering about you all day. What especially pleased me was to hear you sound so happy and full of pep. I am looking forward to a letter from you and an account of all the things that have been happening to you.

I am typing this letter as I seem to have so much to tell even though it was only Friday morning that you left. When the bus pulled out, you looked pretty forlorn and it is needless for me to tell you that I felt sunk. I won't talk any more about that because to recall it makes me want to cry but I am proud to say that I haven't had a good cry yet but have come pretty close to it at least a hundred times already. But have my chin up.

Just as the bus pulled out, Mrs. Bedilion turned around and said, "You brave thing, you." Think of her saying that to me. I just couldn't say a word just then, but yesterday I told her what I thought about her. I think she deserved the compliments. [Mrs. Bedilion had lost her only son, a career Naval officer, just a few months previous to Erman's induction.]

. . .By staying awake all day I had gotten so exhausted that the first night wasn't too bad. You see I just don't let myself think ahead a moment and that way I can give myself the feeling that you will only be away for a few days and that sort of helps me keep going. But I do miss you terribly. . . .

I am so anxious to hear all about what has happened to you and about last night's show and every little detail about everything. I also hope you are lucky enough to be able to buddy up with a typewriter some place.

Darling, have the very best time you possibly can and remember I am thinking about you all the time and loving you and wishing you luck.

With all my love,   Flora

Marietta, Oct. 20, 1943

Dearest Darling:

What a grand letter and how happy I was to hear from you but I couldn't help thinking how tired you must have been when you wrote it, after such a long day and that made it doubly precious. I have carried it in my purse all day and take a peek at it every once in a while.

I was so happy to hear all that you had been doing because it makes you seem so much closer when I can sort of relive your days. . . . The box with your clothes arrived yesterday but I haven't worked up sufficient courage to open it yet. . . .

After lunch I stayed about an hour and then came home feeling as though I had been beaten and aching in every muscle but when I found your letter I got myself a very large glass of wine and read it over and over and felt able to lick the world. Mother said it came in the morning and she almost called me but was afraid I would try to come home at noon just to get it.

I read every word until I knew it almost by heart then Mother and I went through all your experience to date until we had it all in hand. . . .

Shortly before I locked up, a boy came from the High School about the scrap drive and I made arrangements with the kids to move out all cartons, metal you put in the back yard and anything else around so I won't have to bother with it. They even think they can get enough help to move the icebox as the junk man never showed. If they don't take it I shall try and get someone else. . . .

With all my love,
Affectionately,   Flora

Marietta, Nov. 5, 1943

Dearest Darling:

Three weeks ago today since you went away that morning. Well, dear, I might as well admit the truth. I wrote that first sentence and then stopped and had a good cry. (Nobody but just you and I know it.) But the last three weeks have been such an eternity and I am so lonesome for you tonight. When I suddenly thought that it would probably be several more months at least before I shall see you, I just couldn't take it. But don't worry about me I have had my cry and now I shall get my chin up again. You know you always say I am to cry on your shoulder and now I have done it. But I won't do it very often darling. I know you feel just the same way sometimes. I expect most people think I am very heartless about your going away for when they ask me about you I always smile and say you are just getting along beautifully and that you like it and all that sort of thing. Only you know how I really feel inside.

How is your cold? Much better, I hope, for I was a little worried when I heard you had a cold and were getting so much exposure. But in the letter I received today you sounded as though you were better so I feel that maybe you will be all right now. It is a shame you had to have that right in the beginning and I hope you don't have any more. Do you want me to send you some vitamins? Might be very good for you and keep you from getting any more colds.

I know you are not having an easy time and making the adjustment must be hard but I am so proud of you and I know you will come out splendidly. But you know that I am always thinking of you and planning for the day when you will be home again. . . .

Write to me as often as you can darling because I hurry home every day just looking for a letter. I have not written to you as much as I would like or want to but when I finish a day's work I am just too tired. . . .

I have a whole list of things I haven't time to tell you but as tomorrow night is our night, I shall try and write to you then and tell you lots of things about home and what I am planning.

Pleasant dreams, darling,

Love, Flora

Marietta, Jan. 26, 1944

Dearest Darling:

I suppose by now you have gotten the bad news about my illness and giving up my job. But, darling, please don't be upset. It will all work out all right, I know. . . . If they want to consider a leave of absence, that is all right with me. I haven't heard a word from Mr. Frank [the president of the *Marietta Times*] and don't suppose I shall but when I am better I told him I would come in and see him. But I couldn't stay home for an indefinite period and have them keep me on the payroll. I will accept money for value received but not otherwise. One reason for this attitude is that I do not want an obligation that would make you feel that you had to do something at the conclusion of this war that you really would not want to do, in other words, be committed to going back to your old job. You may want to go back for a while, but I don't want you to feel you have to. . . .

I don't know what he [the doctor] will say when he finds out I have given up my job and I really don't care. I am going to get strong this time and then I'll get a job and work but I'm not going to shake around a second time like I did last time and I have made up my mind to that. He says that I am to come down to the office next week for my vitamins. . . .

The grand letter you wrote on Sunday arrived this morning and darling, it really was wonderful to hear from you. I know you are very busy and I certainly do watch for those wonderful long letters. I wish you could write more often but I know you would if you could so don't think I am complaining. When I get a long letter like I did today I just read it over and over until the next one comes. I know your letters almost by heart. Oh, darling, they mean so much to me, to know what you are doing, thinking and feeling. I try to visualize each thing and get into the spirit of it with you. Darling, darling, I love you so much. . . .

It sounds as though the basic training period really winds up with a bang. But the infiltration course gives me the shivers. I don't know why but it just does. . . .

As long as I have your love, everything is all right and remember you always shall have mine.

Affectionately,   Flora

In early March, Erman returned to Marietta on an eight-day furlough. The next letter was written after he was transferred to Fort Campbell, Kentucky.

Marietta, April 7, 1944

Dearest Darling:

I am so unbelievably happy. When I think about how close you are and everything, I just don't really seem able to take it in—oh, darling darling— I love you, love you.

When I heard your voice the other night I was so happy I thought I was going to cry. It seemed I just couldn't think. . . . That telephone call last Tuesday night was certainly a high spot. I had tried so hard to reach the point where I could stand the thought of perhaps not hearing your voice for several years and then to talk to you so soon seemed just like a miracle. If you had not come back east I was hoping you would call me from California. If anything ever comes up suddenly in the future, no matter where you are, call me. . . .

Be a good boy and remember that I love you always more than anything or anybody else in the world.

Devotedly,   Flora

Marietta, May 16, 1944

Erman dear:

Your grand letter arrived this morning and I had a glorious time lying in bed reading it. Our letters mean a lot to us, do they not darling? Somehow, by telling you everything just as it happens each day and reading your letters over and over again I have a feeling of continuity so that when we are together again, even if it is only for a few hours we seem to resume our relationship on a physical basis without any feeling of separation having preceded those hours. It is a glorious state and is one of the precious things about our marriage.

Your letters are also very special. In every line you reveal your love and affection and your observations concerning your own position in this war and the positions of others have always been keen and unusually interesting. The book critic would probably find your letters the most interesting. Because you both give the point of view of a devoted husband and a soldier while my letters only give the account of what goes on in the mind of a devoted wife who tries to describe her emotions to her husband and tell him all the little intimate details back home which she knows will interest him.

However, the thought suddenly went through my mind that just such letters are what the soldier needs. He wants to remain an active force in the lives of those he loves and have a part in their activities even though absent. That is what I try to do in my letters to you. I want you to know every detail in my life and share my emotions so that you will not lose touch with anything about me during our separation. I try to look at everything through your eyes and try to visualize what you are doing and how you are reacting to each new problem and in that way I have the feeling of going with you and being part of your Army life too. Your letters give me such a complete picture of what you are doing and thinking that it makes it possible for me to follow you. When I get a letter from you I try to make a mental picture of all the things you tell me and then knowing you as I do I work out just how you reacted to almost what you said and the expression on your face. It makes me feel so close to you and through every line of your letters is the assurance over and over again of your love and that gives me a safe warm feeling inside. You see, darling, I just love you so much, I don't really recognize any separation from you. They can separate us physically and that is pretty hard to take sometimes but when there is complete emotional and intellectual unity between two people to really separate them is impossible. We know that now.

I often wonder what these poor souls that have little education or people who have had little experience with the written word really do under these circumstances. They must be very unhappy and frustrated especially if the separation lasts for any length of time. I feel very sorry for them. Another case, darling, where we have so much compared to what the average person finds in life. Think of going all through life and never knowing what perfect love and happiness can mean. . . .

With all my love and lots of kisses.

Devotedly, Flora

Marietta, June 6, 1944

Dearest Darling:

Today we have lived history. I can't even describe my sensations when I turned on the radio this morning. Somehow there is a feeling of relief that things have actually started. On the other hand I cannot lose sight of the fact that in all probability there is a long hard road ahead. But, nevertheless, there is the feeling of having a dark cloud lifted. Yes, darling, we are a part of something tremendous. I said to Mother this morning aren't you glad you are alive to see all this and she assured me she would not have missed it for anything.

I guess my old newspaper days got the better of me this morning when I was listening to the radio. I fairly asked to be there and see it all with my own eyes. Even the possible loss of one's life seemed a small price to pay for being part of one of the biggest things in history. If a man survives he will always know that he made history. If he does not he went out in a supreme moment and there is something to be said for going that way. Today I was proud and happy that you are wearing the uniform of your country and my country. I fear if you had walked in the house today in civilian clothes I would have been a little ashamed. As it was, I knew today that you went into the Army willingly and gladly—that you wanted to go— and I am proud that you felt that way.

No matter what the future brings, darling, we can face it and shall face it together for we are never separated except by miles. I fully understand what being a part of all this meant to you and you have always been right about it. In all honesty I must admit that if I had been a man I would have wanted the same things you wanted.

I am not very optimistic about things coming easily but I can face the future with my chin up and I know that whatever the future holds for us we shall face with courage and dignity. I am always with you, Darling, and thinking of you and I am calm and confident about our future whatever it may be. We have a full and wonderful past, although the present is sometimes difficult we now know that we can face it and I have perfect and complete faith in our future. . . .

Later. Just took time out to hear the President and then heard Fred Waring's musical group do "Onward Christian Soldiers." The most beautiful arrangement I have ever heard and thought of you when I heard the tenor part which was marvelous. In one part, the soprano sang the theme and the tenor did sort of an obbligato. . . .

Darling, I shall be thinking of you tonight after I go to bed and praying for you. My love goes with you wherever you are.

Devotedly,   Flora

Marietta, Christmas Eve, 1944

Dearest Erman:

Always remember that I love you more than anything else in the world. No matter what happens you can always depend on my love. In a world where things are constantly changing, it is constant and unchangeable. Though an ocean lies between us we are never really separated. We are the two halves that make a perfect whole. One and inseparable.

Tonight I shall look for the Christmas star and you in France will also be looking for it. Real clouds or the clouds of battle may obscure it but we shall know it is high in the sky sparkling as brightly as ever and bringing its promise of peace and love to all men and women of good will.

The war news has been in the past few days disheartening to say the least and to me it brings the sad thought that our physical separation may be longer.

My heart aches for those who are suffering and dying during what should be a season of gladness. And I have great compassion for those who have lost loved ones. . . .

This Christmas Eve I am strangely happy and I can say to you, darling, a Very Merry Christmas. Darling, we have learned during the past year that true love is indestructible and that time and distance can mean little to a love like ours. . . .

I do not mean by this that I do not miss you tonight and that I will not miss you tomorrow. Altho' you are always with me, I miss the physical you very much. Yes, dear, I miss you dreadfully and long to experience the joy of your caresses. Darling, I want you and need you more and more each day. . . .

As more of the gay and happy things become a reality tonight, I am thinking about that second honeymoon we are going to have when you get home. Let's for a few weeks after you come home be very frivolous and do lots of happy things together. I don't care where we spend it just as long as I am with you. But let's go to lots of parties and have a glorious time. . . .

As a special Christmas gift, I am sending you a thousand I.O.U's for love and kisses.

Devotedly,   Flora

Marietta, April 24, 1945

Dearest Darling:

. . .It must have seemed very desolate to walk down the Paris streets at night and see the flags at half mast. You asked what it was like over here. He [President Roosevelt] slipped away so easily that the first shock was a sort of numbness then the next reaction seemed to be fear. The sort of what will become of us sort of thing. After that was great uneasiness regarding Mr. Truman for most people knew very little about him. Of course, all the pomp and ceremony surrounding his burial. Then something inevitable but very sad happened. The stage was filled with other characters and within one week the wheels of the machinery of government were running so smoothly that it was almost shocking. I suppose the war is partly responsible for this but after twelve years of a most outstanding career it seems incredible that in so many aspects his influence could be replaced so quickly that one would hardly be able to detect the marks of his personality. This is one of those things we shall have to talk over when you get home but already I have given it much thought. Perhaps the necessity for the American people to get acquainted with President Truman very quickly, the progress of the war and conference in San Francisco have all influenced this, and that as the months go on his passing will be felt more and more keenly. Today the American people have their eyes on today and the future. They seem to have little time to look back for even one day. When the war is won they will have more time to look back and ponder. . . .

    With all my love and kisses,   Flora

After the war in Europe ended, Erman returned to the United States and was stationed at Fort Riley, Kansas. Following his discharge in 1946, he and Flora returned to Marietta to live. Erman resumed his work as a journalist with the *Marietta Times,* and Flora became a full-time homemaker. They had one son and three grandchildren. Flora died in 1969, and Erman retired the following year. He continues to live in Marietta.

Chapter 5

Be With Him at Every Mail Call: A Pictorial Essay

It is not too much to say that "Be With Him at Every Mail Call" was the unwritten motto of the United States during World War II. The message which appeared on the reverse side of this widely circulated government poster succinctly explained the importance of the mail in wartime: "Why This Poster Is Important: Mail from home is more than a fighting man's privilege. It is a military necessity, for there probably is no factor so vital to the morale of a fighting man as frequent letters from home."
(NATIONAL ARCHIVES)

As important as letters were in maintaining the morale of the troops, the mail took up space in scarce wartime transport. In an effort to alleviate this problem, the government introduced V-Mail, a process which involved photographing letters which were written on specially designed 8½ by 11 inch stationery available at all post offices. (NATIONAL ARCHIVES)

V-Mail film was flown overseas where it was developed and the letter was delivered to the recipient in the form of a 4 by 5½ inch photograph. Letters with a bulk weight of 2,575 pounds could be reduced to a mere 45 pounds when processed in this manner. (NATIONAL ARCHIVES)

The amount of mail sent overseas increased by 513 percent during the war years. V-Mail facilitated the handling of this huge increase in the volume of the mail. (NATIONAL ARCHIVES)

Despite its recognized benefits, V-Mail was not universally accepted by the public. Many letter writers felt that it was too impersonal and left recipients feeling incomplete—as though they had received only a postcard.
(NATIONAL ARCHIVES)

KEEP HIM POSTED

Make it short

Make it cheerful

SEND IT V-MAIL

FOR SALE HERE

More than one billion V-Mail letters were dispatched during the war years. The process of V-Mail became the basis for modern microfilming.
(SIGNAL CORPS PHOTOGRAPH)

Magazine cover art focused on the importance of writing and receiving letters. Popular magazines carried feature stories on the "dos and don'ts" of writing a good letter, and "Dear Boys" columns, written in the form of letters, were often published in weekly newspapers. (Courtesy of HOUSE BEAUTIFUL, *copyright © November 1943. The Hearst Corporation: all rights reserved. Photographer, Eugene Hutchinson, at R. H. Macy & Co.)*

Advertisers were quick to use the mail and morale motif as a way to promote their products. (COURTESY OF DOLE PACKAGED FOOD COMPANY)

Radio broadcasts frequently emphasized the importance of letter writing. Neal Chapline, known professionally as Molly Carewe, produced a popular, biweekly radio program, "Molly's Boots," for WXYZ in Detroit, Michigan, which was based on her correspondence with hundreds of young Marines. Another well-known radio program, "I Sustain the Wings," which often featured Glenn Miller's Air Force Orchestra, ended its broadcasts each Saturday with an injunction to "Keep those V-Mail letters flying to the boys overseas. Mail from home is number one on their hit parade. They're doing the fighting. You do the writing." (COURTESY "MOLLY CAREWE")

Popular songs also emphasized the importance of letter writing during war-time.

Air Mail for Leathernecks at Iwo Jima, February 1945. As this Marine Corps photograph illustrates, the mail always carried through—even onto the beachheads.
(MARINE CORPS PHOTOGRAPH)

Ernie Pyle placed "good mail service" at the head of his list of soldiers' needs. Men in combat often remarked that receiving a letter was "like a ten-minute furlough." (NATIONAL ARCHIVES)

Mail from home was a G.I.'s only connection with a sane world.
(NATIONAL ARCHIVES)

Prisoner-of-war mail was not delivered with any regularity. However, loved ones at home wrote carefully worded messages on POW stationery.
(AUTHORS' COLLECTION)

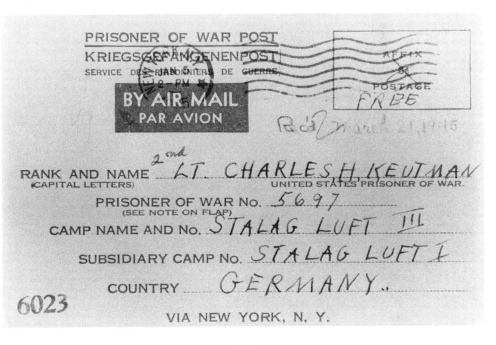

"Mail call" was equally important for the 350,000 women who served in the U.S. armed forces during World War II. (NATIONAL ARCHIVES)

It was also important to "Be With Her at Every Mail Call." (SIGNAL CORPS
PHOTOGRAPH)

Instructions for sending holiday letters and packages were widely circulated. (NATIONAL ARCHIVES)

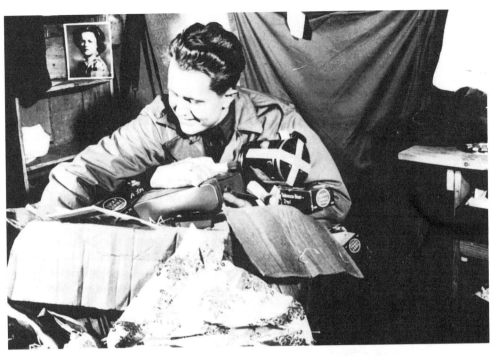

A G.I. in Iceland opening a holiday package. (NATIONAL ARCHIVES)

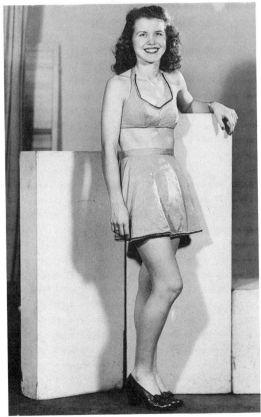

Many women took it upon themselves to devote hours each day to letter writing. In the fall of 1944, Dorothy Heath Clary, a seventeen-year-old freshman at Southern Methodist University, was chosen as the "girl next door pin-up" of the USS Swordfish. After her photograph appeared on the front page of the December 8, 1944, issue of the Dallas Morning News, she received a deluge of letters from servicemen from around the world. She faithfully answered all of her correspondence, and her letter-writing campaign for the war effort became an almost full-time occupation. (COURTESY DOROTHY HEATH CLARY)

Oly Nalevanko, an art teacher from Olyphant, Pennsylvania, drew thousands of cartoons on penny postcards depicting a young woman's life in "an almost no-man's land." This was Nalevanko's way of letting her brothers, sister, and friends stationed overseas know what was happening on the home front. At "mail call," it usually took an

WE'RE GOING TO HAVE A VICTORY GARDEN OR SOMPIN! LOVE, OLY.

hour for a postcard from Oly to make its way to the intended recipient. As the popularity of Oly's cartoon figures spread, servicemen from around the world began writing to her. She answered each of these letters with a cartoon postcard, sometimes churning out as many as one hundred cards a week. (AUTHORS' COLLECTION)

I'M CERTAINLY GLAD I HAVE A BICYCLE!

| Issue No. 18 | Editor: Ruth E. Augustine | Nov. 10,1944. |

About Town

"Will and Jim Mann moved their household goods to town a day last week.
Dorlan Crane orders his address changed from Salem to Albany, Oregon.
Henry Smith circulated a petion for benefit of the Beauchamp family
who lost most of their household goods and personal belongs by fire.
Mrs. Valda Bickford came up from Yankton Saturday for a few days visit
with her parents, Mr. & Mrs. B.R. Tucker.
Pat Wasson 40, scrap dealer at Scotland was accidently killed while
hunting pheasants Tuesday of last week.
John Pavlis recently sold 35 hogs on the Sioux City market, ## wt. 211
and brought $14.45.
Ralph Albright motored up from Lake Andes Monday to business and dropped
into the News office for a brief visit.
We are in receipt of a letter from Dean Scott, who is serving in the
Navy, and enclosed $2.00 for a years subscription to the News. Dean sends
regards to all Geddes friends.
Mr. & Mrs. J.F. Van Gorkom returned Monday evening from a few days
visit with their daughter and husband, Mr. & Mrs. D.R. Snowden at Yankton
and with their son and wife, Mr. & Mrs. Theo Van Gorkom at Vermillion.
Mrs. Gerald Long, Jr. went to Hastings Neb. last week where she will
maker her home while her husband is serving in the Navy.
Hartwig Jensen and son Paul arrived home from Yakima Wash. Tuesday.
morning, where they have been employed in the apple industry. Several
former Geddes people reside there and they report them all well.
Ole Marken was a News caller while in town on Monday. Ole celebrated
his 87th birthday last August and enjoys fairly good health. He can also
qualify as one of our pioneers as he settled in Rhoda township in 1883.
He has raised some good corn in the past years, but none better than this
year.

T/SGT DON MEIS WRITES TO HIS FATHER

Lew Meis received a letter from his son T/Sgt Donald Meis, who is in
the Armed forces somewhere in Italy or France. He writes that they have
been going through some hard fighting but were still on top. "I will be
glad when the war is over and I can come back to Geddes and see my friends
once again. Tell everyone in Geddes 'Hello' for me."

GEDDES BOY COMPANY OFFICER.

According an AP dispatch from San Diego, Calif. - First Lt. Thomas
Dean Scott, 24, a native of Geddes, S.D. is company officer here after
serving 22 months overseas. Hight spots of his overseas experience was
the assault on Eniwetok atoll in the Marshall islands. He commanded a
rifle platoon in that operation. Lt. Scott is a son of Mr. & Mrs.
Tom Scott, formerly of Geddes, but now located at Portland, Oregon.

*One way that loved ones who were scattered around the world kept in touch
with each other during the war years was by producing family newsletters.
"Gleanings," edited by Ruth E. Augustine of Geddes, South Dakota, was
one such newsletter. Ruth enlisted in the Marine Corps in 1943 and was
with the first contingent of Women Marines to serve at Camp Elliott in San
Diego, California. Five of her brothers were also in the service. To solve the
problem of regular correspondence with five different people, she carbon-
copied a "newsletter" once a month. She included family news as well as information which she "gleaned" from her home-town South Dakota weekly
newspaper.* (AUTHORS' COLLECTION)

LEE MESSENGER

Let's get the ☆ before Christmas

School teachers were typically prolific letter writers, making certain that their former pupils did not come away from "mail call" empty-handed. Rusha Wesley, principal of the Lee Street Elementary School in Atlanta, Georgia, located the names and addresses of more than 300 graduates of the school who served in the armed forces during World War II. She and her students sent hundreds of handmade cards and letters to Lee Street School graduates in uniform; she also sent them a school newsletter, the "Lee Messenger," which she produced. (COURTESY OF THE ATLANTA HISTORICAL SOCIETY)

THE BROOKTONDALE BUGLER

Weather - Good for Snow Plows!

January 11
1945

STAFF SUP'VISOR	Mrs. M. Lattin	STENCILOR	Mrs. C. E. Weber
SUPPLIES	Phyllis Lattin	MIMEOGRAPHER	Bert McMaster
REC. SEC'Y.	B. Steenbergh	HON. REPORTER	Harry VanDeMark

MAILING DEPARTMENT
Cholas Compton, Ruby Woodin, Ethel Tulley, Mrs. Harold Hall, Phyllis
Lattin, Grace Savey, Bette Tucker, Bert McMaster, Barbara Steenbergh,
Martha Lattin, Alice Johnson, Lauretta Dalola, Bessie Lynch, Phyllis
Dalola, Bernice Hall.

Circulation - 575

Issue twenty-four

Volume Three

NAMES TO BE ADDED TO HONOR ROLL
Paul Newman
Lewis Murphy
Roy N. Peterson
George E. Drake
******

NEW PATRONS
Mrs. Wells G. Catlin
    32 Grant St., Utica, N.Y.

RENEWALS
Miss Eleanor Howard, B'dale
Mr. and Mrs. Bert Eastman, B'dale
Mr. and Mrs. Percy Yaple, B'dale
Mr. and Mrs. Harold Predmore
    Caroline Depot
Mrs. Bessie Steele, Ithaca, R.D.4
Mrs. Ada Landon, B'dale
Mr. and Mrs. Benjamin Caveney
    Ithaca, R.D.2
Mr. and Mrs. George Bell, B'dale
Mrs. Bertha Metz, Slaterville Spgs
Mr. and Mrs. Harold Hall, B'dale
Mr. and Mrs. Stephen Kish, B'dale
Mr. and Mrs. Alvah Ferguson
    Slaterville Springs
Mrs. Perl M. Legg, Berkshire, N.Y.
****

BROOKTONDALE
The Bugler Staff met at the home
of Miss Bette Tucker on Thursday
Evening, Dec. 28th for the regular
bi-monthly business meeting.

Due to the storm and badly
drifted roads only those from
Brooktondale were present.

We were glad to welcome back
with us, Mrs. Rudolph Tulley, one
of the first members of the Bugler
Staff. Mrs. Tulley is the former
Ethel Hall and Her husband, Pvt.
Tulley is now overseas.

Mrs. Grace Minns Savey, wife
of F/O William Savey of Lincoln,
Nebraska, was a guest. She is
spending several weeks at the
Tucker home.

Mrs. Eloise Phinney has returned
from visiting her husband, Charles
Phinney S2/C, at the Great Lakes
Naval Training Station. She was
registered as a guest at the Hotel
Juneau, Milwaukee.

Mrs. Jane Vandemark recently returned from a weeks' visit with
her husband, J. Thomas Vandemark,
S1/C, of Washington, D.C. Her
husband accompanied her home as
he had a 3-day leave.

CANDLE LIGHTING SERVICE
At the morning service of the Nazarene Church in Brooktondale, Dec.
30th, a candle lighting service
was held in honor of those in the
Service of our Country from our
Community.

Dr. Howard Miller delivered the
message in conjunction with the
service. His subject was, "The
Relationship of Home, Church, and
Country".

A row of nineteen candles was
placed in front of the Altar and
as the Pastor, Rev. Stanford Ernest
read the name of the man or woman
in service, the mother, wife, or
sister, lighted a candle in his
or her honor.

Rev. Ernest offered a prayer
for their safe return and Miss
Betty Miller very impressively sang
"Keep the Home Fires Burning".

Two beautiful flags, the American and the Christian, were presented to the Church by Dr. Howard
Miller and Mrs. Miller at the beginning of the service.

Miss Carrie Hilsinger who spent
the Holiday vacation with her parents, Mr. and Mrs. Clement Hilsinger, made an illustration for the
hymn, "When They Ring the Golden
Bells for You and Me", while Mrs.
Ernest played it. Miss Hilsinger
is a student at Eastern Nazarene
College at Wollaston, Mass.
******

Miss Lulu M. Kio and Paul S. Landon
both of Trumansburg, were married
at 3:30 p.m. Dec. 17, in the First
Baptist Church, Trumansburg. Rev.
Chester V. Zogg, Wolcott, and Rev.
Owen D. Rutledge, pastor of the
Baptist Church, performed the
double ring ceremony.

The church was decorated with
evergreen trees, candelabra and
Calla Lilies. C. Wesley Thomas
played traditional nuptial music
on the organ and Mrs. Harry Morgan
soprano, and Mrs. Leslie Cronk,
alto, sang "Always" and "Thru the
Years."

Mrs. Chester Ingalls, Coopers-
town was her sister's matron of
honor. Richard Pringle, Waterloo,
was best man.

DEAR
DADDY
Bertie Erling
ARE YOU
VERY
LONESOME?
DO YOU
LIVE in
A HOUSE?
SUNDAY We
EAT# VERY
GOOD
Ruth Erling

Children as well as adults understood the importance of writing and receiving letters. Even before they reached school age, young children joined in the ritual of writing to Daddy. Mothers often enclosed the scribblings of their toddlers in the letters which they sent to their husbands. This letter was written in 1943 by six-year-old Ruth Erling of Pennock, Minnesota, to her father, Bertil A. Erling, an Army chaplain who was stationed in the Pacific. (AUTHORS' COLLECTION)

Around the nation, women put together mimeographed newsletters which were sent to the local "boys" in the service. In 1943, a group of young women from Brooktondale, New York, began publishing the "Brooktondale Bugler." Published twice a month between 1943 and 1946, the "Bugler" carried news of local servicemen stationed around the globe as well as hometown reports of sports, weather, marriages, births, and travel. From a four-page letter sent to thirty men, it grew to six pages with a circulation of over 500. A complete run of the "Brooktondale Bugler" is located at the Dewitt Historical Society of Tompkins County in Ithaca, New York. Organized letter-writing campaigns were also sponsored by churches, schools, factories, and community groups, such as the Girl Scouts. (AUTHORS' COLLECTION)

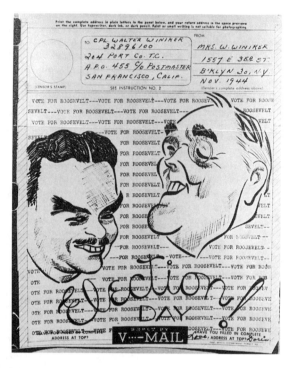

Some women enhanced their letters with drawings. On special occasions, such as anniversaries and birthdays, Doris J. Winiker of New York City often sent her husband, Walter, original V-Mail drawings.
(AUTHORS' COLLECTION)

Mary E. Nutt of Morrisville, Pennsylvania, maintained a steady correspondence with her future husband, John J. Scullin, who served with the Armed Guard in the Navy. She frequently included drawings on the envelopes. (AUTHORS' COLLECTION)

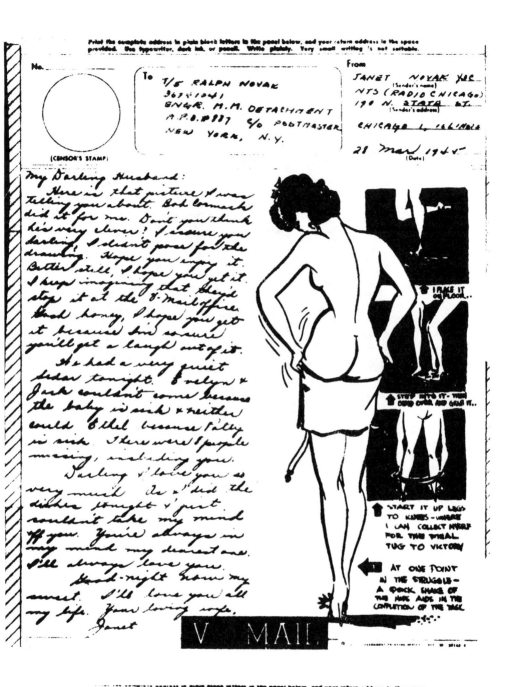

In an effort to buoy the spirits of her husband, Janet Novak, a yeoman in the WAVES, sent this V-Mail to her Army husband who was stationed in Europe. A friend illustrated the letter for her. Janet and her husband had been married for only three days when he was sent to Europe for three years. (COURTESY JANET NOVAK)

Government V . . . -Mail poster.
(NATIONAL ARCHIVES)

Chapter 6

I Took a War Job

THE MOBILIZATION OF THE NATION'S ECONOMY FOR WAR CREATED an unprecedented demand for new workers. In response to this need, some 6.5 million women entered the work force. The proportion of women who were employed increased from 25 percent at the beginning of the war to 36 percent at the war's end—an increase greater than that of the previous four decades.

The woman war worker was highly lauded, and "Rosie the Riveter" became a national heroine. Women worked in shipyards, aircraft plants, and other assembly lines. They were nurses and nurse's aides, served with the Red Cross, were employed in day-care centers, and held a variety of other jobs. Some 350,000 women served their country by joining the WACS, WAVES, SPARS, the Marine Corps Women's Reserve, the Army Nurse Corps, and the Navy Nurse Corps. They also worked as "civilians in uniform" with the Women's Airforce Service Pilots and in civil-service jobs on military bases.

In their letters to loved ones, women war workers expressed pride in their jobs and often were enthusiastic about the new sense of responsibility and independence they were achieving. Their letters remain as eloquent testimonies to their contributions to the war effort.

Polly and William Crow, both twenty-seven years old, had been married ten months when the attack on Pearl Harbor occurred. She was a bookkeeper for the telephone company, and he worked for the Frisco Railroad. William was drafted in the fall of 1943 and sent to New Orleans for basic training. Polly and their nine-month-old son, Bill, moved to Pensacola, where William's parents lived, so that the family could occasionally be together. When William was shipped to Europe in the early summer of 1944, Polly and Bill moved to Louisville, Kentucky, to live with Polly's mother.

In June 1944, Polly took a job on the swing shift at the Jefferson Boat and Machine Company located in nearby Anderson, Indiana. As her letters demonstrate, the demands of a war job and the responsibilities of motherhood created enormous pressures which she, as well as many other working mothers, found very difficult to reconcile.

Pensacola, June 6, 1944

Darlin':

. . . All that's on the radio and in the papers this day is the Invasion. I can take so much of it then I feel like I'd like to crawl in a hole somewhere. Suppose I won't hear from you for quite a while but have gotten so I can take just about anything, come what may—'twill be H—, but I've no choice in such things but just hope and pray you'll be o.k., darlin'. Don't know if you'll get my letters or not but certainly hope so. I'm glad the fire works have started so this thing will be over with, but the way they broadcast it reminds me of a horse race or ball game. I may be a sissy but I can't take too much of it. Radios blare from every direction so you can't get away from it for a even a minute. I love you terribly, Darlin' and can hardly wait to see you again.

Good night, precious,
I love you,   Polly

Pensacola, June 8, 1944

Darlin':

. . . After I get settled in Louisville I'm thinking seriously of going to work in some defense plant there on the swing shift so I can be at home during the day with Bill as he needs me—would like to know what you think of the idea, if you can write. Of course, I'd much rather have an office job but I couldn't be with Bill whereas I could if I worked at nite which I have decided is the best plan as I cain't save any thing by not working and I want to have something for us when you get home so you can enjoy life for awhile before going back to work and Bill and I want all of your time too for awhile so's we can all three make up for lost time.

Gotta scoot as I have several more chores to do.
I love you, Darlin', Polly

Louisville, June 12, 1944

Darlin':

You are now the husband of a career woman—just call me your little Ship Yard Babe! Yeh! I made up my mind that I wanted to work from 4:00 p.m. 'till midnight so's I could have my cake and eat it too. I wanted to work but didn't want to leave Bill all day—in the first place it would be too much for Mother altho' she was perfectly willing and then Bill needs me. This way Mother will just have to feed him once and tuck him in which is no trouble at all any more as I just put him in bed and let him play quietly until he's ready to go to sleep and he drops right off. . . . I finally ended up with just what I wanted. Comptometer [calculator] job—4:00 'till mid-nite—70 cents an hour to start which amounts to $36.40 a week, $145.60 per month, increase in two months if I'm any good and I know I will be. Oh yeh! At Jeffersonville Boat and Machine Co. I'll have to go over to Jef-fersonville, Ind. which will take about 45 minutes each way. Hope I can get a ride home each nite as that's the only feature I dislike but I'm not gonna be a sissy. If I can't get a ride, I'll get tags for our buggy and probably use it. . . . If I don't need it for work I may not get them but will just have to see how things work out. Want to take Bill out swimming a lot this summer so I may need it for that. . . .

Opened my little checking account too and it's a grand and a glorious feeling to write a check all your own and not have to ask for one. Any hoo, I don't want it said I charged things to 'em and didn't pay it so we don't owe anybody anything and I'm gonna start sockin' it in the savings and checking too so's we'll have something when our sweet little Daddy comes home.

Good nite, Darlin'
I love you, Polly

Louisville, June 13, 1944

Darlin':

Just got home from work at 12:30 a.m. Got a ride both ways with one of the girls in the office who lives about ten blocks from here—certainly am glad 'cause I didn't go for the idea of coming home alone. Like my job fine and it was great fun to get going on a comptometer again. I'm figuring the pay checks as everyone with Jefferson Boat is paid by the hour so that makes plenty of work. I haven't sat in one position and an erect one at that for so long that it was rather hard to do so I made several trips to the water foun-tain mainly for the exercise. We have 30 minutes for lunch at 7:15 and go across the park to a little cafe which slings out pretty good hash. At about 9:30 we all give the boss, Mr. Toby, a nickel and he goes and gets all a good old ice cold coke which is most refreshing. Haven't counted the office force but there must be about 20 of us in the nite shift. They seemed very gen-erous with my work last nite and couldn't get over the most legible figures I made. They must be used to sloppy jobs or something. I turned over as much work as the other girls and didn't make one single error which they couldn't get over. . . . Will write you before I go to work each day so's I can tuck me in just as soon as I get home so I get plenty of good old shut eye.

I dreamed this morning that you'd come home on furlough but had to return shortly 'n you were in civilian clothes and had received 4 of ten boxes we'd sent you. I was so glad to see you I almost popped, then I woke up. Shucks.

Good nite, Darlin'
I love you terribly,   Polly

Louisville, June 17, 1944

Darlin':
. . . The gals all got paid last nite. Course I didn't as the week runs from Tuesday to Tuesday. They collect 10 cents from every one and the one whose check numbers show the best poker hand wins the pot, some stuff, eh?

Maybe I'll accidentally win once in a while. Talk about wolves! Baby, the swing shift is overrun with 'em, no one seems to think or care about whether you're married or not, as it evidently makes no difference. However, it does to me. . . .

I love you like H—
Baby,   Polly

As with many war wives, such duties as keeping the automobile serviced and ready for winter weather now became Polly's province. An activity which would have been judged unusual for women in the prewar era was now considered to be routine.

Louisville, Nov. 6, 1944

Darlin':
. . . Have an appointment to take the car in Thursday morning to get it simonized. Have to have it in by 10:00 a.m. and it will be ready about 5:00 p.m. so I'll have to pick it up as I don't want to leave it there overnite. The strip of rubber padding came off the right door so I want to get that fixed also. Will cost about $7.00 but I figured I'd better get it done to protect the finish as it hasn't been done since you left. About time, wouldn't you say? Had 6 qts. of anti-freeze put in it yesterday and it's a good thing I did as it was 26 degrees at 7:00 a.m. and everyone will probably make a mad rush for it now. Have used all my gas coupons now up to Dec. 21st and cain't figure how I did it as I've never run short before. I guess the leak must have lost a lot before I discovered it. . . . That's where my money goes! But I want to take good care of the buggie. . . . After the simonize job, I shouldn't have to spend any more on it for awhile any hoo. 'Tiz worth every penny to have it ready whenever we want to go. . . .

"'Tiz time to go"
Good nite, Darlin'
I love you,   Polly

Louisville, Nov. 9, 1944

Darlin':

. . . The union came in to-nite. Join or else! The gals have all been in a stew since the maids and porters got their raises as they now make more than we do. A fine thing, uh! yeah! We were ready to take up the scrub jobs around in place of ours. They all, of course, belong to the union, soooo, all the office employees all over the yards joined and we had to too. I always said I'd never join one but I sat right here and did. We, of course, are all supposed to get a raise out of it so I figured I wouldn't be losing any thing if we did, so if we don't then I can always get a job elsewhere. I like it here and like the hours so I don't want to quit and am out for every penny I can get while the gettings good, right? We now have about $780.00 in the bank and 5 bonds which sho looks good to me and as soon as I get the buggie in good shape and all the Xmas extras over then I can really pile it away. . . .

Good nite, Darlin'
I love you, Polly

Louisville, Dec. 5, 1944

Darlin':

There's rumors out that by March 1st there will be no more nite shift in any part of Jefferson Boat as work will be completed by then and they're letting men go over in the yards at the rate of 50 a week and expect to have 5,000 gone by March 1. If it's true then I suppose my greatly enjoyed working career will come to an end, as you know we build L.S.T.s [Landing Ship Tanks, used primarily for invasion purposes] for the Navy and I cain't understand how they can cut down like that with the war still going on. One of the boys in New Caledonia wrote his wife that they heard on the radio that the war with Germany will be over in two months and the war with Japan over by the 1st of June. She wrote him tonite asking from what source the announcement came and if it was just a prophecy. Have you all heard any such sentiments? 'Twould be wonderful if it is really true but I certainly won't count on it. They would probably find a place for me on the day shift, if I wanted it but I couldn't do that as Bill needs me too much and it would be too hard on Mother to care for him all day. I have enough savings piled up to last me several months and I know if I don't get it done before you return I never will. However by the time I get all finished and you aren't home by then, or at least have hopes of returning soon thereafter, I'll start pounding the pavements again as I gotta save all the money I can now while the getting is good, but I'll just hope and pray each nite that you will be home by next summer at the latest. . . .

I love you,
Darlin', Polly

While employed by Jefferson Boat and Machine Company, Polly was occasionally called upon to work on the day shift.

Louisville, Jan. 30, 1945

Darlin':

Thought for a while this a.m. I would have to take Bill to work with me, or stay at home. He was evidently dreaming a bad dream and awakened just as I was getting up. He wanted me and no one else would do and while I ate breakfast, he clung onto me like he'd never let me go. We finally convinced him that I was just going to work until 10:00. Going out into the snow at 7:00 a.m. and catching buses wasn't half bad and I really enjoyed it. I was the only one out on our street, and lots of the houses had lights on which looked very welcoming. I liked the feeling of not depending on some one else to get me to and from work. However if I get a regular ride, I'll take it too sometime for it seems like I don't have any time with Bill at all. Got home at 6:00 this afternoon as I had to stop and get the groceries for tomorrow. By the time we ate, did the dishes, I washed out a few things, mended the fur coat again and bathed us both, it was time to go to bed. Bill and I are sitting in bed writing you but he is having a horrible time getting enough stationery, as he has already had three sheets and is yelling for more. Yet, he even scribbled on this [V-Mail] as you can see. He gets a bigger kick out of writing Daddy than anything else he does. I'm going to teach him to say his little prayers for you each nite. Good nite, Darlin'.

I love you forever,   Polly

Mailed your package.

As soon as it became clear that Jefferson Boat would, in fact, be laying off large numbers of workers, Polly began looking for another war job. Because of her skills with computational devices, a position at the Du Pont Chemical powder plant in Charleston, Indiana, was available for her.

Louisville, Feb. 27, 1945

Darlin':

Finished my first day's work at Du Pont's and quit all day long—yeh! isn't that a heck of a start. After being accustomed to modern streamlined offices it was a come down to see the make-shift affair in which I'll work. The worse part is—in the middle of the room is the rest room—a tiny affair just barely large enough to hold a basin and johnny and is used by both men and women—no latch on the door and you either have to hold it shut with one hand and if you need both hands then hold your breath and hope no one comes in on you. They're building our office tho' and it's to be ready in several weeks—don't know if I'll stick it out long enough to see it or not. Then they want to work 12 hours on Monday, Tuesday, and Wednesday—9 each on Thursday and Friday and off all day on Saturday. If you work the 12 hours you get home the best way you can and that definitely isn't for me so when I first heard the plans I went to the supervisor and told him that I would work the 9 hours a day for 6 days a week as was explained to me when I took the job and if they were changing the hours I'd just have to quit—he told me to just go ahead and work the hours I'd planned on. The cafeteria is choice tho'—that is after we finally made through gobs of mud for almost a block until we get to it but then we can take as long to eat as we want— that's the only good thing I can say about it. Yeh! If it wasn't for the almighty dollar I wouldn't show up tomorrow.

. . . Some thing of ours is always broken and I sho wish you'd hurry home to fix everything for us. . . .

Good nite, darlin'

I love you terribly, Polly

Louisville, March 17, 1945

Darlin':

. . . The more I see of war plants the more I believe that they're dragging this damn war out as long as possible on purpose, and no one will even make me believe that politics hasn't every thing to do with the finishing or rather the prolonging of it. Jefferson Boat was bad enough I thought when it came to wasting materials and man hours as they had so many men in the yards they'd practically fall all over one another doing nothing as there was such a great surplus of help but out here it seems as tho' they have so much money they don't know what to do with it and are just throwing it away. They'll spend two weeks putting in water fountains, cooling systems or such and when they're completed they'll decide that isn't what they want and spend another two weeks taking them out, then start all over again. They build a building then decide it isn't what they want and knock out a wall here, one there or even tear it completely down. Hell, if they'd make up their feeble minds in the first place and know what they need and want before they start it blindly they'd save millions of dollars and man hours and get this thing over with—if this is supposed to be the hottest job now the way they are going at it certainly won't help you all much—better stop as I'm feeling so hot I might burn up the paper if I continue.

I love you terribly, Darlin', Polly

Louisville, April 3, 1945

Darlin':

. . . The boss called us all together yesterday afternoon and said when the news of victory came the plant would shut for the rest of the day but if the news came at nite we were to report the next morning as usual. He went on to explain that this plant is making a product which is . . . used or to be used in the Pacific and will continue in full force after the European victory. Every one is expecting the exciting news any minute but I'm beginning to believe it is already over and they just aren't releasing the news yet for fear everyone will go wild with celebrating. I'm not gettin' enthused tho' until I know for true that the word is official. . . .

Gotta go to work.

I love you terribly, Darlin', Polly

Louisville, July 24, 1945

Darlin':

. . . There was another article about the burden on the railroads here in the States since the redeployment started and to lessen the burden the Army is changing the redeployment program and sending the men directly to the Pacific instead of thru the States on furlough—sure hope you aren't being knocked out of a furlough for that reason. Guess I'll just hope to keep on waiting and tearing my hair each time the mail man passes me by.

. . . Think I'll wash the buggie and wax it—since I'm not a workin' gal any more I have to pinch our pennies and I'll try anything once too.

I love you terribly, Darlin', Polly

William Crow returned to the United States in December 1945. After his discharge, he worked briefly for the railroad before taking a position in food brokerage in Pensacola, Florida. Polly Crow worked as a bookkeeper for many years. Their son, Bill, died at the age of 22. The Crows had no other children. They both retired in the early 1980s and continue to live in Pensacola.

Edith Sokol met her future husband, Victor Speert, on a blind date in 1937. He was a junior at Ohio State University, and she was a recent graduate of Shaker Heights High School in Cleveland, Ohio. After high school, Edith attended OSU, receiving her undergraduate degree in social administration in 1942. She and Victor were married on June 14, 1942, and the following month he was drafted. Like thousands of other young war brides, Edith decided to follow her husband to his various military postings. The newlywed couple experienced a "marriage on the move," moving fourteen times over the course of the next two years.

In September 1944, Victor, who had by now received his commission as a lieutenant in the Army, was sent to Europe where he served as an artillery officer with the 84th Infantry Division. Edith returned to Cleveland to live with her parents "for the duration." Her degree in social administration enabled her to secure a job as a social worker in one of the 3100 federally sponsored day-care centers supported by Lanham Act funds. Eventually Edith was appointed to serve as the director of Cleveland's True Sisters Day Care Center. When she received this appointment, she was only twenty-four years old, making her the youngest day-care director in Cleveland. Although she occasionally confided to her husband that her "best service could have been given in the Red Cross or even the WACS," her letters also make it clear that her work as a day-care director was vital to the war effort.

During the eighteen months that they were separated, from September 1944 until February 1946, the Speerts wrote 1300 letters to each other. It was not uncommon for them to pen two or three letters a day.

Edith wrote detailed letters in which she described balancing their budget, car repairs, wartime shortages, and her hopes and dreams for the postwar world. Some of her most perceptive comments concerned the management of wartime day-care centers and the need for continued federal funding of day care after the war.

Cleveland, Oct. 4, 1944

Dearest beloved,

Today seemed to roll very fast at our observation nursery! However, today was the first day I found a "bed wetter" or any kind of wetter, so today marks the first day I have changed a child's clothes since April. Oh me!

At this observation or training nursery school we have two Japanese-American children—a girl and a boy. Both children are very appealing and both parents seems to be very nice. What we "hold against" the Japanese shouldn't at all be held against these American children of Japanese descent. Both these kids play well with the others and are very well liked by the other children.

On the other hand we have Bobby, aged 2 and ½, American child, whose father was a Ranger killed in France. His mother's and grandparent's grief have left a marked affect on the child. He continually cries and wants all the attention. The mother of course is acting unwisely in "pouring her grief" on the child who, otherwise, would be a very normal child. It is a shame that war tragedies must also react on the very young.

Today I spoke to a head teacher who had little or no training in the field except eight months of actual experience. She said that they tell you there is no chance of becoming a head teacher, but that teachers come and go so fast that if you just "hold tight" you're there! Well, I'll "hold tight" until you get back.

My little Japanese-American boy, Wayne, 3 and ½ years, was very cute today. He had to go to the toilet and was "fishing around" in his pants. He said, "Teacher, the thing is very slippery." Also, when he was through, he said, "I'm all peeed out." Believe me, I could write a book on "children's sayings." They are adorable.

My sweetheart, how are you? Have you gained or lost weight? Dearest one, I love you so very much. You know, honey, I thought I loved you after our honeymoon; I knew I loved you about the time we were in Chanute Field; and since then, each day I'm *sure* I love you, and as the days go and come, I love you more and more. When you come back, let's go on another honeymoon and start our life again without any military interruptions. . . .

Good-night, my beloved—until tomorrow!

All my love always,   Edith

Cleveland, Dec. 4, 1944

Dearly beloved,

Now that I've kind of calmed down I can tell you the news of the day! . . .

Went to do Dad a favor on my way to work and got "stuck" on Buckeye and E. 115th. Luckily, Dad has an AAA membership, and so they came and took care of the battery. Of course, I came in an hour late to work! And, of course, Mrs. Lang and Mrs. Yost would be waiting for me on the day I'm late! Also, my watch is on the blink—I'm using a $1.00 one I have from camping days.

When they offered me a head teacher's job at this nursery they're opening on 2916 Mayfield Rd. I nearly fainted! Of course, I remembered to accept the job. Here's the set up: Mrs. Lang, City Supervisor, is turning me over to Mrs. Yost, County Supervisor. However, the county is also run by the Cleveland Board of Education. The federal government put this private nursery at the same address out of business because the owners didn't have a license. Then the federal government bought it and will run it under the Lanham Act. However, True Sisters #30 had a $7,000 surplus and wanted to invest it in a welfare project. They gave it to the Lanham Fund for this nursery plus every month contributing $100. When the war is over, the federal government will step out and True Sisters will be in full charge; which means I'll probably have a postwar job, too.

At present I work only with the Cleveland Board of Education and my check comes from them. I still make my $130 as my contract calls for, but I get $20 more for assuming the head teacher's job. So, plus that $10 cost of living increase wage, I'll make $160 every four weeks. It means $40 weekly. However, the responsibility will be tremendous, as I'm responsible for the health care, children, kitchen, food and buying. I shall have a cook and a janitor and two assistant teachers. . . .

I love you and always will. You are part of me.   Edith

Cleveland, Dec. 9, 1944

My darling,

. . . Since I've taken on this new job, it seems I haven't got a minute to myself. Well, guess this is as good a time as any to give you the full details. . . .

I took the job knowing I was getting into a tremendous project, but not quite realizing how tremendous. The house was absolutely, positively the dirtiest, filthiest place I have ever been in. The people living there moved out a day after we took over. They used to live on the second floor and run a disgusting, ill-equipped nursery on the first floor. You can imagine how dirty it is if the place had to be fumigated, and then, there was so damn much trash in the attic the federal government didn't even think it could be cleaned, so the attic was merely bolted! The basement . . . we finally got cleaned out!

I had to wash and sterilize all the toys and equipment, supervise the going over of the lights, gas, furnace, telephone, plumbing, etc. Had to order food, and equipment, and had to supervise all the housecleaning and keep track of all the bills and the time sheet. Well, honey, I've been working 9 and 10 hours a day. You can see, it is really a job!

Monday morning we opened up with merely 4 children. We will have not more than 10 children for the next 2 or 3 weeks, since there is a lot of work to be done. They are scraping and sanding the floors so that linoleum can be put from corner to corner on the first floor. . . .

The quota of children for this nursery is 35. Although it is considered a large house, it is not a large nursery school except for the yard. . . .

Today, I was supposed to get a half day off, but couldn't do it. I merely ran down and got my hair set, and took some books back to the library. Then, I went right back to the nursery. When I got home at 6:30, I had planned to eat, wrap a package to mail to you, and write letters, but I had so much bookkeeping to do that I only wrapped a package for you, did my bookkeeping and now, I'm writing this letter to you. Honey, I'm really worn out! . . .

I'm thinking of you every hour, every minute, every second of the day and night!

Edith

Cleveland, May 8, 1945

My dearest,

It's late and I'm tired, but it just wouldn't seem right not kiss you "goodnight" even though it's via the mails.

I'm sure I've mentioned a dozen times how wonderful it is to receive V-Mails from you at work. Keep sending them there! . . .

Mrs. Yost came out this evening (5:00 p.m.) and I really opened my mouth and gave forth—Of course, it was merely "a release"—after all, she's got to keep "playing up" all the good points of the job—she's got to keep me there! I realize that my work is interesting —has post-war possibilities; but damn, I am working "like a dog" and I am underpaid! Gosh, there are so many ways to look at it!!! . . .

V-E Day was officially today—heard President Truman speak—but it made little or no matter to me—same old day—same old routine—same old nightly letter when I should be kissing you in order to celebrate!

I adore you, my darling. You are my world! There is no one like you!

All my love forever— Edith

Cleveland, Aug. 14, 1945

Oh darling,

The great news finally came over the radio. I want to write to you and I want to listen to the radio.

I decided to turn off the radio and write you a super-duper letter cause I'm so utterly happy—anyhow, as happy as I can be without you!

At 6:45 p.m. I came upstairs and got in bed to write you a letter. I turned on the radio—and boom—I heard the news and immediately, horns started to blow—there were shouts, etc. Mother had heard the news downstairs and we began to yell wildly to each other. . . .

It seems like a new era has started for me. You see, as far back as I can remember, there has always been a war—Oh darling—if only you could come home now—right now! I love you so very much. Do you think that this may speed up your homecoming?

Honey, before I forget, there is a Maternal and Child Health Bill #1318 before the Senate, and if public pressure would help, perhaps we could get it passed. Please drop a V-Mail to Senator Burton or Senator Taft asking him to vote for the bill. This bill would continue federal day care centers when Lanham Funds stop. Get some of the boys to write to their senators—please. I've bought 25 cards and passed them around and mailed them already! I'm getting more too!

Dearest—I'm so "hepped up" I can hardly write! We have been waiting so long for this news! . . .

I love you very much.   Edith

Cleveland, Aug. 21, 1945

My darling,

. . . Well, honey, this morning's papers came out with the announcement that Lanham Funds have ceased and all the day care centers all over the country will be closed by October 30, 1945. Everyone knew that Lanham Funds cease 30 days after the emergency but they were hoping for an amendment to the bill or something. Anyhow, Senator Lanham is only out for the business interests and therefore doesn't care what happens to all these mothers and children. All that he originated the bill for was to get women in industry—after the war—the hell with them! Anyhow, the nation as a whole is excited (I hope). It really is a lousy deal for servicemen's wives with children who are using these centers in order for them to work and supplement their husbands' allotment!

Mrs. Yost called me to tell me that our center would be one of the last to close—and officially it would close October 15th—only, at that time, True Sisters would step in and take over at our place.

You can't imagine the excitement around the center all day! Mothers kept calling in—people and staff kept asking me—as if I knew it all. I'm really going around in circles!

Anyhow, everyone thinks that some other agency will cover the operation of these centers in Cleveland. In the meanwhile, all my mothers have written to Senator Burton and Senator Taft to hurry up and pass Bill No. 1318—Maternal and Child Health. Many of the women have written to their husbands to write in too! Please darling, cooperate with me, and get all the boys you know and yourself to write to their respective senators to vote for Bill 1318. I just called your folks and told them to all send in cards! . . .

Sweetest boy—I adore you madly—I'm tired of being brave and good and honorable—I want you home!

I love you,   Edith

By the way—this "galls me": The city of Cleveland is raising thousands of dollars to build a fountain in Public Square as a memorial to soldiers of World War II. Wouldn't it be a really swell thing if they donated this money to housing for veterans or for day care centers for servicemen's children—but no—why bother—everyone will go look at a fountain—ha! ha!

Congress extended the Lantham Act for an additional six months. However, in March 1946, federal support for child-care facilities ended. Edith continued to serve as director of the True Sisters Day Care Center until February 1946, when she and Victor were reunited.

During the last six months of the couple's separation, Edith frequently took the opportunity to tell Victor that she had received a great deal of satisfaction from her work. Her busy and challenging days at True Sisters had made it easier for her to endure the long months of loneliness when she and her husband were apart. Just as important, the responsibilities of her job had contributed to her becoming a more mature and independent woman.

Cleveland, Oct. 21, 1945

Darling,

Lately I just haven't had the time to sit down and write you all of what I think and feel, but I think I've given you a smattering of my moods in all my letters. . . .

In a way I'm disgusted with everybody and everything—all I want is for you to come home so that I can really live! . . .

Last night Mel and I were talking about some of the adjustments we'll have to make to our husbands' return. I must admit I'm not exactly the same girl you left—I'm twice as independent as I used to be and to top it off, I sometimes think I've become "hard as nails"—hardly anyone can evoke any sympathy from me. No one wants to hear my troubles and I don't want to hear theirs. Also—more and more I've been living exactly as *I* want to and I don't see people I don't care about—I do as I damn please. As a whole, I don't think my changes will effect our relationship, but I do think you'll have to remember that there are some slight alterations in me. I'm pretty sure that holds true for you too—am I correct? . . .

I love you. Edith

Cleveland, Nov. 9, 1945

Darling,

At last a bunch of your letters came through—airmail 10/28 through 10/31 and V-Mails 10/28 and 10/29. Believe me I was "tickled" with the "haul" I made! . . .

Sweetie, I want to make sure I make myself clear about how I've changed. I want you to know *now* that you are not married to a girl that's interested solely in a home—I shall definitely have to work all my life—I get emotional satisfaction out of working; and I don't doubt that many a night you will cook the supper while I'm at a meeting. Also, dearest—I shall never wash and iron—there are laundries for that! Do you think you'll be able to bear living with me? . . .

I love you, Edith

Cleveland, Nov. 18, 1945

My darling sweetheart,

. . . This "waiting for you" seems so endless! Sometimes, when I'm working, or when I'm plain not thinking about my troubles, it doesn't bother me too much, and I think that I can patiently wait until you get home; but sometimes, like this morning when I was ready to get up and thought that this is only November, I thought my heart would burst out of it's shell—I just didn't think I'd live through another day without you! And sometimes, like when I'm driving to work in the morning sunlight I don't think I can go on much longer without you—I feel as though I don't care whether I live or die—all I want is you! I buy clothes to keep up my morale, but each garment only keeps up my morale for the space of buying it! I miss you horribly—nothing can substitute for you, although I've tried very hard to make some things do the trick! No go!

When you come back, there are so many things I want to do together. Although I want to settle down, and although there's a whole future together to plan, I still want to do the little ordinary things I've missed doing with you in the past 14 months! I want to smile at you across the table at the Statler's; I want to hold your hand at the Playhouse and the Hanna; I want to walk proudly down the aisle with you to the dress circle at the Music Hall; I want you to watch me try on dresses at Halle's; I want to stroll down Euclid Ave. with you; I want to love you madly each night; I want you to meet every child in the school; I want to ride with you in the morning sunlight past Shaker Lakes; I want to take a shower with you; I want you to kiss me good-morning and good-night; I want to watch you shave. Oh darling—I want you so very much!! I love you more than I can ever put into words—I wish my heart could spill love on you, like my mouth can water yours with kisses! . . .

All my love ever and ever,   Edith

Cleveland, Dec. 2, 1945

Darling,

. . . We're having a big Xmas party at school, and at present we have asked each mother to donate 50 cents and we take the kids shopping and let them buy a present to put under the tree. Gosh, we took seven kids to the dime store yesterday and they had a wonderful time deciding what they wanted. They chose everything from clay sets to cars to irons, etc. I think it was as exciting for the child as the teachers. We let them pay their own money and they saw exactly how much their money could buy! . . .

Yesterday, on the busy intersection by the Highbee-May Co. stood girls with baby carriages holding signs reading "Bring the Boys Home. Don't use the Ships for Profit," etc. Anyhow, they had a big petition which they are sending into Washington and I was about the 900th person to sign. I'll eventually send you the little bulletin they handed out. They were from the original "American Youth for Democracy." They were telling the public that public opinion is what gets these issues across to the men in Washington.

Many people were afraid to sign, but believe me, I made my own mother sign and some of her lady friends we "bumped into"! . . .

Sweetheart, I love you very, very much. I can hardly wait for the days when we are together forever and ever.

All my love always,   Edith

Cleveland, Jan. 7, 1946

My dearest darling,

. . . Altho' I spend quite a bit of time writing to you, I hope you never receive these letters because you are on your way home.

Boy—I really love my job! I felt 100% better today after I got to work and got busy. Nothing like work to keep your mind off your troubles. . . .

If you do get this letter before you leave (hope not) call me, if you can, when you dock. Call me at work or at home. However, and God forbid, if you come in later than the end of February call me at home, since the entire program *may* "fold up" the end of February. If you can get a hotel accommodation, fine, or, would you like me to get it? We can decide when you phone me. Would love to meet you at the Terminal—please plan on that! I *definitely* don't want our folks to know. If you call me from N.Y.—and even if you call at home—no one needs to know *when* I'll meet you or *where*, because, you see, I have a suitcase at work for just such a "happening." I can just call home and say I'm staying at Gallaghers or some such thing. I want just *one*—just *one complete* day and night absolutely alone with you!

Darling—I, too, have gotten to the point where I don't care about writing letters to friends or anyone. All I want is for the days to just fly by—For my part this could be the 27th of January instead of the 7th—I'm still hoping you'll be home around the first of February. . . .

Dearest—it can't be much longer before we'll be talking instead of this silly writing.

I love you,   Edith

Following their reunion in February 1946, Edith and Victor settled in San Antonio, Texas, where he enrolled in St. Mary's Law School. Upon receiving his law degree in 1949, Victor established a private law practice in San Antonio. Over the next few years, Edith devoted much of her time to raising their three daughters. She also attended Trinity University where she received the M.Ed. degree in 1964. For twenty years, she taught social studies in the North East Independent School District in San Antonio. She retired from teaching in 1983.

After forty-four years of marriage, the Speerts were divorced. Edith continues to live in San Antonio, where she coordinates book discussions for the Institute of Lifetime Learning and serves as a docent for the Institute of Texan Cultures. She enjoys traveling, attending elderhostels, and visiting with her five grandchildren.

Marjorie E. La Palme, a twenty-one-year-old registered nurse from Greenfield, Massachusetts, volunteered for the Army Nurse Corps in April 1942.
She was one of approximately 350,000 American women who directly assisted
in the war effort by serving with the armed forces. In June 1942 she was sent
to England where she worked at a military hospital. Following the D-Day
invasion of June 1944, she was transferred to an evacuation hospital which
followed the 9th Army through France, Belgium, Holland, and Germany. She
was stationed overseas for thirty-nine months.

Marjorie's mother, Ethel M. Pendlebury La Palme, was a native of Derbyshire, England. She had come to North America as a World War I war
bride. During the Second World War, she spent hours each day writing to
her daughter as well as to her three sons in the armed services. She also
corresponded with her mother in Derbyshire, whom Marjorie was able to
meet for the first time when she was stationed in England.

During Marjorie's many transfers from one battleground to the next, there
were often long periods when she did not receive mail from home. Eventually, her mail would catch up with her and, as she has recently commented,
"all was right with my world again."

Greenfield, Nov. 28, 1944

My Dear Marjorie,

Received your latest letter yesterday written November 12. So now you
are right in the front line. Oh Dear! I will be worrying over you from now
on. That's where you are going to see the sad sights of the poor boys.

I hope and pray it will soon be over. They seem to be getting terrible
weather over there in France by the radio. Rain and snow and mud. It must
be discouraging.

I don't know whether I told you in my last letter about our Thanksgiving
dinner. I guess I did though. I write so many letters I forget what I write
half of the time. Only Pa, I, Joan [Marjorie's younger sister] and Ronnie
[Marjorie's younger brother]—it was a very quiet dinner. After we had dinner, I had the dishes all done by 2 p.m. . . . . It was a far cry from our old
Thanksgiving Days when we always had a big crowd around the table. I felt
pretty lonesome though . . .

Do you want me to send your box of underwear over? I have had it
packed so long but hated to send it when I knew you were going from place
to place. It would have perhaps gotten lost.

We are all well. Take care of yourself, and try and rest all you can. I
know you must be pretty busy with all those poor wounded boys. I will
write again in a day or so. Pa sends his love. . . .

We are all thinking of you every minute and are very proud of your
wonderful self.

All my Love as always,   Your Loving Mother

Greenfield, April 23, 1945

My Dear Marjorie,

Received your latest letters since you crossed the Rhine. . . . You must be very busy now. The 9th Army is about to link up with the Russians by radio news. The Russians are fighting in the streets of Berlin right now. I'm kind of glad they got there first because they won't show any mercy. The news of those horror camps the U.S. Army is coming across is sure horrible. It seems incredible that so called Christians could inflict such horrors in this day and age on helpless people. . . .

I received the letter with the snapshots, taken in your fatigue suits and the armful of shoes. Of all the pictures you have sent home, I think you are the prettiest girl in the whole lot. They're either too plain or old maidish looking types.

Now you are right up in Germany. Watch out for those damned Germans now. Don't eat anything as I hear everything they offer to the troops is poisoned. . . .

Take care of yourself and let's hope you will be homeward bound pretty soon.

Love from Pa, Ronnie, and Joan.

All my Love and God Bless you my Dear,   Your Ever Loving Mother

In the fall of 1945, Marjorie La Palme returned to Greenfield, where she worked as a maternity nurse for the next five years. In 1950, she married Wilfred Faneuf. They had five children. Marjorie's mother died in 1967. After the Faneuf children reached school age, Marjorie resumed her nursing career. Her husband died in 1982, and she retired from nursing three years later. Marjorie lives in Greenfield and is an active member of the local senior citizens center, where she tap dances with the "Golden Dancers."

———————————

In 1942, at the age of 40, Anna Rachel Russell, the first black woman to graduate from the Philadelphia School of Design for Women (now Moore College of Art), volunteered for the Women's Army Auxiliary Corps. She was the first black woman from the eastern district of Pennsylvania to join the WAACS. She spent most of the war years at Fort Huachuca, Arizona, a training post for black recruits. During her three years in the Army, she worked as a graphic artist, producing wartime posters, cartoons, brochures, diagrams, and maps. What follows is one of the many letters of congratulations she received after she enlisted in the WAACS.

Philadelphia, Sept. 27, 1942

Dear Miss Russell:*

Today I learned of your undertaking and how proud I was to learn of your efforts.

When I arrived home I went in search for your picture in the record. My mother had already seen it and read it and told me about it. I have cut your picture out and placed it on my wall. And while I write I can look at your picture.

Oh, I do praise the Lord for you and I pray his blessings upon you. I praise Him for several reasons—

1. Because you are willing to make the sacrifice.

2. Because you are willing to help in the crisis to make a better world for our children to live in.

3. Because you know the Lord and women like you are needed to help in this war.

I cannot go but I shall be praying earnestly for you.

I don't have money to give you as I'd like but I will put you on my prayer list for success.

Please remember me in prayer and write me once in a while. I shall be anxious to hear and know how you are making out. Don't forget the words of Jesus as He said, "So I am with you always etc."

And also, I'll never leave nor forsake. And oh you can trust Him for He never fails. Is there any little thing I can do for you?

By By,   Minnie

Following the war, Anna Russell Jones continued her career as a graphic artist. She did graduate work at the Moore College of Art, and she also studied medical illustration at Howard University. In 1952, she married William Albert Marsh Jones, Jr. She received an Honorary Degree, Doctor of Fine Arts, from Moore College in 1987. She lives in a retirement home in Philadelphia.

Nineteen-year-old Alvira "Pat" Vahlenkamp of Grand Island, Nebraska, was working as a civil service employee for the Air Corps in Grand Island when, in 1942, she began dating Charles "Chuck" Melvin who was attending Army automotive school at Fort Crook in Omaha. Pat was also enrolled in the Civil Air Patrol and had begun flying lessons. Following a twelve-month courtship, Pat and Chuck were married in September 1943.

---

*This letter is located in the Anna Russell Jones Collection, Afro-American Historical and Cultural Museum, Philadelphia. Printed by permission of the Afro-American Historical and Cultural Museum.

Chuck was shipped overseas in the spring of 1944. He landed in France at D-Day plus six and was involved in very heavy combat. After her husband left for combat, Pat enlisted in the Women's Army Corps in July 1944. Following basic training at Fort Des Moines, Iowa, she was posted to Rosencranz Field in St. Joseph, Missouri, and then to the 14th Ferrying Group in Memphis, Tennessee.

Pat joined the WAC because she felt that this would free a serviceman to go overseas, for personnel in her area of speciality, supplying equipment for planes and crew for overseas duty, were in short supply. Initially, Chuck was not happy with her decision to enlist in the WAC, although he later found it admirable.

Fort Des Moines, Aug. 13, 1944

Darling Hubby:
Didn't have as much time today as I expected, but have more time tonite. And am feeling much better tonite. My arms aren't even sore any more.
Sunday was just another day here for we G.I. gals. Only, we were able to sleep until 6:30. Ate at 8:00. Drilled until noon mess. Lecture at 3:00 until mess. Then we were off. We all have our uniforms now. So five of we girls went to the P.X. and Service Club. Didn't stay longer than an hour. . . .
I'm ready for bed and am laying on my bunk. The gals are all over. Susie, a redhead from K.C., said to tell you she stills loves you and the Army was fine. She's really a scream. . . .
Tomorrow nite everyone is restricted to the barracks because of an inspection by Col. McCaskey, Post Commandant, Tuesday morning. . . .
Darling, please, keep on loving me. Will you? That's all I want. That's all I need. I miss you dreadfully and I think of you constantly. I dreamed last nite that you didn't love me any more. It was awful. Made me feel awful all day. Please, darling. If only right now you were with me and we could live our lives together alone, I would be so happy.
Until tomorrow. Remember eleven months ago tonite? I'll never forget it, darling, as long as I live. How could I? Or, why should I want to. I have a darling husband, and I want only him.
Love,   Pat

Fort Des Moines, Aug. 16, 1944

Darling:
A break, I don't know for how long but I know it won't be long. Pretty hot today and we have been darn busy. Have been in Boomtown [a new section of the base] for two days now. I didn't get to write last nite. Seems all we do around is fall in and fall out.
I am in the second platoon of Company 18. Incidentally, I have an upper bunk. But it is nice and cool up there. We have three barracks, a day room, supply and orderly room all in one building.
Thought sure when the mail orderly came around I would get some mail tonite, but no mail. . . .

Golly, we were really rushed today. Our really first day of basic. Classes, marching, marching and classes. Our new company officers are all new at the game. So are all the N.C.O. Personally, they aren't very good at directing a bunch of women.

. . . Crazy, isn't it, Sweetheart. That we have to have a life like this and can't be with the one we love so dearly. Darling, I miss you so much, it's awful. More than ever it seems. But, Darling, it seems to me my love for you is growing much more stronger every day, darling. It seems every day draws me closer to you, darling. I mean it with all my heart. Someday I'll tell you exactly why I left the Air Base at Grand Island and joined the Army. It has nothing whatsoever to do between you and I. Darling, please believe me when I say no one can or could ever take your place in my heart. Nothing can ever replace those fourteen wonderful days and nites we spent together eleven months ago. Darling, we will have many more of those days and nites, won't we? . . .

Until tomorrow nite darling;

Your wife loves you dearly, and you alone always.

Yours forever,

(if you still love me)   Pat

Fort Des Moines, Aug. 23, 1944

My Darling:

Another nite, another nite in which I miss and love my darling only as much as any two people could possibly miss and love each other.

Am in the day room, half hour to bed check. . . .

Tomorrow I and the little gal next to me are lucky. We have K.P. going on duty at 10:30 until 10:30 Friday. Am glad to have K.P. over with. We only have it once during basic here.

Friday nite we will have to G.I. for our Saturday inspections. So Darling, possibly I may not have a chance to write again until Saturday nite. But don't worry, you are constantly in my mind and thoughts and dreams. I got a letter from Mom today. She said you were always in her thoughts too. . . .

We received the news today of the capture of Paris and Marseilles. I wonder just where my darling is.

Darling, I am feeling fine. We have very good food and I always have an enormous appetite. Don't believe I've gained a bit. I am thinner than I was when we were married. Things are getting better and easier every day and I love it, Sweetheart. . . .

Yours only,   Pat

Fort Des Moines, Aug. 27, 1944

My Dearest Husband:

Sunday nite, 9:15, twenty minutes to "lights out" and I must write to my darling. I am fine, Sweetheart. Miss you and love you as much as ever. Maybe I should say more because my heart aches for my husband, darling. . . .

I survived K.P., Darling, and it wasn't bad at all. The army in my estimation, darling, is getting better every day. I like it, Chuck. Of course, I know what my husband thinks of the WACs. But, Darling, always remember your wife is still your wife. WAC or no WAC and she loves you and you alone. Honestly, Sweetheart. . . .

Received a nice letter from Mom Melvin that I have already answered. She is quite proud of me, darling. I only wish that my husband had a good opinion. Please trust me, hubby. If you ever lose your trust and faith in me, then it's no go. Then nothing would count. That I couldn't take. Because there is only one man that I love and I want him alone. NO other man ever will touch me or any part of me but my husband. . . .

Until tomorrow nite, Sweetheart,

Yours,

Only forever,   Pat

Chuck was severely wounded in September 1944 and spent the remainder of his Army career in various hospitals. After returning to the United States on a hospital ship, he was sent to the hospital at Camp Atterbury, Indiana. He was then transferred to Kennedy General Hospital in Memphis. Coincidentally Pat was stationed in Memphis at the time. Pat's commanding officer was notified by the hospital commandant of Chuck's arrival. Chuck was suffering from severe psychoneurosis and placed in a locked ward, but because Pat was in uniform she was able to visit him in the hospital.

The next letter, addressed to Chuck in Indiana, arrived in Memphis after he and Pat had been reunited.

Memphis, Feb. [?], 1945

My Darling Hubby:

Monday nite, and not a solitary thing to do. It's raining outside, has been all day. So most of the girls are staying in tonite. I sure hope so because I didn't get much sleep last nite. I woke up at every sound.

Miss you dreadfully, darling. Received a wonderful letter from you today. You said you were leaving there Wednesday for Memphis, darling. I'm surely hoping you get here. I've counted on it. Of course, if you don't, I'll understand. . . .

I hope your darn headaches stop soon, Sweetheart. Maybe I can help that though when we are together. . . .

They've changed my K.P. from tomorrow until Wednesday. Here I was already for it tomorrow, then they change it. But I guess one day is as good as another.

Wish you were here tonite, Darling, I miss you so, Sweetheart, and love you so much.

Will close now and may we be together before many more nights pass.

Yours alone forever,   Pat

In May 1945, Pat assumed the responsibility of checking her husband out of the hospital in Memphis as the doctors told her that they could do no more for him. The only alternative was for him to become permanently confined.

Pat and Chuck were immediately discharged from the service. The couple moved to Pontiac, Illinois, to be near his family. They had three children. Chuck secured a job as a foreman in the building trades and manufacturing. Pat worked as an office manager. After many years of treatment, Chuck has recovered from his disabilities, although he still makes monthly visits to the Veteran's Administration hospital. Pat and Chuck retired in 1981 and moved to Grand Island, Nebraska. In 1986, they moved to Clarkdale, Arizona, where they presently live. They have six grandchildren.

Audrey M. Davis grew up as a Marine "service brat." She graduated from Cornell University in 1940 and from Columbia University Library School in 1942. She met her future husband, Carleton Kelvin Savell, in the spring of 1944, while working as a "civilian in uniform" for Army Special Services at Camp Kilmer and Fort Dix, New Jersey. He was a career Navy man who had recently returned from two and a half years in Samoa. They saw each other nine times during a fourteen-day period before Kelvin had to report back to his Navy base at Coronado, California.

In September 1944, Audrey resigned from her job in New Jersey and traveled across the continent by train to be with Kelvin. In early October, the couple was married. They had three months together when Kelvin's shipboard duties on the USS *Colorado* began in January 1945.

After working three months for the San Diego Public Library in early 1945, Audrey accepted a position at the Presidio in San Francisco, where she was appointed Chief of Training and Inspections for the Army 9th Service Command. Her letters to Kelvin provide details about her various war jobs as well as the problems she encountered in locating appropriate housing.

Fort Dix, July 5, 1944

Precious:

. . . I am at work, and am gold-bricking most fiercely. My conscience is pricking a little, because I have Mrs. R. hard at work, and I must at least give an impression of business or the morale of my staff will be shot. She knows right well that this is no business letter! After I typed the monthly book order, I started this as a deserved ten-minute break—but it has lengthened into well over half an hour!

Strange. There is exactly one person in the library now, and it is only 8:30. Every one who didn't ship today is shipping tomorrow. Thirty-eight books have been returned tonight, 55 people have been in, at least 30 free books have gone out—and three books have been borrowed in the entire day! All this shop talk must be fascinating to you. I'm really not going to talk about libraries all my life, Darling—I'm just glad there is no one here, so I can write you again. . . .

All of that stuff that makes the world go 'round, and then some.

Guess Who?

Audrey Savell regularly reviewed books for library publications. She was asked to review Barbara Klaw's best-selling book, *Camp Follower: The Story of a Soldiers's Wife* (1943). In the next two letters, she offered her opinions about it.

Fort Dix, July 11, 1944

My Precious Darling Sea-Daddy:

. . . I got a new proof to review yesterday, and of all things, it's entitled "Camp Follower." It seems like a pretty readable number from the 10 pages I've tried, and naturally it hits pretty near home, so I'm anxious to get on with it. The deadline is one week from yesterday, so I *have* to get on with it. It starts out with the woman leaving Union Station in Wash. to go out West to join her husband—well, the difference is small. . . .

I love you, Darling   Me

Fort Dix, July 12, 1944

Dearest Darling:

It is now 9:30 a.m. and I've already put in an hour's work! Unusual, to say the least. It's this way—at 4 p.m. yesterday I got a typical G.I. order to list every book I've ordered since April 1st, and all the free ones that have come in too, and have said list ready by 10 this morning! I may have thought I was a lady before, and may even have fooled a few people into sharing my view, but by the time I was through swearing, I'm sure no one remained with any illusions, including myself! It's all in connection with that asinine drivelling law of censorship, of which I disapprove but completely. I was about to depart . . . so I departed anyway, leaving the whole thing in Mrs. R's ample lap. She managed to mooch a typist from one of my boy-friends, so got rid of the buck nicely. This morning all I had to do was list the free books, fuming the while. I ended the list with "short history of the American democracy." Made me feel a little better, and writing to you will cure me of anything. . . .

. . . After we got home, did I have sense enough to hit the hay? Oh, no, I had to sit up 'til 11:30 reading my proof "Camp Follower." Those girls have one terrible time, no kidding. I never had any respect for the silly women who had to upset all the economics of the country by following their husbands around like little puppies, just because they didn't have the guts to take a separation like the thousands who *have* to because their husbands are overseas, and probably in danger besides. I've probably exposed this theory before—but I find it's just a theory, for I'm afraid that in the last analysis I shall have to do the same thing. . . .

I love you,   A.

Coronado, Jan. 5, 1945

My Precious One:

. . . I had to move this morning which was no little task, tho' Peace and Mrs. J. [neighbors] helped. That box is wonderful! I have all the books and aluminum ware in it, and it isn't half full, also your wood box with table legs. So I'm going to repack the foot lockers again and put all the linen and presents we won't be needing 'til you get back and we have a home in the box too, and pop it into storage and maybe one of the lockers too. Mrs. J. says she will move me in her car. I gave her the 2 gas stamps we had left. She told me of a woman to call about a room in S. Diego, and I am to call her back after she talks to the manager of her house on 3rd St. to see if she has a vacancy. . . .

This room has a very nice large kerosene stove which heats it in a jiffy and doesn't scare me so much as the gas. I still have your picture frame and lamps to make the place as homey as any place could be without you—(still not too homey!). . . .

That blessed job! I don't particularly adore it, but it has saved my sanity the last two days, I guess. I weeded three drawers for expired registrations today, a task that keeps me busy while leaving my mind free to think of you. My new assignment is to weed my information file, which consists of throwing nearly the whole thing out. Don't know what Miss Dysart [her supervisor] will think of my method, but for my money most of it is worthless. It's not as engrossing a job as I might wish right now. . . .

I love you more than life,

Your Adoring wife, A.

Coronado, Jan. 31, 1945

Angel Darlin':

. . . First the U.S.O.—gad, what a rat race! Still haven't recovered completely from running the check room from 6:30 to 11:15, most of the time completely alone and unaided. The girl who was supposed to be on duty hooted off to dance at 8 and I never saw her again 'til 11 when she stopped to get her coat. I wouldn't mind being stuck like that if there were any kind of organization around there, but the whole thing is just hit or miss. No one had told me a thing about the joint so I couldn't answer any questions, and twice I had to page someone on the loud speaking system and expected to get electrocuted before I discovered how to work it. Fingers crossed for next week. . . .

All my love, A.

Coronado, Feb. 11, 1945

Darlingest One and Only:

. . . Old Lady Coulter [her landlady] came fuming into my room this a.m. saying "I can't stand it, just can't *have* it. Those people making so much disturbance at night." "Did they make any noise?" lied I. I'm just by the bathroom and naturally heard them going in and out until about midnight, but I was awake anyway, and if I hadn't been I wouldn't have heard them. The poor girl works 'til 8, and then comes home and cooks their dinner, so naturally they're in the kitchen 'til real late, and that bothers Coulter. . . .

Your ever loving Wife.

Coronado, March 16, 1945

Darling:

I'm so terribly excited I can hardly hold the pen! This afternoon Mr. Xenophon Smith from [the Presidio in] San Francisco phoned and wants me to take a job up at headquarters, in his office—and what a job! I'm positively shattered when I think of the responsibility of it! It will consist equally in training new librarians to replace the 24 on this command who are already going overseas and more to follow, and travelling all over the Service Command giving the libraries a technical inspection. Gad, *me!* I'm thrilled and scared all at once, but I just can't see turning it down. . . .

Mr. Smith says they need me at once and to beg Miss P. to let me go without 2 weeks notice. He said she is a friend of his, and to say if she did him this favor, he would try to repay by a favor in the future, so I phoned her. All hell broke loose. She can be a regular she-devil when she wants, and this time she really wants. She did all but threaten me with complete professional disgrace, insisted this work was every bit as *vital* (imagine!) as anything Mr. Smith has to offer, and had the nerve to say that even if I gave a month's notice it wouldn't be enough since I've been there so short a time. She said I'd be leaving them in a terrible lurch, and that I had no *business* to apply for another job after I had joined their staff in a professional capacity. She insinuated that I could never expect any kind of recommendation from them, and that my chances of ever getting another job in this part of the country should be absolutely nil. If I hadn't already made up my mind to take the job if it will wait two weeks for me, that would have decided me, for that sort of browbeating is just the kind of thing I won't take from anybody. Never will I stay anywhere by force, so I *must* go now. . . . For my mind is made up, even if the San Diego Public Library has to go lurching around for the rest of its mortal life. . . .

Of course taking this job would not solve my housing problem which is what I had hoped, but Mrs. C. says she and the Andrews know someone who has a large home there and might rent me a room temporarily or permanently. . . .

Love and then some, Me

San Francisco, April [?], 1945

Hi Angel:

Big news today I'm going to share an apartment! Today Mrs. Frisby [a co-worker] saw an ad in the Post Bulletin and brought it in to me. I told her I didn't *want* to live with a stranger, then, on second thought I decided it wouldn't do any harm to look it over. So went down tonite. The girl is about 35, works at the Presidio, and has been sharing the place with a girl she works with for nearly two years. They're the best of friends and that's a good sign. The other girl is now going to share a house with another friend. Anyway, it's a very nice apartment house—the kind you have to buzz to get in—right on some of the town's main car lines and within two blocks of restaurants, stores, etc. . . . There is only 1 main room with a double bed that comes out of the wall (the one disadvantage, having to share a bed!) but a grand kitchen and dinette (that did it!), a nice bath with shower and tub, and a whole room for a closet and drawer space. There is a large entrance and vestibule so the effect isn't the least crowded. We will fix our dinners together, and keep breakfast and lunch provisions of what we each want. The rent will only be $22.50 per month, and it will be my place as much as hers. . . . She expects to be away often on week-ends, and I'm supposed to be travelling half of the time once I get started, so I'm confident the whole thing will work very nicely. . . . I'm to move over this Sunday. Won't give you the address until tomorrow—I still have no faith in people and someone might change her mind!

All my love,   Me

San Francisco, April 18, 1945

Darling:

Honey, I'm a success. I got sheets! Such a time—went to four of the biggest stores first and was turned down cold. Finally ended up in the basement of J.C. Penney's looking for seamless stockings for Mrs. Frisby [a co-worker]—another extinct item - and saw some bedding so on, the off-chance, I asked. The girl said, shhh, and sneaked in to a back room and brought out some carefully wrapped—didn't even know what I had bought, until I got home. I felt like someone buying hooch during Prohibition—Anyway, we now have two double sheets!

Towels are also very hard to get. I bought one really nice bath towel and two hand towels, and our crummy one I can leave here when I go. We can always use some extra towels. Purchased also a Pocket Book Cook Book, I can't face a kitchen unarmed! . . .

Often I wonder just who the devil I think I am, parading around as teacher, authority, and expert! Mr. Smith called Mrs. Frisby into his office yesterday and told her about a job in the *Berkeley Public Library*—hardly a subtle hint! And at less salary than she gets on his staff. I feel awfully sorry for her, and who knows, if those are his tactics, and he doesn't fancy the job I'm doing, it might be me next! Wonder what he will do if she decides not to take it. She's always pestering him about every little thing, and I think that's the reason. If he wants to see me he has to request an audience.

Forever yours,   Aud.

San Francisco, Sept. 14, 1945

Precious One and Only:

. . . Mr. Smith suggested I might want to stay in San Luis Obispo most of the next week to give my course to the librarian, who is new, then go to Cooke over the weekend and the first part of the next. He asked me if I was in a hurry. Goodness knows, I don't expect to be. Ann will forward my mail to Cooke and I'll try to put off setting the day of my return until I get there and see what the mail has to say for itself. Smith intimated that this might be my last trip as he doesn't know how much longer the Depot as now set up will last—said he might have to transfer me to book selection (or something else). However, I don't give a damn at this point—it's not the principle, it's the money of the thing. He wanted to know what my plans were. . . . I guess tomorrow is the first Saturday "since the duration began" that we haven't had to go to work. . . .

All my love with all my heart, Me

Audrey and Kelvin were reunited in October 1945 when he returned to the United States for a two-week leave. He then went back to sea on "magic carpet" duty, bringing home the troops. Kelvin remained in the Navy after the war. He and Audrey established a home in San Diego. They had three children. After fourteen years of marriage, they were divorced. Audrey continued her career as a librarian, retiring from the library at the Naval Training Center in San Diego in the mid-1970s. She has three grandchildren. Since her retirement, she has traveled extensively. Audrey lives in San Diego.

Velma Berryman was born in 1918 on a Wyoming homestead. Her parents were farmers, and she was able to attend nursing school in Billings, Montana, using funds she earned form harvesting crops. She graduated in 1940 and was working at the County Hospital in Billings when the war broke out. She met her future husband, John Kessel, who was from the Billings area, on a blind date in January 1941.

In October 1942, Velma began working as a nurse at the Heart Mountain, Wyoming Relocation Camp, where some 10,000 Japanese-Americans were interned. About this same time, John enlisted in the Army. After basic training in Utah, he was sent to school in Lincoln, Nebraska, where he received training as an airplane carburetor specialist. They were able to see each other occasionally because of the relatively short distance between Lincoln and Heart Mountain. Velma's letters to John include significant descriptions of her work at the relocation camp.

Heart Mountain, Oct. 27, 1942

Dearest John:

It's cold again tonite and the wind is sure howling around the end of the wards. Rite now I'm waiting for my first Japanese baby. Little did I think I'd trade my Mexican babies for a different race. They are kinda cute, tho. . . .

Guess Hank [a friend] has really turned into a rolling stone. I wanted to be one but guess I'm fixed now until the war is over. Since you have to be, better I stay here so you will know where to find me when this is all over.

Boy, do I rate. I have a big table in my room now. Before I just had a dressing table made out of orange boxes with my mirror hanging above it. Now I can write to you without sitting on the bed.

The head nurse got a telegram saying her father died back east and she left this evening. If that doesn't change things too much around here I will keep my date with you Thursday. I only hope nothing keeps me around here later than 11:30 Wednesday evening.

I'm most unhappy. I don't agree with some of the Jap[anese] doctors around here but then who am I to disagree. After all, it's their patients.

I started this letter at 8 and now it is 10:00. So you see I've had a busy evening. We had one accident case. Some Jap[anese] let a box fall on him down to the ware house.

. . . One of the nurses just wrote my name in Japanese. Perhaps I should show it to the F.B.I. How do I know she isn't writing something different. . . .

Honey, goodnite now,
Love   Velma

Heart Mountain, Wyoming, Nov. 23, 1942

Dearest John:

. . . [A] visiting nurse had me in conference most of the day Saturday and from 3 to 11:30. I was the only nurse in the whole hospital with just nurse's aides and orderlies to help me. If the intern hadn't helped me I think I'd gone nuts, 'cause we were pretty busy and had several sick patients getting oxygen and what not. This nurse decided to give me a raise of 300 more a year and promotion as assistant chief nurse. Under Civil Service, you can't be Chief Nurse without special training. Seems like I get it whether I want it or not. . . .

A little Japanese beauty operator came over this morning and waved my hair and tomorrow I'm going into Powell and have my picture taken. . . .

Lots of love,   Velma

Billings, Dec. 14 [?], 1942

Dearest John:

What a day. But maybe I should start back to last nite when we got a telegram to go for the patient in Sheridan. Dr. Irwin asked me to go with him and we left camp at 6 this morning. After we got to Billings, he called Sheridan and found the patient wasn't able to stand the ride so he left me here in Billings while he went on to Sheridan to straighten things out. So here I sit in the hotel waiting for him to get back. . . .

Last nite at camp we had a black out. It was perfect. Because the lights all connected with one switch. Just the same, I don't like being alone in the dark. Scared cat! . . .

I sure wish that man would hurry up. I hate like —— to wait for a man.

All except you, honey. I'm willing to wait for you. But then, you're extra special. . . .

Lots of love, Velma

Heart Mountain, Dec. 17, 1942

Dearest John:

. . . Tonite we are going to give a party for the Jap[anese] R.N.s. We had to call it off Tues. nite because Dr. Irwin and I went to Billings that day.

Last nite the wind blew something terrible. The sand was on the floor in the hall this morning a good half inch thick. The electric line to the hospital blew down so we had another blackout and the electric line burned the wire fence in a couple places. This is the funniest place when the lites are out. No like.

We have Xmas trees for all the wards. I don't know where they will get decorations for them tho. Time to pass medications. . . .

Lots of love tonite, Honey, Velma

Heart Mountain, Dec. 28, 1942

Hello, Darling:

. . . One Japanese R.N. quit. She got mad and left the nurses' quarters and everything without telling us anything about it. We certainly get very little cooperation from these Jap[anese] and they're so darn sly with so many little under handed things. Yesterday, they put me in charge of a Ward and I asked for all new nurse's aides and got them. So I put up a sign on the door saying all people not working in this ward stay out. One of the nurse's aides who had worked there before came along and tore my sign down. I put it back up and this morning then they had this girl up in front of the head office. She lied like a trooper and got out of it. Makes me so unhappy, for 2 cents I'd join the Army. At least, all my efforts wouldn't be for nothing. Don't mind me. honey. You know I always have to explode every so often or I'm not happy. . . .

All of my love, Velma

Heart Mountain, Jan. [?], 1943

Dearest John:

. . . Yesterday, I got a paper from Washington, D.C. saying my raise went thru and also my grade in Civil Service. Honey, if this wasn't Civil Service I wouldn't stay but since in the years to come I might want to work again for the government I'd better stay put for a while. It seems ages since I've been home and it's only been about a week now. Boy, this being so close to home is going to spoil me. But then you aren't here to spoil me so I don't mind being spoiled a little. I was perfectly happy in Billings and I didn't get home too often but then you were there.

Last nite we had an emergency operation and I scrubbed for it. It's the first time in a long time I had helped in surgery but guess I made it all right. I hope! Anyway the Japanese doctors are very nice to work with but a trifle slow.

The soldiers coming up to Soldier Clinic in the afternoon now wear gas masks, or I should say, carry gas masks. They are expecting troubles here but I wouldn't think the hospital would be in on it because it's their own people. Anyhoo, I'm not worrying. . . .

We are getting two mental cases on this ward this afternoon. Who-opppee, won't that be fun.

Darling, I must close now. I'm sending a snap shot a school teacher took of me as I was coming from the mess hall.

Forever yours,   Velma

Heart Mountain, Jan. 20, 1943

Dearest John:

What a nite. I've really earned my board and room this evening. We have some real sick patients and as usual I'm the only R.N. on.

The other day a chief nurse came and there is really going to be a few changes around here. I asked over to the administration office a leave and they said it was possible if I had a good reason. But would have to go thru the chief medical officer here first. So, maybe around the 15th of Feb. Uh! I think this new nurse will probably want to make changes and I want to see the reactions. . . .

Today we heard over the radio at noon that it was 28 below zero in Billings. Bet it's really cold there tonite. The ambulances froze up and now they haul the nurse's aides to and from work in an open truck and it takes an hour or two to thaw out the nurse's aides after they get here. . . .

Well, darling, I hope in the near future to be able to tell you something definite about me coming. After I hear from you, I'll know more what I should do. Until then, I'm still missing you.

All of my love,   Velma

Heart Mountain, Jan. 30, 1943

Dearest John:

. . . I asked our new chief nurse about a leave and she said I was foolish if I didn't take it. You see she has a boy friend in the Army and understands how it is with me. I'm going to ask Dr. Irwin again in the morning and I'll add a p.s. on the end of this.

I go off nites the 9th and 10th and will be there Sat. the 13th and stay until the 22nd. That will give us 2 weekends together. Honey, won't it be wonderful to be together again.

I'll find out what time I will get there and send a wire or something. So, you can meet me if you aren't busy that day. If you aren't there guess the next best thing to do is go to the Corn Huskers Hotel until you come. You know I've never traveled very much and I'm kinda scared.

The chief nurse made the suggestion that I have you find a room for me ahead of time so we wouldn't have to waste valuable time walking around looking for one. But, from what I hear rooms are hard to find. You do what you think best. The way Faith [her sister-in-law] worked it before they were married she gave her name as Faith Ames and it was up to the land lady to guess Miss or Mrs. That way Ivan could come to town, and they could sit in the room and talk instead of standing on the street. John, I certainly hope you don't think I'm crazy for suggesting these things.

Lots of love, Velma

Heart Mountain, Feb. 25, 1943

Hello, Honey!

. . . Last nite I came up here about 9 p.m. The nurses had painted a face on my pillow and put a long veil made out of gauze on it. They had the sign, "It's only for the duration, Velma. Johnny will still come marching home." One of the nurses put a sign on the door, "Welcome Home Mrs. Kessel." It's still there and I think I shall leave it there. You know, honey, I love that name. . . .

So much has happened since I left. The Jap[anese] got up a petition and had the chief nurse kicked out. In fact, they only gave her a few hours' notice or else. Tonight a new chief nurse came. Here's hoping she makes a success of things. . . .

There's some soldiers here trying to get the Jap[anese] to volunteer for the Army. They are certainly meeting with opposition. 125 said they would be willing to fight if they could go to Japan and fight against us. Nerve, don't you think. Only a few have signed up to go. . . .

Must close now,
All my love, Velma

Heart Mountain, March 9, 1943

Dearest John:

Two letters from you yesterday, John. Gee, they each had a package of gum. Honey, that was such a cute trick. If you'd been here I'd really given you a kiss. The gum supply is holding out fine. Thanks to you. . . .

One of the Japanese nurses made me a small bouquet of flowers for a gift. They are made from paper but certainly look real. . . .

I must put a uniform together and wash my white soxs so I'll write more tomorrow.

Goodnite, Darling Velma

Heart Mountain, March 25, 1943

Dearest John:

. . . The chief nurse said she would give Sunday off for this week and Monday for next so I would have two days off in a row. Very nice of her, I would say. Now, if you were only home, I would be the happiest girl in the world. . . .

All the little boys around here have made kites. They certainly know how to make them fly too. Last nite we drove down to the Canteen, about a mile from this area, and there were at least 50 kite flying. Little Japanese boys around 4 to 5 years old holding on to the strings. . . .

All my love,   Velma

On John's first furlough home, in April 1943, he and Velma were married. After a three-day honeymoon, John was sent to the Gold Coast of Africa for three years. He was unable to save Velma's letters after he was sent overseas.

Velma worked at Heart Mountain as a nurse supervisor while John was overseas. He returned in the spring of 1945 and was sent to Morrison Field, Florida. Velma joined him there until his discharge in December.

Following the war, the Kessels returned to Wyoming, settling in the small town of Powell. John bought into the O.K. Tire Store, where he worked for thirty years. Velma continued her career in nursing, working at the hospital in Powell and also serving as the school nurse. They both retired in 1978. They divide their time between their home in Powell and their winter residence in Overton, Nevada. They have two daughters and four grandchildren.

Margaret "Peggy" Meeker of San Pedro, California, was seventeen years old at the time of Pearl Harbor. Shortly after the United States entered the war, Peggy's father joined the Navy in order to do his part to win the war. Peggy, her mother, and her younger sister often entertained servicemen in their home as San Pedro was the major embarkation point for the Los Angeles area. Their house was a "home away from home," both for those going to their ship as well as for others returning on leave.

Peggy and her family sent many letters and packages to their friends in the service during the wartime period while also keeping up a regular correspondence with her father. There were times when Peggy wrote as many as twenty letters a week. In the fall of 1943, she also began writing to a twenty-three-year-old Navy officer named George Hooper, whose ship was part of the Pacific fleet. He had grown up in southern California, and they had met when he had visited the Meeker home with a friend.

During the war, Peggy held jobs as an "incoming inspector" in two different aircraft plants. This involved keeping time sheets and inspecting materials. She worked by preference on the midnight shift and most of her letters to George were composed on her rest and "lunch" breaks. Her letters describe her great satisfaction with and immense pride in her war work.

San Pedro, Sept. 2, 1943

Hi!

Found this paper in my box so decided to write a few more lines. I really have been working. I just finished your letter when the papers came, what a rush and I haven't even neared the end. Oh well might help to take off the excess weight.

I just finished a very light but satisfactory lunch. I have a pint of milk to drink during my next rest period, "to keep up my strength," as Mother says. . . .

One of the girls I ride with just came in to see me. She is very nice. Her name is Nita and her sister's name is Judy or Julie. There is also Agnes and Kenny who is a she and drives the car. I didn't get to work last night because they couldn't get transportation for me. But, tonight here I am. I'm now making ninety cents an hour, and five cents of that is night shift bonus. However, bonus or not, it comes in handy. I now have about a hundred and fifty dollars to pay off to Mom, the dentist, *and* the jewels for my watch. It shouldn't take long 'cause my expenses aren't great and since you have already been here I won't have any use for new clothes. Maybe by the time it is all paid off I'll be so used to not spending it so freely that I'll be able to put some in the bank for a change. That would be something. Probably the bank would cave in under the strain. Oh, well wishful thinking. Back to work now.

Bye

Back again and this time it's the last rest period. The next time the whistle blows it means to go home. That will be wonderful. I really am tired tonight. I guess I should be with the amount of work I have done. . . .

I can't do a thing until the lead girl comes so I will continue to write. I am the only inspector on nights and also my own leadman, but when something comes up that stumps me I send for the lead girl and if she can't figure it out, why we put a note on it and leave it for days so the Chief Inspector can see it.

Bye now,   Peg

San Pedro, Oct. 2, 1943

Dearest George:

. . . I have some news about that up and coming Inspector at the Douglas Plant in Long Beach. It seems that she was the first of her group that came to the Plant to get her Inspector's stamps and own number which is good and she is mighty proud about the whole affair and I don't know whether you know about it or not but the Long Beach Douglas Plant was awarded the Army-Navy "E" for Efficiency and I am sporting a pretty little pin that says so, so you can see I guess I am capable of learning something that I never thought I would be able to do in a thousand years. Oh I know you didn't say anything to discourage me but I was proving it to myself more than anything else so forgive for bragging a little will you? . . .

About that ninety dollar food bill, there are a lot of things attached such as rising costs and such and we did have such a lot of company and no ice so that everything that we tried to keep spoiled and it was in the hot weather and there are lots of cokes and beer and stuff like that . . . besides the prices of food are nearly double nowadays and you really can't get by with much less now so you don't have to worry your serious little head about it anymore. . . .

Lovingly yours,   Peg

P.S. I do love you and send all your firing this way please 'cause I think I make a very interesting target, don't you?

San Pedro, Dec. 2, 1943

Dearest George:

. . . We are having a little party over at work tomorrow night. About seven of us and we are all bringing something different so it will be kind of like a picnic. Anything to break the monotony of the meals. I get so sick of taking my lunch that I started to eat in the cafeteria and now even that doesn't appeal to me so I just eat jello and two glasses of water each night, but I try and eat more here in the morning 'cause I lost seven pounds some place but have gained two back in the same space of time I lost all seven but I feel very healthy 'n I'm not worrying too much about it. . . .

Lovingly yours,   Peg

San Pedro, Dec. 10, 1943

Dearest George:

. . . First I want to tell what I did that I am so proud of and then on to answering your letter. I am now the very proud owner of a little gold pin which says that wearer is a blood donor. Barbara [Peggy's sister] and I went down together the other night and although she had given before they wouldn't take her because she wasn't 18 yet. It made me a little weak and I hadn't eaten very much that day and had slept but two hours so I missed work that night but I didn't mind awfully losing the work when I consider the cause. However, enough of stuff about me and onto a more interesting subject. Yes, I mean you so don't be looking around 'cause around here we all think you are pretty wonderful.

Lovingly yours,   Peg

San Pedro, Feb. 13, 1944

Dearest George:

. . . You mentioned [in your letters] about me thinking of quitting my job, well, there're several letters already in the mail telling of my troubles in that line, and I'm now back in the job quite happy and contented even though I won't get my raise in March as I expected but then we can't have everything. George, this is the best shift I could be on to spend the most time with you when you get leave. You see, I don't have to go to work until midnight and get off at seven in the morning and only need about five hours sleep, or maybe a little more and I can spend all the rest of the time with you. And there are the weekends. I get off at seven Saturday morning and don't have to be back until Sunday at midnight. So, you see, we could spend a lot of time together. . . .

You know, George, after being gone so long, I can't even remember what your voice sounds like. Honest, I know it sounds funny, but at times I have to stop and think and then look at your picture hard to make the memories come real. . . .

Lovingly yours, Peggy

P.S. Just Waiting.

San Pedro, March 15, 1944

Dearest George:

. . . Gosh, we have been working hard at work lately. Just rushed to death and never getting through. Our production schedule has been doubled and still we work harder and put out more all the time. . . .

I had a very busy weekend Friday night. I took Mother to a radio broadcast. It was the show "People Are Funny" [a very popular radio show during the war and after], and was broadcast from Long Beach for about 5,000 of the Douglas workers. They gave four pairs of tickets to each department in each shift and held a drawing for them. My name was the first one drawn in our department. After the broadcast we met Barb and went to dinner and then to a show. . . .

You had better be careful how you talk to me 'cause I have developed a big muscle in my right arm and a good strong in my left arm, so take it easy, kid. . . .

Lovingly yours, Peg

San Pedro, June 15, 1944

Dearest George:

Another night of work is half way over. Yes, this is my lunch period and I just finished eating and I thought I would start your letter anyway. Tonight is another of those lousy nights where I don't think I'll get through. I have to leave some of the work for the day girls 'cause it is too heavy for one person and I'm kind of babying my back ever since I hurt it again. It still kind of aches when I do too much heavy work so I try to plan the work so as to have some hard and some easy. Doesn't always work but it helps. . . .

I rather like my job too much but I am not making a decision 'cause I don't think it is going to last long. You see they have already laid off over half the personnel but the Inspectors haven't been touched and I think they are going to start on us this next week. In a way, I'm glad 'cause if I get let out here, I'm going to work for the Navy. That's what I would really like to do. . . .

Well, George, I will have to call it quits now as work calls. Write as often as you have time and have a good time, the hell with being good. It doesn't get you anywhere anyway. You might as well have the fun as the reputation. Bye for now.

All my love, Peg

In July 1944, Peggy took a job as a clerk-secretary at the Naval Shipyard in San Pedro.

San Pedro, July 15, 1944

Dearest George:

I've been home from work long enough to have a good, big breakfast and sit down to write to you. Do you mind? I really put in a night's work last night 'cause we had an extra report to get out besides our or rather my regular work as I am the only clerk on nights. I did manage to get it done, but I am four days behind in the swing book. The swing book is the record book for swing shift. We keep a record of how much work a welder does and how much rod he uses and believe me it is a job to keep up with and I was behind the eight ball to begin with 'cause when I went on graveyard the book was several days behind. I think I'm going to work Sunday night sometimes to keep up. In the ship yard the graveyard shift works Saturday night instead of Sunday night but I'm going to talk to Mr. Gonzales, my boss, and see if I can't work Sunday instead of Saturday 'cause with my job it doesn't make any difference when I do the work. I just post from the work sheets.

We had a swell program last night during lunch. A band played several pieces and a couple people sang and the music was really groovy. Kind of makes you feel good so that you go back to work with a new zip about you. . . .

Gonna quit now.

All my love,   Peg

San Pedro, Nov. 10, 1944

Dearest George:

. . . I am out on a limb and this time I had nothing to do with it aside from being a female. Some fool in this yard decided that all the women both production and clerical workers are to go on another shift or be terminated and I guess I will be in the last category as I can't work another shift with Mother as sick as she is and will be for a long long time. [Her mother had recently had a serious operation.] I only need to work until January and then I will be twenty and will be able to go into the service. Yes, I am going to join the WAVES. I think I can pass the physical now and they are sending them overseas now. The first contingent is leaving for Hawaii soon. Then they will be sending them to Alaska, Panama, South America and several other places. Until that time though I don't know what I am going to do. My boss said he is going to plead to keep me, but I don't think anything can be done. . . .

I love you and am just waiting until that day. Bye now.

Love,   Peg

Fortunately, Peggy was able to remain on the graveyard shift for a few more months.

San Pedro, April 11, 1945

Dearest George:

. . . I tried to write to you today, but it's just no go 'cause there is always some interruption. If it's not some one at the window I have a report to make out. They can't possibly terminate many more people or there won't be anybody working there. Gosh, we average between 70 and 80 terminations a day. . . .

Bye now.

I love you, Peg

Within a week, Peggy began attending a modeling school, in preparation for a new career.

San Pedro, July 22, 1945

Dearest George:

. . . Yesterday at work was spent entirely on saying goodbye to people, not really goodbye but so long for awhile because I hate to say goodbye. I kept telling people I would see them later so I wouldn't have to even say so long. Oh, some of the people I really didn't mind because I just knew them as acquaintances but those I made friends with I really hated to leave. Annie was so sweet to me and made it so much easier because she went around to all the places with me to say goodbye and that made it a little more normal. She waited until the last minute before giving me a very nice and thoughtful gift she had for me. It was a bottle of Balalaika Cologne which is one of my favorites and she had remembered me saying so quite a long time ago. That made me feel very weepy so I left in a hurry and then called her up just before I left the termination office to say why. She told me she understood and not to worry about hurting her feelings.

I couldn't even say goodbye to Ivan because I knew I would cry if I had to do that. He understood very well because as I got out of the car, he said as he does every day, "So long, see you tomorrow." All I could do was run to the house. . . .

Bye now,

I love you, Peg

In August 1945, Peggy went to work for a fur jobber in the Los Angeles area. The position involved some modeling and some office work. She also began freelance modeling. She and George were reunited on October 25, 1945. They were married six days later.

George was called back into the Navy during the Korean War and remained in the Navy until his retirement in 1967. Peggy worked for a decade in various jobs for the University of Virginia. The couple has three sons and six grandchildren. She paints in oils, plays the organ, and is an active member of the Vienna Arts Society. Peggy and George live in Falls Church, Virginia.

Chapter 7

For the Duration

DRAFT NOTICES AND WAR CONTRACTS WERE ORDINARILY ISSUED "for the duration and six months." The phrase "for the duration" quickly became a shorthand way of referring to the period of the war—however long that might be.

Rationing, shortages, war bond drives, blood drives, blackouts, and air-raid drills became a way of life for women on the home front. Women rolled bandages for the Red Cross, joined military mothers' clubs, volunteered their time at the local USO, and planted victory gardens. The Allied demand for foodstuffs placed enormous pressures on American agriculture, and the workload for farm women significantly increased as sons and husbands departed for the military. As part of their support for the war effort, women also worked in the fields, cared for the livestock, and canned and preserved food.

Most Americans readily adjusted to the demands created by the war. In their letters to loved ones and friends, they often described these changes. Even for those persons who found themselves isolated from mainstream events, writing letters to loved ones was useful in helping them to endure the "duration."

Saidee R. Leach of Edgewood, Rhode Island, regularly corresponded with her son, Douglas, a "Ninety-Day Wonder" ensign in the Navy who served with the USS *Elden,* a destroyer escort operating mostly in the Central Pacific between 1943 and 1945. She penned many of her letters from the Providence, Rhode Island, shop of the British War Relief Society where she worked until April 1944. Her husband, Arthur, operated a small jewelry business and was a volunteer air-raid warden. Her daughter, Marilyn, was married to G. William Schmid, a chief petty officer in the Coast Guard, who was stationed at various ports in New England. Marilyn spent most of the war years at her parent's home in Edgewood.

In her letters to her son, Mrs. Leach often wrote about the changes which the war had brought to the American home front. Her letters were filled with information about food and fuel shortages, rationing, air-raid drills, and her work at the British War Relief Society. As an active member of the Calvary Baptist Church, she was also careful to include descriptions of the many special religious services which were held in honor of the Calvary men and women in the service.

British War Relief Society, Providence, Dec. 21, 1942

Dear Douglas:

. . . Dad could not start the car this morning (he has just received his B card) so after two busses had passed us because of being loaded to capacity, we managed to get to work. My shop is so cold that I have put on a furlined overcoat that has been left here to send to England but I shall continue to make use of it until the box is ready to go! Of course we keep comfortable at home, although over the week-end we lived in the kitchen as it was impossible to feel comfortable in the rest of the house even although we had plenty of coke and the furnace responded nobly. . . .

I do hope your Christmas box reaches you by Christmas Day. We shall be thinking of you and wish we could send you much more but of course we were limited by what you could have. . . . As yet we have bought no tree but hope to get a smaller one than usual and put it at the left of the doorway between the living room and dining room beside the desk. We will take the rocking chair upstairs temporarily. I will write you a list of what we receive. So far, I can't think of a thing to give Dad. I have tried to get him a certain golf stick which he mentioned but so far have failed. But I'll find something for him. . . .

My fingers absolutely refuse to work any longer. We all hope that you have a very pleasant and unusual Christmas and you know that you will be in our thoughts many, many times during the day.

Love from
Mother

British War Relief Society, Providence, Jan. 11, 1943

Dear Douglas:

The Government has taken my shop typewriter and I am using a "Royal" which formerly belonged to a Howard Johnson which has had to close because of the ban on pleasure driving and as I am not used to it, this letter may be full of mistakes.

We evidently are going to have a severe winter but we keep very comfortable at home, with Dad and I away all day, we can keep the house about 65 except for the kitchen, and as the sun comes in there it is always warm for the cat and dog, then at night we trip up the thermostat as soon as we get in and by the time we are ready to sit down, the rooms are comfortable. . . . We are still able to use the car to get back and forth to work, but Saturday night we attended a birthday party for Tom Buffum, Senior, and walked down and back. . . .

Our love to you and Dad will write later in the week.

Mother

Mrs. Leach's account of the birth of her first grandchild is an example of how wartime circumstances necessitated that grandmothers throughout the United States share experiences that had previously been the bailiwick of fathers.

British War Relief Society, Providence, March 29, 1943

Dear Uncle Douglas!

Daryl Anne Schmid arrived Sunday morning, March 28th, at quarter of the eight in the morning, weighing 6 pounds and a half. She has quite a little black hair but that will rub off and I think she will be a little blondie. Marilyn is feeling fine and very happy and we have been able to reach Bill by telegram and he has answered with a telephone to his mother. Marilyn was most ambitious on Saturday, made a cake, cut out a dress for herself, and went to a wedding but about an hour after supper we started for the hospital with the happy result. I spent a most interesting night in the waiting room with six expectant fathers acting in the traditional manner and saw six tiny bundles brought in one at a time by a nurse accompanied by the doctor and presented to the relieved and happy father (five girls and one boy). After that first glimpse you cannot see the baby again except through the glass window of the nursery because of the danger of infection to the baby and I was so disappointed not to see Daryl that way. I waited all night and about 7:30 the desk nurse told me it was a good time for me to go out and get some breakfast as everything seemed to be "quiet on the Potomac" and she was born 15 minutes later while I was out hunting for a restaurant on Smith Street! She evidently is going to be a lady of quick decisions. . . .

Marilyn will probably be at the hospital for eight days, then I can take off a few days from the shop and then Marion Butler will stay with her until she feels real strong again. . . .

Dad and I have been thru the horrible ordeal of having our picture taken and the finished article is being mailed to you today—hope you like it and that it is the right size. It is difficult to get two people to look equally well in a photograph but I think this is quite satisfactory and particularly good of Dad.

Our best love, Mother

British War Relief Society, Providence, April 26, 1943

Dear Douglas:

Easter week-end is over and it proved to be a very pleasant one for our family. Dad and I went to the Thursday night communion service in the

Temple—a large congregation and many received the right hand of Fellowship including Mr. and Mrs. Brown—the choir sang beautifully "Were You There" unaccompanied. Our British War Relief Society shop was closed for Good Friday and that day Marilyn took Daryl Anne for her first carriage ride. . . . Marilyn had a chance to buy a very good second hand carriage for twelve dollars. We met many of her friends along Broad Street at the first National Store. . . .

Saturday I went down town with Marilyn for her first trip and we were glad to get home for the crowds were terrific. I stopped at the Piggly Wiggly but could not get fresh meat of any kind, so found that Spam fried in butter made a very tasty Easter dinner. We took Daryl to the Schmid's about ten-thirty and then Marilyn, Dad and I went to Church (this of course, on Sunday). Marilyn looked so pretty and young, wearing her last year's blue suit which makes her look so slim, and a frilly white hat and gloves. . . .

The work of the British War Relief Society is calling so I must away. Will be looking for a letter and hope you had a pleasant Easter.

Lovingly,   Mother

British War Relief Society, Providence, May 10, 1943

Dear Douglas:

Yesterday, Sunday, was one of our few gorgeous spring days. Dad has been working on the yard and it begins to look very fine. . . .

We had an exhibition of pictures of every man in service at the church yesterday. They were arranged alphabetically at eye level all around the chapel and of course we thought yours was the handsomest one there! At the close of the church service every one went into the chapel and theoretically started along the wall at A and proceeded around to Z but you know women! But nevertheless everyone managed finally to get around and we had a very pleasant time greeting all the parents. During the church service the large service flag which was hung at the center of the platform had each star designated for a particular service man and eventually you will receive a picture of it showing which star is yours. . . .

We still are having fun getting our food. Meat seems almost non-existent although last Friday Mrs. Buffum and I happened to be in the Piggly Wiggly just as five hams arrived so we pooled our ration points and bought one together having it split down length-wise so as to have it evenly divided. Potatoes have entirely disappeared and we are substituting macaroni, rice and very often R.I. Johnny cakes but nobody seems to mind. . . .

We often wonder what you are doing at a particular time. . . . Keep a plugging and write us when you can.

Ever so much love,   Mother

British War Relief Society, Providence, May 17, 1943

Dear Douglas:

Just time for a few words with you before the day's work starts. It is a beautiful spring day, just a little sharp in the morning but by noon it will be quite warm. . . .

A state-wide air raid was scheduled for anytime between seven in the morning and four in the afternoon [on Sunday] so Dad felt that we must have the alarm set for seven o'clock so it was "good-by" to any thoughts of late sleeping! But it was lucky we did for the signal was given at 7:03! Dad grabbed a glass of milk and took some cookies with him and with his five men drove out to the Scituate barracks. We saw none of the excitement but theoretically the Edgewood Yacht Club was burned, as well as several houses, and many of the enemy were intercepted at Reservoir and Park Avenue. . . . Dad came home about two o'clock. . . .

I was able to buy a toothsome looking roast on Saturday but as both Dad and Marilyn were not to be at home for Sunday dinner we are having it for tonight. It is quite an event for red meat has been rather scarce. . . .

The first customer of the day has just departed so I think I will consider it as a signal to get busy. . . .

Lovingly, Mother

British War Relief Society, Providence, Nov. 15, 1943

Dear Douglas:

We have enjoyed your many letters and have had fun trying to guess where you have been. . . .

Glad that you have Thanksgiving birds on board. The newspapers seem to doubt that there will be many turkeys in the market locally. The local dealers absolutely refuse to kill their flocks for the prices allowed by the O.P.A. [Office of Price Administration] and distant birds are not expected to reach the eastern market and for the first time in my life I have won an order for one! To please one of the men who came into the shop with a punch board I took two chances for a quarter and won a five dollar order on the Weybosset market! . . .

Mrs. Wriston is just stepping out of a taxi with her arms loaded with bundles for us so this is

THE END

All our love and good wishes, Mother

Edgewood, May 1, 1944

Dear Douglas:

I promised you an extra letter last week and then didn't write it and apologize but somehow the week seemed very full, mostly of housework and sewing and there seemed little time to write, so the extra will have to be another time. By the way, we are constantly being urged over the radio and press to write the service men more often and I wonder whether you would prefer that I write you several short notes each week or the one long letter as I have been doing. I have the feeling that your correspondence is so large that you always have mail whenever a batch reaches your ship—am I right or do you sometimes hang your head in sorrow and slink away to your bunk to gnaw your fingernails? Tell me truly for I can do either way you prefer. . . .

In the broom closet in back of the stove, I reached in to find a rag that had fallen down and my hand discovered a black rubber ball, you know they are impossible to buy now. I don't know its history but it had no teeth marks in it so it must have been there before Chip's time. He hasn't had a ball for months and went nearly wild, but do you know, he hadn't had it more than ten minutes than he remembered about putting it under the piano the way he used to and had us almost crazy getting it out for him! What a memory! Daryl loves to help us throw his toys but we can't let her play with him alone for he is too rough and is quite jealous of her. Bing is more tolerant and it is funny to see Daryl climb into the basket with him under the stove. Bing will stay for a minute or two then get up and go under the dining table to finish his nap. . . .

Love from us all,   Mother

Edgewood, Oct. 23, 1944

Dear Douglas -

. . . We, too, have our maps in the "bulkhead" over the kitchen radiator. I have just put up the new geographic map of your part of the world and have just put the pins in Leyte. Last night after the 11:00 news broadcast we heard General MacArthur direct from the Philippines, as the flag was raised and he put the islands back under legal rule. It was quite thrilling to hear. . . . There over on the opposite wall, between the windows and the cupboard side of the sink, I have "Germany" and have just put the pin in Aachen. It looks marvelous and yet the unconquered territory still looks huge! . . .

Heaps of love,   Mother

Edgewood, Dec. 19, 1944

Dear Douglas—

. . . No, I am not envious of your eating steak, for we want you men to have the best. We are not suffering by any means and in fact it is quite interesting to see how we can get along. Last week I bought a piece of beef called Utility Grade which is so far below Grade A that no points were required and by adding catsup to the kettle which helped to tenderize it, we had one of the nicest stews I ever made, but often we will get a pot roast that no amount of working can make tender. . . .

When I comment on your not saying anything in your letters, don't think I am tempting you to tell anything—I wouldn't have you do that for the world—in fact—I say with pride that you have never disclosed a thing to us and you have never even hinted where you have been or are going. So many people "boast" my son and I have fixed up a code, as tho any fool couldn't think of that, and I know many an officer who has done that very thing. . . .

This will probably not reach you before Christmas and we hope you had a pleasant Day.

Lovingly,   Mother

Edgewood, Jan. 28, 1945

Dear Douglas—

. . . Possibly you have been reading of the severe cold and fuel short-age. We are very comfortable, have not had to shut off any rooms and Mar-ilyn is still sleeping upstairs. We can only have a ton of coal at a time and ours had just been delivered and since then, the only way to get any is a bag at a time from the municipal coal yard and bag it yourself! I remember when Grandpa Raybold had to do that in the last war. It still is very cold but I can't tell you just the degree for our "out-door, in-door" thermometer has been on a strike for several weeks. But the weather should warm up in a week or two and that will ease the situation. . . .

I hope your work is easing a little and that your health and the weather conditions are good. Yes, I too feel that all the time you are away is making the time for the homecoming so much nearer. The allies are moving forward in all theatres and we hope it continues that way. . . .

All my love,   Mother

Douglas Leach returned to the United States in the spring of 1945 and was discharged from the Navy in 1946. With the help of the G.I. Bill, he began graduate work at Harvard University, receiving his Ph.D. in History in 1950. Saidee Leach remained active in church and community affairs in Rhode is-land until her death in 1970 at the age of 77. Douglas Leach recently retired from the history faculty of Vanderbilt University. In 1987, the year after he retired from teaching, he published *Now Hear This: The Memoir or a Junior Naval Officer in the Great Pacific War* (Kent, Ohio, 1987).

Jack Gunter, one of six children, was raised in Phenix City, Alabama, near Fort Benning, Georgia. Three of the four Gunter sons served in the Navy during the war. The oldest son was exempted from military service because he had an essential job with the railroad. Their mother, Mary Gentry Gunter, was very active in volunteer work for service people in the nearby area. This single surviving letter to Jack tells him about her volunteer work with a Navy mothers' club.

Phenix City, Jan. 1, 1943

Good Morning, Sugar Boy:

Here it is Friday and the beginning of a New Year. Here's wishing you the best of everything. . . .

Well, Dad and I sat up last night and heard the bells and drunk drivers ring out the old and ring the new. . . .

Sugar Boy, I've joined a Navy mothers club in Columbus [Georgia], and they are giving a big Navy ball tonight for all the boys home on leave, and are bringing 300 [Navy men] from Auburn University who are there study-ing radio. You bet, I'll be in my glory to be among all those sailors. . . . I'm taking about 35 of my girls [from the local USO] over. I think I'll be giving a dance at the club house for them too as Auburn isn't far away and entertain sailors for awhile, for I've certainly given my time for the soldiers. I carried a bunch of girls down to Fort Mitchell the other night. . . .

I'm sending you oceans of love. Be sure to write soon. Loving you al-ways.

As ever,   Mother

Jack was discharged from the Navy in 1947. His mother died in 1956. Jack still lives in Phenix City and runs an insurance and real estate agency.

───────────────── ✌ ─────────────────

Joseph L. Barrow of West Point, Georgia, was single, living at home, and employed at the local water works when the war broke out. He enlisted in April 1942 in the Sea Bees. After training at Norfolk, he was sent to the West Coast and was then detached for school with the Marine Corps. In March 1943, he was shipped to the Southwest Pacific and landed on D-Day at Bou-gainville Island. He was sent back to the United States in May 1944 and was shipped out again in October to Alaska. He was discharged in October 1945.

Prior to his enlistment, Joseph had lived with his mother, Margaret "Mag-gie" Barrow, and his grandmother, who passed away while he was overseas. Joseph's father had died in 1936.

His mother's letters are filled with her love and affection as well as news of his family and acquaintances. They skillfully convey the day-to-day life on the home front in small-town America.

West Point, Dec. 20, 1942

Dearest Jodie Boy:

Well, just back from Long Cave, after a most delightful day. Went up with Jan. Reg and Bobbie brought me back. There was a lovely dinner (bas-ket lunch) at the Long Cave Methodist Church, served in the "Hut."— Baked chicken, fried chicken, country ham, dressing, salads, cakes, every-thing else you could think of and want. Pretty tree and gifts for everyone. Can you imagine it, I got a large box of roasted pecans—Just save me the trouble of picking some out—Wish you had them.

You should see what I brought home, backbone and spare ribs, sausage, liver pudding, butter and turnip salad (doesn't that sound natural?)—Oh, yes, I almost forgot my Xmas presents—two nice gowns, a Jergen toilet set, lovely toilet soap, wash rags and candy—So Santa Claus came early this year. Everything useful as well as nice. The gifts were from all the folks.

Before I forget, Dona and Grandmother C. each sent you a dollar which I will include in the money order (seventeen dollars in all). I am so glad you wrote for the money with such a marvelous opportunity to attend the Rose Bowl game, it would break my heart if you did not get to go, that near and everything. I want you to go and enjoy every minute of it, just write and tell "Mom" all about it. . . . We can well afford for you to have fifteen and more if you need it. Please do not hesitate to write for me to send you money or anything else you may need. Heaven knows you have earned it. As I have said before, I do not want you to "mope" around camp, when you have leave, take in the sights and enjoy every minute you can. You are certainly entitled to have all the fun you can.

Your trip to the zoo and Botanical Gardens sounded most interesting. Parson said he was glad you were seeing things like that because it is so educational as well as a wonderful way to pass the time. Your friends sound like such nice fellows, so glad you have been able to make nice associates like that. I also like the idea of you spending this time with Webb, the water works operator. All of that will come in mighty well some day. . . .

Know you did appreciate and enjoy your Xmas box from the "Jaycees." Think it was lovely of them to remember you. Bet they bought [it] at Neal-Shaefers. One day recently, Steve hinted that some one was sending you a nice toilet set. Hope you have gotten my boxes, at least two of them by now. . . . Guess you will have enough candy for once, but just tuck some of it away to enjoy after Xmas is gone if you can. You had better save some of these boxes to send some of those things home that you cannot take care of out there. Course keep all you need and want. . . .

Well, Honey guess this about is all the news for this time, will write you again soon. Hoping you will have a nice Xmas. Mother will be thinking of you, and wishing you the best of everything. Enjoy the football game and remember every man in this town would like to be right there with you. All the folks send love and best wishes for Merry Xmas.

With lots of love. Again best wishes for a nice Xmas.

Lots of love,   Mother. .

West Point, Jan. 1, 1943

Dearest Jodie Boy:

Well, this is my first letter of the New Year. I will start it off by writing to you.

So the "Big Rose Bowl" game is over with a score of 9–0 [the University of Georgia beat UCLA]. I listened to it all, could just imagine My Sweet Boy there. Know you needed a few more eyes to take in all the sights, the queens and princesses. Bet they were beautiful. 92,000 people are an "awful lot" to see at one time. In all that tremendous crowd did you by any chance see anyone you knew. I was really worried about Frankie [Sinkwich] and our boys. UCLA must have been better than we thought. Was so happy when Frankie finally did make that touchdown. . . .

Charlie Cooper said if he were stationed in Calif., he would almost rather go to the Rose Bowl than come home. That he could not think of anything more beautiful, thrilling or exciting than being there today. The people, the flowers, the bands, the cheer leaders and best all, "The Game." Novatus spoke up and said, don't worry, Old Joe will not miss a trick. Just wish I could hear him tell about it. . . .

Here's hoping the new Year will bring peace and you boys back home again.

With lots of love.

Lovingly,   Mother

West Point, June 10, 1943

Dearest Jodie Boy:

Received your V-Mail of May 19th today. Always so happy to hear from you. Hope you have gotten lots of mail too by now. This is the first one in about a week from you. Have been writing, so I know you will be getting them eventually.

Gosh, the whole town is "agog" over our surprise air raid alert Monday night (June 7th). About nine o'clock during a terrible electrical storm, the sirens started blowing, got mixed on their signals, but eventually people realized that it was a black-out. Then a truck of Mylands caught on fire in their store's back yard. Then the fun really started. Mac was put on guard duty on this side of the bridge, but no one would stop when he gave them the signal to. He got so mad and "cussed so loud" Hugh A. heard him from the theatre, so Allen put on a raincoat and went out to help him. Of course Tom Roberts who was supposed to be on the east side of the bridge never did show up. . . .

No one here had any warning until the flash came. Naturally the rumor is going this was the real thing, an enemy plane had been sighted near one of our coast towns. Anyway it shook a few of them out of their complacency for awhile anyway. Well, today, this afternoon to be exact, Mrs. R. E. Smith invited me to go out to Lanett Ball Park with them to attend the American Legion Flag Day celebration. It was one of the most colorful and elaborate exercises this community has witnessed in a long time. The parade led by the 124th Infantry Band of Ft. Benning, local Legionnaires, The Valley and West Point State Guard Companies, visiting soldiers and sailors in uniform, the W. Pt. Mfg. Co. band, the W. Pt. High School Victory corps, Boy and Girl Scouts, the Lanett Girls Drum Corps (you should see their snappy uniforms) (and majorettes strut) fancy drill team of Girls, Red Cross, War Service Secretaries and many more.

The military exhibit from Ft. Benning includes Jeeps, Amphibious tanks, overseas equipment, parachutes, and paratroopers. The young man with the 30 cal. machine gun was so nice and friendly. He explained the method to us. Many types of tents and equipment were on display. The men were more interested in the WAACs though. Not bad looking either. It was quite an exciting and thrilling afternoon and thoroughly enjoyed it. . . .

Almost forgot to tell you the most important thing about the parade, and Mac told me to be sure and do so. Someone in the Lanett Guard made a sarcastic remark, about it just being too bad that the W. Pt. Guards did not have any helmets to wear in the parade. Some of the boys told Novatus about it, so he just got in his car, and went to Atlanta, Monday and got some helmets, also some brand new packs, fully equipped with everything a soldier needs. Oh, boy, were our boys happy, and they did "strut their stuff." Really looked like the "real soldier," and not just Home Guard. Have a nice number of recruits. Put on some fancy drills, looked as good as the soldiers from Ft. Benning. Old Mac really has what it takes. . . .

By the way, about 2 or 3 thousand German prisoners who were captured in the Tunisian battle were brought to a concentration Camp located between Fairfax and Apelika, in the Beulah community. Many of them I hear are mere children about fourteen of fifteen years of age. Said they had been told in Germany that New York had been bombed like London and that we Americans were starving to death. . . .

Another thing I meant to ask you before, do the natives there speak English? And how do they make a living? Are they farmers? Do they have any modern conveniences? . . . .

Hope you are well these days and not worrying too much. Sometimes things seem awfully hard to understand. But the Bible tells us that all things work for good. We must have faith.

Remember always that Mother loves you so much, misses you terribly. Be good to yourself.

Will write again real soon. With all my love,

Lovingly,   Mother

West Point, May 14, 1944

Dearest Jodie Boy:

Cannot find words to express my joy to know my sweet boy is actually back in the U.S.A. Still have to stop and think at intervals if it is really a fact, or am I dreaming.

Know I never received a message that made me quite so happy as the one telling me that you had arrived. Had hoped and prayed for such a message such a long time.

Course I am terribly sorry you have been ill and that you will have to stay so long in a hospital. But, after all, your health is your first consideration, and it does seem that the Navy does try to give their men the best of medical care. You are still a young man with a long life ahead of you, so we want to try to get well above everything else.

Received the seven hundred ($700.00) dollars last Thursday morning. Deposited it in the Bank subject to check as I do not want so much money around the house. Gosh, bet you never drew that much money at one time before. At one time it would have been considered "a small fortune.". . .

Bet you are confused and mixed up about the "states." All of the boys coming in from the Pacific area seem to be. It must be very primitive and rugged out there. It will seem wonderful to be back in civilization again after you get "adjusted" to we queer beings, the "civilians" you know. . . .

Never realized before how many friends you and I have until now. The whole town are rejoicing with me that you are actually back in the States

and are coming home (what a magic word). Everybody are eagerly awaiting
your coming, cannot go to town without everybody wanting to know when
is Joe coming home and tell that rascal I want to see him. Guess you will
just have to go into every store and place of business and say "Hello" to
everybody. Honestly, it makes me so awfully proud of you. You really and
truly have friends galore.

Have been up in the "clouds" ever since I knew you had your feet back
on good American soil and are coming home.

Can hardly wait to see you. Know it is going to be a happy reunion. Am
so delighted now that I have not rented the room, because [we] can really
enjoy each other, all we like, without some one always in the way.

Did not know what to do about writing you so I figured would probably
be home by the time this reaches California. You have loads of mail waiting
for you. Know you will have a "field day" reading it all.

Again let me say how very happy I am that you are back in the States,
but best of all that you will soon be home. Can hardly wait I am so happy.
Have the "old red rooster" (frier) up and everything ready. . . .

Lovingly,   Mother

Following his military discharge in 1945, Joseph Barrow returned to Georgia
to live. He resumed his position at the water works, and at his retirement in
1976, he was superintendent of municipal services in West Point. His mother
died in 1983 at the age of 90. Joseph married Mary Margaret Barrow in 1951.
They have two children and one grandchild. He lives in Lanett, Alabama,
where he is active in the local historical society.

⎯⎯⎯⎯⎯⎯ ✍ ⎯⎯⎯⎯⎯⎯

Farm work and life can be very demanding of people's time and strength.
This was especially true of the 1940s when the family farm was still in its
heyday. Farm families and farm communities generally had very close bonds.
Work in the fields, especially at planting and harvest times, was frequently
shared or exchanged while farm machinery and draft animals were often hired
from more affluent neighbors.

The small farm villages near Deerfield, Michigan, were no exception to this
way of life. The Ricica family, whose father was a Czech immigrant, moved
to Deerfield in 1938 and bought a small twenty-acre farm. The six Ricica
daughters, prior to their marriages, all worked on the farm.

Rollin "Pete" Zilke, who lived on a neighboring farm, received many letters
from his future wife, Frances, one of the six Ricica daughters. Their first
meeting came in 1938, when she was fifteen and he was nineteen. After he
was inducted into the Army in March 1941, he and Frances conducted a
courtship by mail which eventually led to their marriage in the spring of 1946.

Pete also received weekly letters from his sister, Marion Zilke Miller, who lived with her husband and children on several different tenant farms in nearby communities. Her husband, Bert, was granted a deferment because of the essential nature of his farm work. Marion's letters to her brother provide important information about what the World War II experience meant to many farm women across the United States.

Adrian, May 25, 1942

Dearest Brother Pete:

. . . I've been trying to clean house a little. I cleaned the paper in the living room and dining room, so now I've got to wait until I can take my stove down to clean the rest. I want to get done this week. I'm washing today and this afternoon I've got some potatoes to hoe. . . .

Bert and Cal got all the corn in that they could. Bert is plowing the other 10 acres today, then he has got about 15 acres of soy beans to plant. He has the ground all plowed. Boy, it's hard to get fertilizer. We couldn't get any at Jasper and at Deerfield they were all sold out at noon Saturday. . . .

Well, I really must close and get dinner. It is near eleven thirty. Loads of love.

As ever,   Marian

Adrian, July 24, 1942

Dearest Brother Pete:

Oats are all combined, had better than 300 bushels off of 5 acres. So that wasn't too bad. Corn is all tasselling out. Looks nice and green. . . .

Boy, you should see little Norman Lee [Marion's son] drive our tractor. He can steer the thing. Bert let him steer it across the oats field with a load of oats on behind it. His little eyes were as big as apples, he was so tickled. . . .

We have our back porch mostly done. Is it ever going to be nice. Bert sure has done a good job on it for never doing anything like it before. . . .

Loads of love,   Marion and all

Adrian, July 30, 1942

Dearest Brother Pete:

Thursday, around eleven o'clock and I just came up from the flats where I've been pulling grass and hoeing my late potatoes. The folks were up last night. They had been threshing Monday at home until it rained. They had 186 bushels out. They said their wheat was nice and turning out pretty good.

Bert is going to have another job now driving milk truck. Our milk man has to go if he passes at Detroit so Bert is learning the route. He will get $75 a month and he doesn't have to leave home until around 8 and he can be back home again by 11 or 11:30, so that isn't bad. That will give him time to do up his work. I guess he is going to cut hay this afternoon. . . .

We wormed our pigs last night. They are growing but aren't fattening just as they should. . . .

Well, must close and get dinner as Bert just got home.

As ever, Loads of Love, Best wishes,   Marion and all

Adrian, Aug. 7, 1942

Dearest Brother Pete:

Cloudy, damp and trying to rain some more. . . . Bert got his hay all up again so that is done for this year as there won't be any third cutting.

We took our little heifer over to Bechtel's and put in pasture. I've been pulling onions. I got quite a few pulled. I'm going to take 2 bushels into town this morning, and see if I can sell them. I've got to go and register for some canning sugar again. . . .

Bert was going to rake up our straw and put it in today but it is too wet. So he is going to work and fix up the rest of the porch if he can. . . .

Well, Pete, as there isn't any news that I know of, guess I'd better close and do up some of my work so I'll get home from town in time to get dinner.

As ever. Loads of love,   Marion

Adrian, Aug. 28, 1942

Dearest Brother Pete:

Well, it is almost noon and I sure haven't got much done today. I'm trying to can some sweet corn and it seems to go so slow. I've got one cooker full on cooking and another one ready to go about 18 pints altogether. . . .

My chickens must know that eggs are high because what I have left sure are laying good. . . . Dad would like to get some pullets, but they are so high. Over at a sale near Halloway a week ago today, some 4 months old brought $1.10 a piece.

We have been having a lot of nice ripe watermelon lately out of our garden. Gee, they sure tasted good. The muskmelons don't seem to ripen as they should.

Well, I guess I better close now and get at my work. My house looks like somebody's hog pen. So until next time.

Loads of love,   Marion and all

Adrian, Sept. 9, 1942

Dearest Brother Pete:

How is this wicked old world been treating you lately. Fine, I hope. Well, after tomorrow, we will know how Leon comes out. He goes to Detroit tomorrow. [Leon, Marion's brother-in-law, was to report for his physical.]

We are having some trouble with the neighbor's cows. They get in our corn all the time. Bert is holding one so he can collect damages. The sheriff told him to. He said he'd try to get everything fixed up today. I sure hope so because it's been better than a week. . . .

Thanks a lot, Pete, for offering us your money for the payment but we

made the grade o.k. And are getting a few other debts paid up. We owe
$40 on the car and $260 or $240 on the tractor so that isn't so bad. Maybe,
some day we'll get it paid.

I guess Bert is going to go back to town [to work] as soon as he gets his
corn husked. It will be o.k. for the winter, but not next spring. Well, I
really don't know any news as there doesn't seem to be much going on
around here. Bert is going to cut hay over to Bechtel's next week. He didn't
think he'd get a 3rd cutting but says it looks as if there will be more than
there was in the second cutting.

I must close and get around to find something for dinner.

Loads of love,

As ever,   Marion

Adrian, Sept. 23, 1942

Dearest Brother Pete:

I guess I better write before you think we have forgotten you.

I've been busy canning chili sauce and pickles and such.

Well, Sunday night old Jack Frost hit here. There really was a white
frost but far as hurting anything, I don't believe it did. Bert says beans over
on Bechtel's are nice. Each pod has got 3 nice beans in and a lot of pods on
a stalk. . . .

Well, maybe Bert will get his hay bailed today and then get his corn cut.
It rains so darn much you can't get much done. . . . Bert says Dad's sugar
beets look just grand, nice big ones. The sugar beet factory along with all
the rest are having a hard time to get men.

Bert has decided to go back in the shop again. Thinks he may get rid of
the big cows and keep just the six heifers. They should bring in quite a milk
check then.

Well, this is Thursday, cold, damp and windy. Bert got some of his hay
baled also some corn cut now it rained again. He is trying to cut corn today
but the darn old binder doesn't work very good, so he doesn't accomplish
very much. . .

Loads of love,   Marion

Adrian, Oct. 6, 1942

Dearest Brother Pete:

I'm laying flat on my back in bed trying to write, so if you can't seem to
read this you'll know why.

Well, it is sunshining today and not too cold, rather warm. Yesterday, it
tried to rain.

Fred Albright is out helping Bert. They are fixing a corn crib. I guess
maybe they'll start to husk corn yet this week, maybe tomorrow. Fred wants
Bert to go pick apples a day and then they take apples for pay. So, I guess
maybe they'll go this afternoon.

Bert went and got Uncle Louie to come last night. You can't find anyone
to help out. I hated to take him away from the folks but they will manage
for a few days, I guess. He probably can go home again Sunday.

Boy, our little girl is cute. She has blue eyes and her hair is darker then the boys quite a little. It may be light though. The doctor is to come again today. I sure hope he tells me I can get up Saturday. I hate this staying in bed, when I'm not really sick.

The baby has got so many cute things. Margaret got her a nice blanket and the sweetest pair of bootees. Then Edith and Percy got her a baby bunty, a pink one. The little hood is just like a hood and coat together. It's so sweet. Elmer and Madeline brought her a big pink and white blanket, also the cutest cake of soap. It is like an elephant and red ears and a hat on. It's really cute.

I'm going to try and have Norman and the baby baptized a week from Sunday. I'm going to have Elmer and Madeline be the sponsors, so Madeline is going to get the baby a special dress for it. Norman has a little blue serge suit with a white blouse so he should look cute too.

Boy, does Norman ever like the baby. He just loves her. Stanley [Marion's other son] was so disappointed because it wasn't a boy that he wouldn't even look at her at first, but he likes her now. . . . Dad gave Florence Mary a dollar, so I think she is fixed up pretty good. She is stout as the dickens. Holds her little head right up straight without wiggling.

Bert got all of our late potatoes dug that was fit today. The cut worms worked in them and they rotted awful. We were supposed to go to a birthday supper tomorrow night now here I am in bed. If I had been sick on Sunday like the Doctor said then I'd been able to have gone. Now I get cheated out of it. . . . Well, the doctor was just here and I can get up Saturday a little he says and Sunday all day so it isn't so bad.

Bert and them got the corn crib fixed and have husked a little corn. Well, I guess I'd better close for now and rest for awhile. . . .

Loads of love,   Marion

Adrian, Nov. 30, 1942

Dearest Brother Pete:

. . . We are moving back to Deerfield again in the spring. We rented the Lou Thuke place that Ernie Piotter worked on share rent. We have to keep six cows and 4 sows and all the chickens we care to raise.

My chickens are beginning to lay now. I sure hope they hurry up and lay a lot, the way the price is. . . . We have sold five of our cows. One man bought our 2 new big Durhams and old Black and Blue roan and dad is getting another one. We still will have 4 and our little heifer we raised. One we are going to butcher a little later on. She is not with calf and we can't get her that way. We tried 4 times or 5 so that should be enough. . . .

Dad got his milk check today and his milk tested 5.2 [percent butterfat]. Wasn't that good. Milk also went up another nickel. We won't get our check until Tuesday as our milkman gets in too early to get the checks and they don't give them out on Sunday so we'll have to wait until Tuesday. . . .

Florence Mary is growing. She weighed 12 lbs. Friday.

Well, I guess I'd better close and go to bed so I'll be able to get up in the morning. So for now.

Loads of love,   Marion

Marion continued to write weekly letters to Pete throughout the war years. After the war, she and Bert operated farms in and around Deerfield, Michigan, where they live today. Pete and Frances Zilke also farmed. They had three sons. Pete died in 1976. Frances recently retired from farming, and the Zilke farm is now operated by tenants. Frances has ten grandchildren.

Catherine DeMers lived in rural South Dakota during World War II. She wrote many letters to her stepson, Donald DeMers, a corporal in the Army. Donald, who had enlisted in February 1941, was on a ship bound for the Philippines when the attack on Manila and Pearl Harbor occurred. The ship, USS *Holbrook*, was then diverted to Darwin, Australia, and he spent the war in various parts of the South Pacific.

Because of his combat situation, Donald was only able to save a few of the letters which his stepmother wrote to him. These letters demonstrate the strong bonds that can develop between a stepmother and son. They also describe life on a remote South Dakota farm during wartime.

Elk Point, Nov. [?], 1941

Dear Don:

Am so sorry to hear that you're leaving this good old U.S.A. I've been thinking of you so much I forget what I'm doing. I'd give my life to keep you from going if it could be arranged, because I lived thru the other war and I really know what it's all about. I only hope that you won't have to really get into it—just patrolling will be very tame wherever you go. I hope this letter isn't censored because where ever you are, I want you to let us know in code whether things are too bad by saying, "Well, Mom" for poor food or not enough to eat and "Well, Pop" for poor conditions. Now please don't forget this, 'cause I really want to know and I'll have prayers said for you.

Did you get your candy o.k.? If I thought I would have time I would send you some other stuff, but I'm afraid it would arrive too late. If you can sneak a letter to us out of camp so we'll know where you're going, do so, because we are really worried about you. . . .

This is all for now. God Bless you, Don, and be careful where ever you go and do not pick up diseases because if you go to a warm climate—disease is much worse and I know you've been a model son whether you're my blood or not and I want you always to remain that way. Your self respect means more to me than you'll ever know. Oceans of love and good luck.

Mother

Elk Point, Spring 1945 [?]

Dear Don:

Yours truly rec'd and it's about time we had some news from you. First of all, I want to thank you a million for the wonderful plant. It's the most beautiful thing I've ever seen and it must have cost you a young fortune. It's still in blossom and there's two more buds on it. The color is deep pink. Thanks, thanks, and thanks. . . .

We've certainly had the rotten weather here. It's been so cold up until today. We've had lots of rain, too. Have the garden in and we've had radishes twice already altho' I can't eat them or, in fact, I can't chew anything. Remember how I suffered with my mouth. Well, my lower plate cut my gums so bad that I doubt if I will be able to wear them all summer. So, I won't eat much fried chicken. . . .

Dad is planting corn to beat the dickens. He has about 175 acres in and that's wonderful for what little they've been able to do in the field. Hope it stays decent so they can finish up. Next thing the alfalfa will be ready to cut.

Dad sold a team of horses. Got 150 bucks. Also sold his cattle and they lacked a very few dollars of doubling their money. So, all in all, we've done pretty good and I hope we got a few breaks now.

Hope you know whether you'll get out by the time you receive this. . . .

This is all for now, and don't say I wrote about *pitch* [a card game]. Thanks again for the gift.

Love,   Mother

Donald returned to the United States suffering from malaria in March 1945. After recovering in a military hospital, in Hot Springs, Arkansas, he was discharged.

Elk Point, July 3, 1945

Dear Don:

We really are ashamed of ourselves for not writing you sooner. We really have been working so d——d hard that the bed really feels good. Dad's been in high all the time. Honest, this weather would drive any one nuts. We have a bad wind storm right now. Dad just came in, it's 15 min to 8. He really wanted to get thru our field but I guess we aren't supposed to have any crops this year. You, nor any one else has ever seen such crazy weather. I saw it coming so I got my new chix in just in time. It's thundering and raining right now.

Do you know they've done very little field work on account of so much rain. I took gas and water out to Dad at 3 p.m. and when I turned around I was mired. I got out and put some dry straw under my wheels. I finally got out. So much for that.

I think Vida [Donald's sister] told you we are re-decorating the house. I don't think I'll ever get thru. Have 2 rooms painted, the walls and the floors and stairway, but there's all the furniture to move back and that's a real job. Vida helped me at first, but she has enough to do now. I raised chix for her in exchange for her helping me. I hope by the time you get home, I'll have everything done. . . .

Honest, Don, I just can't write. My arms stick to the oilcloth because I have all the windows and doors shut. I think the storm is letting up a little.

Are you planning on getting out or not?

Let's hear from you,

Love,   Mom and Dad

After his discharge in 1946, Donald met his future wife, Bonnie Bauer. They were married in 1947. The couple operated a farm in Cherokee County, Iowa, and raised a family of three children. Catherine DeMers remained on the family farm in South Dakota until her death in 1980. Her stepson died two years earlier.

Occasionally work on the home front, especially in isolated farms and ranches, could not be accomplished after young men in the family were drafted. Some service personnel, as in the letter which follows, were given discharges in order to return to the farm or ranch to work.*

Forrest, New Mexico, Feb. 3, 1944

General MacArthur:

I have want to write you abut my son. He has ben over seas 2 year in Feb. And them take him off the farm and that all he knows how to do raise on the farm. We have 25,000 acre of farm land whitch we plant in wheat oats and corn feeds stuff and we had to rent our farm out since they take our son.

we run cattle all the time hve 200 acre 300 cotton all the time we have a lots of grass land we run our cattle on and we havlf to take our land out another year.

No body here But Mr. Best and I who is his wife.

Mr Best is 55 years and I am 50 years.

And we cant get help to run this ranch and farm.

Look like our son has done his part bin army 3 year and we need him so bad. General MacArther dont you think 2 year is long enough one boy to be oversea.

When it so miny here in State that have already train

The Mother here cant under stand ever thing that happen.

Us Mother have heard you was for the boy, but to stay longer than 2 year over sea and we were wonder if you feel that way about it.

---

*This letter is located in the MacArthur Memorial Archives and Library, Norfolk, Virginia, Record Group 3: Southwest Pacific Area, Commander-in-Chief Correspondence. Reprinted by permission of the MacArthur Memorial Archives and Library.

General Mac Aruther do you think it change we could get our son out to farm our land we have and look after the cattle

My son address is

Sgt. Charley R. Best

Serail no. 38012757

Co, C 46th Engineers

Unit no. 2, APO 928 of Postmaster

San Francisco Calif

I am hoping and prayes you so I can tell us you the truth. Like for you to get reach of my Son have a talk with him.

Us Mother prays for this war to end and God be with you all all boys I do Prays.

Mrs Ray Best

———————————— ✎ ————————————

While he was in Army Air Corps, Jack R. Sage of Sprague, Washington corresponded with a number of female relatives and friends. His correspondents included his mother, his sweetheart/wife, Dawn Dyer, Dawn's younger sister, Dawn's mother, and several young female friends from the Sprague area. During much of the war, the Sage and Dyer families maintained residencies in Sprague as well as in nearby Spokane where various members of both families were employed as war workers. Jack entered the Army Air Corps in June 1942. After his basic training, he was stationed in Las Vegas, Nevada. Jack and Dawn were married in June 1943 in Las Vegas. In the late summer of 1943, he was transferred to Yuma, Arizona, and remained there until the end of the war.

After Dawn and Jack were married, she wrote relatively few letters to him because they were together much of the time. However, Jack's mother and mother-in-law wrote to him frequently. Their letters were filled with local news, much of which had to do with how Sprague met the demand of the war.

The following two letters were written by Jack's mother, Helen Davis Sage.

Sprague, July 25, 1942

Dear Jack:

Well, to begin with, I must tell you about the excitement we had just before noon today. The fire whistle blew. I went outside to see where the fire was and saw a lot of smoke. . . . The grass in that back lot back of those houses [nearby] got on fire in some manner and it burned over to the barn and then the barn caught on fire. It was burning up one side and on the roof and it was surprising how fast it spread over the entire building. The fire department got there in a hurry and had it under control in short order. Dad and Hank were on the nozzle. . . . If there had been a wind, we would have had a wild time around here. . . . The barn is pretty badly burned. It was so very dry and the fire spread all over so fast. . . .

So you can really make a bed. I suppose when you come home you'll show us just how the job must be done. Then there's the cooking. When you come home I'll just take a vacation and let you show us how the job should be done. You'll make some girl a good wife some day.

It's sure hot weather now, and there are country fires nearly every day. I sure do hate to see that happen. Last night there was a big wheat field fire near Wilbur and today there is one near Ritzville. The first of the week there was a big fire near Kohlotus and it burned one house and barn and wheat fields. . . .

I made around 7 gallons of kraut this week. It will take about 2 weeks to work and then I'll can it in jars for winter. Our cabbage was lovely but I had to get it used up. We still have several heads to use and when that is done the second and third batches will be coming up.

I canned 43 qts of apricots. Now, I hope I can get a crate of boysenberries and then later the peaches. Our boysenberries are lovely but we don't have many this year. The plants are only a year old. Next year they should be very good. The grapes look so pretty on the vines. They won't be ripe until September. California grapes are being sent up here now.

We surely have a lot of sweet peas this year, first time we've ever had any luck with them. I pick them nearly every other day. . . .

Well, I hope I've remembered to write all I had intended. If I didn't I'll write it next time. Hope this finds you fine.

Love,   Mother

Spokane, April 22, 1943

Dear Jack:

. . . I suppose you know by this time that I went over to Sprague. It is pretty over there now but the trees have not leafed out yet. I hope this frost didn't do any damage over there. . . .

[The] Dyers are fine. Mr. Dyer is feeling better than he was and looks better. The rest are the same as usual. Dawn is worrying abut her weight but she doesn't look fat, she just thinks she does. . . . Bill [Jack's brother] and I ate dinner at Dyers on Sunday. It was very good and Dawn made a lovely angel food cake. We sure did stuff ourselves, but Dyers wouldn't let us quit until we were in misery. . . .

Well, I suppose you want to know what we think of you and Dawn getting married. Well, whatever we say won't make any difference but we should think that it would be better to wait 'till you get your next furlough. Then you could get married up at Dawn's. Also you could have something saved up and would have your higher rating by that time. If you get married now you'll find the financial part of it pretty difficult. We can't help you now because we are trying to get this place fixed so it will be decent to live in. It's taking all the money we can spare just now, and we are having to wait on a lot of necessities. Of course you will have to decide for yourselves, we don't object to your getting married but we are looking at it from a practical side. . . .

Well, I must get this out to be mailed if it is to go today. We hope that you are feeling fine and in good spirits. Let us know what you intend to do.

Lots of Love,   Mother and Dad

The next letter was written by Jack's prospective mother-in-law, Stella Dyer.

Sprague, Autumn 1942

Dear Jack:

. . . [Dawn] went up to Spokane early this morning on the train. Ray [Dawn's father] was to meet her and they planned on trying to find some typing work for her. And tonight she will stay with Dorothy so I suppose they are having a regular talk fest by now. . . .

Well, it's time to turn on the war news again. Dawn complains that's all I listen to. But somehow we're always hoping for some good news. Doesn't seem quite so black today except for the loss of two more destroyers. Well, we'll build four more and see how they like that. . . .

Think Lincoln County will come out about third in the scrap drive contest. Not too bad. Imagine about the next work for the Scouts will be to collect tin cans. We are supposed to save them now.

I feel rather like a slacker now. With school being later I don't have to get up till 7 or sometimes 7:30. Just in time to scoot son off to his work at the bank. Bill turned it over to him last week. Can't even take any credit for keeping my defense worker well fed. Tho' he does fill up in grand style on Sunday. We always wait breakfast until he gets home.

Love from us all,   Stella Dyer

Stella Dyer wrote this letter to her future son-in-law shortly before her daughter and Jack were married.

Sprague, Spring 1943

Dear Jack:

. . . We are really having summer I guess. Three days in a row now without rain. The lilacs and spinea are just coming out. Really awfully late. . . .

Yes, Jack, Dawn will likely be homesick, but she's never been a cry baby and should be able to conquer it. Help her all you can and she'll be all right. I'm not going to do any worrying about it but will be glad when you are able to live off post. And working should help. She won't have so much time to think about it. Some time this will be over and you can get back to normal living, but just now do the best you can. . . .

Love   Stella Dyer

In the fall of 1945, Dawn Sage, who was now pregnant, returned to Sprague for the impending birth. In a letter of October 18, 1945, Stella Dyer reported to her son-in-law about the arrival of his daughter, Meredith.

Sprague, Oct. 18, 1945

Dear Jack:

I'm groggy but will try and write a few words and then have a sleep. Want to go back to Ritzville for a while this afternoon. I do hope I got those telegrams all straight. I sent one to your folks and Bill, too. Yes, I really meant it, an 8 pounds 8 ounces girl. Any way that's what the nurse said. I haven't seen her yet. Saw Dawn for awhile but she was all tired out and half asleep. She had a pretty tough time of it for awhile but the Dr. said she was fine. I stayed with her until about three thirty and then they took her to the delivery room and kicked me out. But baby wasn't born until about 5:45. I heard her cry and the Dr. say "a big fellow" and tho't that Dawn would be disappointed but when Dr. came out he said a big girl and he really meant *big*. The nurse said she was pretty. . . .

All the rest of us are fine and I'll write again later. I'm awfully sleepy now.

Love, Mother

Jack was discharged from the service in January 1946. His mother, who is 90, lives just outside Tacoma. His mother-in-law, who is 92, still lives in Sprague. Jack and Dawn have lived in Stellacomb, Washington, since 1952. They have four children and four grandchildren. Jack has served on the Stellacomb town council for the last thirteen years. He was recently appointed Washington state lobbyist for the American Association of Retired Persons.

———————————

Almost everyone wrote letters during World War II. It was part of the war effort. Names were passed around or exchanged to encourage writing between those on the home front and those on the war front. Casual correspondence of this type often provided news of dances, movies, and popular songs, while also offering the opportunity for mild flirtations.

Lawrence Neuerberg of Wadena, Minnesota, entered the Navy in the spring of 1944. After he left for boot camp, he sought pen-pals from his former high school acquaintances and his cousins. By the end of the war, he had received more than 450 letters from twenty different young women.

Minneapolis, April 19, 1944

Dear Lawrence:

I suppose if you want a letter by Friday, the only thing to do is sit right down and answer the one I received this evening. I guess I'll have a few spare moments between now and "bed-time." We had dinner quite early tonight, after having so much company, it seems rather nice to be just like four of us again.

I was indeed sorry to hear of your having to leave for the armed services in the near future, especially so soon after a new acquaintance! It surely would be nice if this would all come to an end pretty soon. Gee, it would be super if you could be stationed down here for a few weeks—and even months. Do you know your way around the city? If not, perhaps I could arrange to meet you at whichever depot you arrive at. That is, of course, if you haven't any other arrangements. You possibly have friends or relatives that will meet you, and I surely wouldn't want to be a hindrance to anyone!

Speaking of Sammy Kaye [a band leader], I plan on seeing him some time before he leaves. I'm a little undecided which night I'll go, as I have quite a bit to do the rest of the week.

However, I hope to manage and tuck him in somewhere, as I'm very anxious to see him. My cousin and sister went tonight with friends of theirs. (By the way—they were a bunch of girls.) My other cousin and I are both writing letters, which will help to pass the time away.

My hours at work are from 9:00 until 4:30. I surely can't kick on them, can I? We get every holiday off that comes along; also an hour off for lunch and at least a half-hour for relief periods. Our association works on a banking schedule as we handle savings accounts etc. Walking is really beautiful in the mornings and it helps to keep one awake throughout the day. My telephone number at work is At 3264 and at the house Ge 8274. They are very nice in letting people have personal calls at the office. My phone surely was heavy today with *business* calls! I hope it isn't that way tomorrow. . . .

I believe this coming Sat. night we four girls and approximately 3 or 4 others may go roller skating. I wished you could be here with us, but am afraid I'm making a rather big wish. My heart will be in Wadena, even though I'm not there in person!

Since news is scarce and dry, I'm afraid I'll have to close with "So Long for Awhile."

Love,   Ramona

P.S. Be sure to write soon again, won't you?—How would you like going out to Wold Chamberlain sometime? (Gee, I'm beginning to sound like a wolfess!!)

Seattle, June 30, 1944

Dear Lawrence:

I didn't expect to find you in the Navy but swell going, kid. I know you'd rather be home, as who wouldn't but down deep doesn't it give you a good feeling to know that you're doing your duty.

Just got your card this morning so thought I had better answer immediately as who knows, I may never have as much leisure time as I do now.

I don't blame you for having a good time before you left. Speaking of dances, we have also taken in quite a few. My boyfriend, a pre medical student just left Sunday so we went everywhere possible. He is getting a great deal out of it as he will be able to continue his studying thro the Navy and from what I hear they give excellent training. Darn it, if you would have come a little sooner, I could have given you his address and maybe you two could have gotten together. He is loads of fun. Full of the devil, etc.

Did you have a special girlfriend back there? Tell me all about all of them.

Had a bacteriology exam today. Gee, I sure have nurse's training. Have such a swell bunch of friends etc.

Daddy is a lot better now. At least he seems to be but he still must continue with his treatments. How were your folks when you left?

Would it interest you if I rattled on about my work on the floor? Well, you're getting it regardless. I am working on a Men's Orthopedic floor— Amputations, Fractures, spinals, etc. It is all very interesting and La Rayne [is in] her glory.

Anything new back in Wadena. Think I'll call Clara Hankens one of these days. Sure miss her. Tomorrow is my day off so I think Mom and I are going shopping. Right now I feel as tho I could sleep forever as you know Nurses never get much sleep.

Well, Lawrence, you should have a lot to write about so come and tell me all about it.

As ever,

your cousin,   La Rayne

Eagle Bend, Aug. 13, 1945

Dear Larry:

I received another letter from you today, so will sit right down and answer it immediately.

Was glad you and Herbie got to see each other even though it was only for a few hours. I can well imagine how surprised and yet "tickled" he was when he awoke and found you lying there beside him. I've got to have a good conversation with the fellow when he returns. However, next Sat. night is my last one to be spent around here. I'm expecting to make my return to the cities next Sunday p.m. so if you'll start addressing my mail at 1822 Park again, I shall appreciate it very much. Hope Herbie will be back by then. I can imagine what was said about me, possibly some of it wasn't too good. I know Herbie has seen me with different fellows, but I feel the same way as you do. I wouldn't want you to be sitting out there and begrudging you of a good time, and I know you feel the same. After all, I've been going with kids just 'cuzz I don't wanna stay. It's your privilege to go out with whomever you please, Larry, and I shall not and will not *ever* be angry at you for that. I would think it perfectly ridiculous to show such a selfish attitude on my part. It's human nature within one to envy the girl a *little* that gets to go and with such a grand fellow and gentleman as you, but that's given as a compliment. Please take it as such! I've never had any complaints to make long as I've known you, Lawrence, and that's been for a good long while now. Bet Herbie thinks I'm off the beam as the way I kid with him sometimes. There really isn't any alternative. Hope he knows how to take me by now.

We're just about through shocking [the grain], but have had quite a delay due to the considerable rainfall during the last two days. Am glad I can go back as soon as this, 'cuzz with such grand war news, I'd better get busy and look for a position. I won't quit looking till I really get a good one this time. I mean something "brainy" and high pay etc. I gotta make this good.

Mom says to help her with supper, so you know what that means. Write again soon. Am glad you liked the pictures. Don't worry about my persuasion in obtaining *yours*. Won't leave 'em alone 'till I get it!!!!

Love and More Smooches,   Ramona

After the war, Lawrence went to the University of Minnesota with the assistance of the G.I. Bill. A week after graduating, he married a classmate from the university. She was not one of his World War II pen-pals. He and his wife live in Rock Island, Illinois.

Mabel Opal Miller, a stenographer and bookkeeper from East St. Louis, Illinois, was one of a group of friends who, during World War II, volunteered as a hostess at the local USO. She and her friends met many servicemen stationed with the Air Corps at nearby Scott Field in Belleville. As happened elsewhere, correspondence sometimes followed. In addition to her USO work, Mabel also volunteered as a nurse's aide.

Among the persons that Mabel met at the USO was Ivan Johnson, a young airman from Michigan. They became friends in 1943 and when he was transferred, in January 1944, they began to write to each other. Over the course of the next year, their correspondence grew more important to each of them, especially after Ivan was sent to Europe in the spring of 1944. Both Mabel and Ivan had been raised in foster homes and both had been forced to go to work at an early age. Mabel had also experienced an unsuccessful marriage. Their letters served as morale boosters and also enabled them to share experiences with one another during a stressful time in their lives.

East St. Louis, May 14, 1944

How's the G.I. who was here for so short a time?

Whoever coined that phrase, "short and sweet," anyway? They surely couldn't have been talking about furloughs, could they? Those were the fastest two days I ever lived through. It seems I should be able to turn away from this typewriter and still see you in the room. . . .

I went to church. I had hoped when you came Tuesday night that you would be able to stay at least til noon on Sunday, for you see we had special Army-Navy Services along with Mother's Day Services and there were a lot of men in khaki and blue there. I got up with the blues, and I don't mean Navy blues, and I still have them. The church services didn't help any. Well. . . .

Don't forget Father's Day, June 18th. Remember he is concerned about you too. Also, I don't believe that you didn't write your mother for a whole month as you said, but regardless, of how often you write her, you still should write more often. I don't know how mothers feel, but from my observations in this house, they must have a yearning, aching, anxious feeling in the pit of their stomachs most of the time. If I ever read one of your mother's letters, I would know what she wanted from you. . . .

Lots of love, Mabel

East St. Louis, May 20, 1944

Dear Ivan:

You said you were shipping out Saturday. I hope you didn't leave until Saturday night, so you would be there for mail call, because by Saturday you should receive the lengthy letter I wrote over Saturday and Sunday and mailed Monday night. I had the four leaf clovers and I had soaked them so well before I wrapped them in the waxed paper because I wanted them to be fresh when you rec'd them. But if they have to follow all the way to the desert [in Nevada] trying to catch up with you, I'm afraid they will be dead or mildewed. I wanted you to press them. You could cut little sections of that isinglass container, just large enuf for one clover and each of you in the crew could carry a good luck clover with you. Anyway, that's what I had in mind when I bought the container. . . .

So long, Mae

East St. Louis, June 14, 1944

Ivan:

. . . In regard to the Red Cross course I'm taking. Do you know what we will be when we get thru and are eligible for our caps? Something like yardbirds. We won't be assistants to the graduate nurses, oh no, we'll be assistants to the *student* nurses. I'll have to do away with the long fingernails; have to keep them down to the flesh in order not to scratch the patients. We have to furnish our own uniforms, buy nurse's shoes and get a watch with a second hand. All our labor is donated. We got our uniforms the other night, and you should see them. Heavy blue denim, the smallest size is about 3 sizes too large. What a sloppy looking piece I'm going to be. The patients will take one look at me and have a relapse. We finish our classes this Friday night and take our last typhoid shot, start work on the hospital floor Monday night, that is practice work for 45 hrs. Wonder what kind of a nurse I'll make. I could put my hot hand on your cool head, I mean my cool hand on your hot head, or hold your hand. . . .

Well, I've got to be running along. I am on my way to the hospital for class. Left home early so I could get a letter off to you, meaning this one.

Lots of Love, Mae

East St. Louis, July 15, 1944

Hello, you old meany!:

. . . At the present writing I am wondering where you are. It's awful, this suspense. I can't believe that you are thru with your training. You haven't been taught how to bail out yet, have you. I'll finally get to go to church again tomorrow. By the way, that's what you ought to do. Try some spiritual nourishment for a change instead of all that liquid nourishment. Don't any of your buddies go? You never answer me on this subject.

When you get overseas and there is anything you want that you are permitted to have and it is possible to send from this end, let me know, I'll see what I can do for you. . . .

This is about all for now,

Love,   Mae

East St. Louis, Aug. 15, 1944

Dear Ivan:

Yesterday evening when I reached my boarding house, I found another letter from you waiting for me. My, was I surprised! Almost too good to be true. I had rec'd the one you wrote from French Morocco Saturday and then Monday eve, the one from Italy was waiting for me. The letter was postmarked Aug. 8 and I rec'd it on the 14th. How's that for service.

This morning over the radio we rec'd the first news that our troops had made beach landings at Marseilles. Now, I know why you are in Italy. If it is permissible to tell me what air force you are in, tell me, then I'll know when you go out or have been out on a mission.

I am glad they sent you where they did rather than down in the So. Pacific. You may end up later on fighting the Jap[anese], but by then I hope the Jap[anese] won't be as maniacal as they have been. Do you know what is good for that tired feeling? Can't think of anything better right now than to receive a letter. It certainly would have been a boon today.

Lots of love,   Mae

In early September 1944, Mabel visited friends in Little Rock, Arkansas, for a brief vacation.

Little Rock, Sept. 6, 1944

Dear Ivan:

. . . She has a lovely home on a 12 acre farm. Has 3 cows, 1 horse, another on the way, 2 little cows, one a boy, another a girl, a pig called Abigail and ten little piglets. We all retired at 9:30 p.m. which was quite early for me. . . . It was grand sleeping to the tune of cows mooing and chickens crowing. I was awfully tired at first, change of climate and the let down from the hectic rush at E. St. Louis. Such a relief to get away from it all. And talk about food! I'm not telling you this to make your tongue hang out, but I had all the good fresh milk, buttermilk, butter, cream, ham and eggs I wanted. The real McCoy! The home grown ham was delicious.

I noticed on the farms, mostly the little ones with just a shack for a home, there seems to be no one but the women left to do the work. You see them out taking care of cattle, etc. It makes one proud to see how the women have picked up where the men left off and are keeping the home fires burning. One of Mr. Haussner's [Mable's foster father] sisters is running an up-and-coming bakery which she and her husband had before he left for the service. In addition, she has her own home to run, a daughter to raise and is taking care of her mother who is almost an invalid. . . .

Yours, as usual, Mae

East St. Louis, Sept. 22, 1944

Dear Ivan:

Our [St. Louis] Brownies are only one game in the rear of your league-leading [Detroit] Tigers. They play again tonight. I'm keeping my fingers crossed, hoping my team will win. "Hold Those Tigers." [The St. Louis Browns did win the American League title in 1944, the only time in their history.]

. . . Re: Promotions. It doesn't seem fair that you should again be bringing up the rear, but have patience, my dear, who knows but what that class before and after you . . . which was shipped out ahead of you, via furloughs, may not have also entered the fighting front ahead of you, and got in on that killing invasion of Normandy? It isn't just the G.I. who gets screwed, Ivan. There is many an officer who has the same complaint. . . .

As ever, Mae

East St. Louis, Dec. 21, 1944

Dear Ivan:

. . . Skies are clear here. I wish to goodness the skies were clear on the Western front so that our bombers could work on Von Rundstedt and his supplies. What a massacre that's going to turn out to be. Have been turning in on all the war news today, and it is so heartbreaking. I can't seem to get my mind on what I am doing. Tried working on the books and gave up— made so many mistakes. I wish to goodness the higher ups would stop coddling us civilians and really put everything on a war basis—make us do things or else. I always did say back in '41 when they started conscripting the boys, they should do so to everyone. When you hear the reports of how the Germans have been ordered to shoot all Americans taken prisoner, it makes your blood boil. Think of what that means. Already they claim they have taken 20,000 of our men prisoners. I wish they'd close all the night clubs and shows. Am going to the Haussners', but dread going since all the bad news from over there. The last time they heard from Bill, he was in Belgium. Your brother was there too, wasn't he? I do hope they are safe. . .

What I wish you most is that you are well. Mae

Early in 1945, Ivan returned to the United States. He spent part of a furlough with Mabel in East St. Louis. He was then posted to the Santa Ana rest camp near Hollywood, California. Mabel used her vacation time to go to California so that she could be with Ivan. When she returned to East St. Louis, however, the correspondence dwindled. After Ivan was discharged from the service in the autumn of 1945, he and Mabel met for a final "hello and goodbye." With the tension and anxiety of the war years over, they were ready to break off the relationship. They both felt that they had benefited by the experience.

After the war, Mabel continued to work as a stenographer and bookkeeper, retiring in the late 1960s. She lives in Prescott, Arizona.

For many women, the phrase "for the duration" directly related to the amount of time that a loved one served in combat. In the case of bomber crews, this meant the completion of a set number of missions.

Blanche Lindemann Sowers, living at home with her parents in Norwood, Ohio, wrote the following letter to her husband, Charles G. Sowers, a ball turret gunner who flew fifty-one missions over Europe. It expresses her relief and ecstasy upon learning that he had successfully completed his missions.

Norwood, Nov. 24, 1944

Hello, my darlin':

Honey, right now I'm so happy all I want to do is bust out crying. I got your wonderful letter telling me you finished up today and got such a deep down feeling of happiness, darlin', I can't put it in writing. I feel like laughing and crying at the same time, just like all women so much in love with their hubbies feel when something so wonderful happens to them. Honey, I came home from work hoping all the way I'd have a letter from you and telling myself I probably wouldn't cause I just got one Monday. But when I opened the door and saw 2 letters I couldn't believe it. I should have known something was fishy cause mom and pop were both sitting in the front room and they told me to come over there and read 'em. So I did.

I opened the skinniest one first and it was written on the 9th of Nov. Then, I started opening the other one and mom said, I betcha $1.00 there's good news in it and I said no, it was probably an old one too. But then pop bet me $1.00 too and by that time I had it opened and honey, I just breathed a big sigh of relief and I felt like a ton of bricks fell off my heart.

And Mom said she just knew there was good news in that letter when it came cause it had a 6 cent stamp on it, so she went and called your pop and told him I had a letter from you and it looked *important*. So right away, he said, *open* it up, but mom didn't want to and he said he'd take all the blame.

So she opened it and read the first line and that was *all* she had to read cause your pop got so excited she said he almost cried. Gosh, honey, you sure are an important guy cause everyone wants you to come home real quick. Kathryn is supposed to call tonight so I can tell her and Lloyd's going down to your house and he can tell your mom. Gosh, honey, I'm so happy for you, and I love you so!

Bye now,   Me.

Blanche and Charles were reunited in 1945. They settled in Norwood, Ohio, where he worked as an operating engineer and she as a homemaker. They had three children. Charles retired in the early 1980s. They continue to live in Norwood where Blanche runs a babysitting service. They have seven grandchildren.

———————————— ∾ ————————————

While most wartime separations occurred when loved ones were inducted into military service, the events of the war resulted in forced separations of a very different type for a minority of Americans. In 1942, the 120,000 Japanese-Americans living along the West Coast were evacuated to camps located in remote areas of the United States. This relocation process sometimes resulted in painful separations.

Sonoko U. Iwata was born in Los Angeles, California, in 1911. Her husband, Shigezo Iwata, was born in Japan in 1900 and immigrated to the United States in 1924. The couple had been married for four years at the time of Pearl Harbor. When the war broke out, they had been living in Thermal, California, for six months where Shigezo had recently taken a position as the secretary of the Thermal Farmers' Cooperative Association.

Following the entry of the United States into World War II, Shigezo came under suspicion as an "enemy alien," even though he was married to an American citizen. In March 1942, he was taken by the FBI to Santa Fe, New Mexico, where he was given a hearing and eventually moved to the Lordsburg, New Mexico Internment Camp.

Sonoko and their three small children remained in Thermal awaiting the impending evacuation of the Japanese who lived in the area. In May 1942, they were sent to the Colorado River Relocation Camp near Poston, Arizona. After several appeals to various government agencies for reconsideration of Shigezo's status, he was allowed to join the family in Poston in July 1943.

Sonoko Iwata's letters are remarkable documents which discuss the children and their reaction to their father's absence, the events in Thermal while awaiting evacuation, and the help she received from many friends and neighbors. Her letters also discuss the conditions in the Poston relocation camp where they lived. Many of her letters were marked with a war department censor stamp: "Detained Alien, Enemy Mail, Examined." Mrs. Iwata has translated those letters which were written in Japanese.*

_____

*The letters of Sonoko Iwata are located in the Iwata Papers, Balch Institute for Ethnic Studies Library, Philadelphia, Pennsylvania. Printed by permission of the Balch Institute for Ethnic Studies.

Thermal, March 15, 1942

Dear Shigezo san:

It is nine o'clock now and I've just finished putting the children to sleep. They played well and are so tired today. I managed to take them for a little ride down the road and they were so happy. First several days they were very lonesome and kept going to the neighbors' following the lady as she irrigated the pea patch and even going down to their house while I was busy attending to Miki [the Iwata's one-year-old daughter]. . . .

I wonder where you are and what you are doing just now. I won't know till Tuesday perhaps just where you are located. Johnny was going to San Francisco to-day although he knew that the former group had already left for Santa Fe, New Mexico, and he stopped in to see if I had anything for you, in case you might be there. I packed a suitcase for you but Johnny returned just a few minutes ago with the same suitcase. You were not there and moreover, you might be among those picked up in San Bernardino while the former group was on its way to New Mexico the day after you were taken in custody. If you are already in New Mexico, I am terribly sorry you had to go with practically nothing. I'll send you some things right away.

Your income tax report was filed yesterday. Jimmie took it to the bank and I had it notarized there.

You won't have to feel uneasy about us at home. I'll take good care of the children and I'll keep hoping you will return.

Please take good care of yourself in your new surroundings. Will you write when you can?

Always,   Sonoko

Thermal, March 16, 1942

Dear Shigezo san:

It's Monday and no word from you or the F.B.I. office! But I do know now you are in New Mexico—a telegram was received by one of the families here and some one came to tell me that in the message it mentioned you as being with the group in New Mexico.

It was too late today to send your things so I'm asking Yeji to take the suitcase to the Express Office tomorrow morning. I do hope you can have it by Sunday. You must be badly in need of everything. I can't imagine how you might have managed the past week. There are some more things I must get in town to send to you—envelopes and shirts, particularly. Jimmie took me to town but I forgot to get some of the things—and at the time I didn't dream you would be in New Mexico yet, and I thought there might be a chance to get in touch with you.

I hope it won't be too difficult to settle down in your new surroundings. It is rumored here that a certain skin disease due to the soil conditions prevails in New Mexico. I do hope it is just a rumor.

Enclosed are two typed letters. Will you affix your signature and return one for me to give to the bank? This is what I'm supposed to do, isn't it?

The two cartons of Lucky Strike were given by Johnny. He took them to Tujunga, not knowing you had already been sent to the present camp. . . .

Do take good care of yourself and be pleasant with all. Will write again. As ever, Sonoko

Thermal, March 18, 1942

Dear Shigezo san:

Well, Miki is exactly one year old today and she still doesn't show any signs of teeth! We celebrated today in our own quiet way and the children were well pleased. Miki was just all smiles as we sang our greeting to her. Can you imagine what we are having for the little birthday dinner? Green peas, squash, and mashed potatoes, and apricots for dessert—we're turning vegetarian around here. . . .

We're practically going without meat nowadays—just bacon and eggs and some fish. I've been going without tea or coffee. It is no effort on my part since I've been used to it before marriage, but perhaps it's because I don't want to bother about brewing coffee just for myself. But at any rate, it's economical too. We take plenty of milk and water, and I'm watching the children's diet, so you won't have to feel uneasy about us becoming malnourished. . . .

There was a meeting here tonight to meet the adviser of Federal Reserve Department (U.S. Agriculture Department and U.S. Employment Service too) stationed at Indio [California] office. He will help us with evacuation problems. . . .

I don't know how long I can continue writing every day. If it should embarrass you in front of friends you know, say so. Till tomorrow, good night.

Sonoko

Thermal, March 22, 1942

Dear Shigezo san:

. . . Today was a beautiful Sunday. During the day it is very, very warm nowadays, but still in the mornings and evenings it feels chilly. Grapefruit and lemon blossoms are beginning to open and they fill the air with their fragrance; pomegranate buds have unfolded, too, and are showing their pretty, bright flowers; grape vines are just about shooting forth their buds and the longest vine is already, nearly a foot. They were only about an inch or so when you left, wasn't it? You remember the young eucalyptus tree at the corner of the fence? Young leaves are showing on that, too. Just now I went out near the lemon tree and the bees were just buzzing around. That certain fragrance reminds me of the drives we used to take into the Whittier hills. . . .

Sonoko

Thermal, March 30, 1942

Dear Shigezo San:

. . . The other night, I sat up to sort out all the letters and cards we had received. I made up my mind to forget the past and look toward the future but it was the hardest thing to throw away all those letters, except a few from close friends. . . . Even the letters between the two of us, I destroyed because I felt that we could remember those days, anyway, without tangible reminders. . . .

Love, Sonoko

Thermal, April 18, 1942

Dear Shigezo san:

. . . I know that our stay here has been but a little over six months and no one would be able to vouch as to your character here. Even during our four years' stay in Los Angeles, we kept pretty much to ourselves, meeting very few people because we could hardly afford social life and so I couldn't think of many whose reference might aid you in any way. . . .

Yesterday afternoon, for the first time, we went over to Bob's for a visit, taking some cup cakes I made for Dickie and Umi-chan. It had been so long since I'd seen their mother. . . . When we were returning, Michiye san loaded our car with everything she could think of—grapefruits from the two trees they had saved, lemons, eggs including one turkey egg, bananas for children, tomatoes, and squash. We returned by the back way. . . . When we approached the point where it seems as if the hills end and also later when we were passing through the road that dips into the ditch just a little ways from Hikei san's, Masahiro [the Iwata's three-year-old son] remarked that we'd been here before with you. They mention you in that way often. Since they saw you leave with the authorities, they say that you are with men who look like the mailman. A few days ago they wanted me to call you over the 'phone and ask you to return. I had to tell them you were so far away, I couldn't reach you. When I receive words from you, I let them know. At other times I do not speak of you unless they mention you first because I don't want them to know how I feel. . . .

May you be strengthened in the trials you must face.

Love, Sonoko

Thermal, April 27, 1942

Dear Shigezo san:

. . . You are having quite a weather, aren't you? You might feel at home in the snow but how about the *older folks*. I do hope they are not taking it too hard. Are you sure you're warm enough with the clothes you have?

Your khaki pants, I'll order with the Sears. I think you will be able to have it within a week. I am also ordering more clothes and tan shoes like you had before and will send them all in that rather small suitcase of yours. In event of evacuation, I'm afraid I'll not be able to take along your clothes with me. And, since there's no telling how long the present condition will continue, I want you to have enough clothes for at least a year or so.

I don't see how you got along all those days with just the amount you mentioned. I hope you are not always receiving favors from your friends. I'll send more of your allowance? Will that be all right with you? In the meantime, I'll send the Chesterfields which you asked. . . .

Many more from Los Angeles will have to vacate their homes by the 29th of this month—day after tomorrow.

Will write again. Till then,

Lovingly,   Sonoko

Thermal, April 28, 1942

Dear Shigezo san:

Everything is well with you, I hope.

Out our way, the pump went on the blink again since yesterday morning and because one of the small parts was broken almost beyond repair and a new part had to be sent from Los Angeles, we were without water until this late afternoon. My, it was some experience. Yesterday evening at about six o'clock, we went over to Sakamoto san's and got one kettlefull and another gallon of water and that held us over till the pump was repaired. It was windy, moreover, and everything was dusty. Our dishes piled up and the whole house was a sight. I was certainly thankful when Mr. Bendel told me at about four o'clock that the water will run again.

Masahiro has begun to be curious about everything. The other day we were out in front looking at the cedar-like tree which right now has a mass of purplish pink flowers and is really pretty. He asked who made these pretty flowers and the pomegranate, and the like. When I told him God made everything in the first place, he asked where God went after making these things. So I told him He hasn't gone any place but is still every where— only one can't see Him. He didn't say anything after that and then the next morning he went around pointing at the different trees saying, God made this and God made that. I had to explain again that God made them in the first place but after that people like Daddy and Ojisan have learned to raise and care for them, so that they could help, too, in having more trees. He asked where all the water comes from and whether the mountain is soft or hard. You remember how the little boy in the theater was asking his father about everything? Now at little over three and a half, your own son has started to ask questions. . . .

Please extend my regards to your friends whom I know.

Yours,   Sonoko

Thermal, May 4, 1942

Dear Shigezo san:

In the papers, they say that all Japanese in the military zones will be evacuated by May 20. So, even if we should be among the last group, we have less than three weeks to go. It makes us all feel so rushed. . . .

This house where we live right now will be entrusted to Mr. Pfost to be rented to someone. I will take an inventory of the things we leave here like the office furniture, refrigerator, range, and chairs and tables and the like and a copy of it and important association papers will be placed in a safe deposit box which Bob will rent. Whatever could be sold, we'll try to sell. At first, the empty building next to us was going to be used as warehouse, but the Federal Reserve Bank owns a garage in Coachilla [California] and it is said, whatever one needs to store, can be stored there. . . .

Yours,   Sonoko

Thermal, May 6, 1942

Dear Shigezo san:

. . . Registration for sugar rationing commenced yesterday at the Oasis school. I went with Tayeko san, with the children tagging along, and received the first war ration cards for each one of the family. We were among the first four registered and so it took a long time before we finished—about an hour even though we had necessary information written out. . . .

Lots of things came up yesterday, it seemed. A representative from the Federal Reserve Department came around to many of our houses including ours. He was a very kindly person and the way he talked made everything encouraging. He wanted to know what arrangements we had made about our property. I don't have much and our car is already sold, but I did mention a few things I wanted stored to be sent later to whatever camp we go. He told me that things can be shipped to me later if I wish it and have it prepared to be sent. Now I can be sure that I won't have to carry Miki [who had begun to crawl] all the time. I think that I should have the baby bed and the buggy sent to me later, don't you think?

Will write again,

Yours,   Sonoko

Poston, May 26, 1942

Dear Shigezo san:

It's fifteen minutes past nine o'clock and it is just getting dark. Our room which is on the west end of the building gets the sun from two o'clock or till it sets at about 8:20, making the room intensely warm. Iron posts of the bed become heated right in the room. There are now two cases of measles in our block of over 200 hundred people. Miki is under observation now as a suspicious case. Dr. Iseri who is Alice Sakema's father and an old friend is among us and administers to the sick. I certainly hope Miki will not come down with measles, but if she does, it will be all right. Don't worry. Each day finds us a little more adjusted to our new living.

Love,   Sonoko

Poston, May 28, 1942

Dear Shigezo san:

It's been almost ten days since we've come here and thanks to the efforts of those responsible, many improvements have been brought about, making it much easier for us to adjust ourselves to our new surroundings.

There are three separate settlements which are three miles apart and capable of housing 20,000 people. We are in the northern settlement which has facilities for 10,000. I don't know how many blocks there are here but I know there are more than fifty and each block has a little over 200 residents.

We from Indio and Thermal and Palm Springs are more or less grouped together here in Block 42. In every block there is Dining Hall, Recreation Hall, Block Office, Laundry, and Men and Women's restrooms. So, you see, each block is like one community and it's up to those of us who comprise the community to make it better, through cooperative efforts.

First two days when our block kitchen was not yet ready to serve food, we went over to our neighboring block which is across a wide field. We had to stand in line under the hot sun and when inside we had to again stand in line with our plates and cutlery. Honestly, it made me think of what might be in a cheap restaurant. It was like survival of the fittest, too, as small babies and grown ups had the same chance. On top of all that, there would be just sauerkraut and wienies and rice. Miki couldn't very well eat them and then I couldn't be sure that I could get milk. So, things were pretty awful for a few days. Now that our own block kitchen is working, conditions are much better. There isn't much standing in line and the atmosphere is more like that of a dormitory and more often than not, we have good food. . . .

Love, Sonoko

Poston, June 18, 1942

Dear Shigezo san:

Through several people who have returned to their families from where you are now, I have heard that you are getting along well and there is nothing about which I should feel uneasy. I also received the little souvenirs you sent. It was very thoughtful of you and we all liked them very much. . . .

Since I have no income now and I don't know when I'll be able to work, I have tried to cut out all expenses I possibly could and at present, I don't even take the papers and try to catch up on news by visiting neighbors who have papers.

This coming Sunday is Father's Day and our thoughts will be with you especially. We certainly hope and pray that you will be able to join us soon. . . .

With much love, Sonoko

Poston, June 28, 1942

Dear Shigezo san:

Today being Sunday, there's something in the air that is quiet and peaceful. . . .

I've just given Miki her bath, Masahiro and Misao are playing outside with Dickie Yano and Jackie Kitagawa; some of the young people are playing cards and many of the mothers are resting outside in the shade.

In my first letter to you from this place, I remember telling you that this place was barren and without any trees but upon closer inspection we did find a few along the stream that runs just outside of our block, and those few trees certainly look beautiful. The stream, or perhaps it's large enough to be called a river, runs so slowly and is so muddy that you could hardly tell it is flowing. Even though small, it's deep and the banks are steep so that we mothers with young children have to be careful. No one has fallen in yet. . . .

The heat is quite intense but now that June is almost all over, we'll have only two more months to endure. The other day in the house the thermometer registered 114 degrees and was in the neighborhood of 110 degrees for several days, but now it is a little better. No one in the block has been any worse for it. It was actually cold this morning and we all had to have sweaters or jackets for breakfast. Personally, I think the sudden cold after the heat will hit us hard, and we will have to be prepared with plenty of warm clothing.

Today, our neighbors gave us some melons which were brought in from the valley. It certainly was a treat. Like others, I'm saving the seeds for future use. . . .

You wrote interment camp on your letter. I think interment has to do with death and burial. You have your dictionary with you, haven't you?

Until tomorrow,

Yours with much love,　Sonoko

Poston, July 22, 1942

Dear Shigezo san:

. . . I am enclosing a copy of the letter of appeal I wrote to the Attorney General Francis Biddle in Washington, D.C. and to United States Attorney William Fleet Palmer in Los Angeles.

Perhaps if I had written with the assistance of others, it would have been better but every word came from the bottom of my heart and I did the best I could.

Yours,　Sonoko

Poston, July 21, 1942

Sir:

I am taking this means to appeal to you for a reconsideration of the decision against Shigezo Iwata, my husband, who was taken into custody on March 11 from Thermal, California; given a hearing on May 15 at Santa Fe, New Mexico where he was detained; and transferred to Lordsburg, New Mexico on June 19 as an internee of war and now identified as ISN-25-4J-110-C1 and located at Barrack 4, Camp 3, Company 9, Lordsburg Internment Camp.

I am an American citizen of Japanese descent and I believe in the government of the United States. I am grateful for the privileges I have been able to enjoy and share as a part of democratic America.

The decision you have recently rendered against Shigezo Iwata, my husband, must have been reached after a careful consideration, but I am making this appeal to you in the hope that there might be room for reconsideration.

I solemnly affirm that Shigezo Iwata, my husband, has at all times been loyal to America and has always cooperated with our government, observing all regulations and trying his best to add constructively to the welfare of the nation. In the almost five years of our married life, I have always known him to practice simple honesty. He has been open-hearted, too, though markedly reserved. Our life has been a struggle on a small income but always there was hope and ambition for a higher living and we were slowly but surely attaining it. If Shigezo Iwata is returned to his family now settled at the Poston War Relocation Camp, I can assure you that he will cooperate and unite in efforts to build-up this city of Poston which we know is a part of democratic America.

This appeal, I make, not because of our three small children who undoubtedly will receive more adequate care if their father could be with them nor for my own desire of keeping our family together since I know that countless number of homes are being permanently broken because of this conflict, but because I firmly believe Shigezo Iwata, my husband, is a loyal resident and has never been or never will be dangerous to the security of the United States. Moreover, to be considered as such is a dishonor we cannot bear to face.

Whatever your final decision, I shall still have faith in God and in our government, but I keep praying that you will be able to give Shigezo Iwata a favorable decision.

Any word from you will be greatly appreciated.

Respectfully yours,   Sonoko U. Iwata (Mrs. Shigezo Iwata)

Poston, Aug. 17, 1942

Dear Shigezo san:

I've received a reply to my letter of appeal I recently sent to the United States Attorney's office in Los Angeles. I was told I should submit substantial factual information and references of the persons who vouch for alien's conduct. Then, they could take some action. So, I've been working hard last week trying to prepare my affidavit for you and getting references for my reliability to vouch for you.

Everything was ready to be notarized Saturday but when I went, the Notary Public was still on leave and was expected the first of the week. So, this morning I went again, but again, she wasn't in. Here I am so anxious to send my letters out and I just have to wait. I only hope she will be in tomorrow. She was due at 8:00 this morning, I was told.

Your card reached me Saturday. I ordered a replacement of Mother Goose and it also came. Children like it so much that I'm glad I got it for Masahiro.

Yours,   Sonoko

Poston, Oct. 5, 1942

Dear Shigezo san:

Today is the beginning of school here in Arizona. Since the school buildings are not yet ready, recreation halls in the different blocks are being used as class rooms temporarily. Some children have to go quite far and some to classes within their own block. Masahiro is being registered today in the nursery school which is just across the road from us. Misao is still too young to go. . . .

My mind and my heart, too, are occupied wholly by you and I really have no room to think of anyone else.

I do wish you could join me, though. It really would dispose of a lot of heartaches and unnecessary rumors. Even Masahiro has his grief when his playmates say, "My daddy came back. You're daddy isn't coming back." Then I'd have to tell him you will return—some day. Isn't it awful? Don't worry about us. I'll manage somehow.

Love,   Sonoko

Poston, Jan. 1, 1943

Dear Shigezo san:

Happy New Year and Happy Birthday! I hope you are having good time, though away from home.

All through December I didn't hear from you at all. It must be because of censorship. Nowadays, letters are usually about a month old by the time they reach us. I wait and wait for a word from you and yet when it doesn't come I also fail to write. It's really awful of me. . . .

This stationery or rather writing paper is a Christmas gift from Miss Griffith, my Sunday School teacher whom I hadn't seen for five years. She and Miss Jacobs, another Sunday School teacher, and Miss Cox, my high school teacher, you remember, all remembered the children with interesting toys and books. . . .

Miki is beginning to talk in sentences and is at her cute age. Like Misao, she wants to say hello to everybody she meets. He likes Mrs. Sugimoto so much.

There has been talk about the internees' families being able to be united at a family camp. Although I'm still hoping you might be given a second hearing, I thought it best to be ready to join you. When there is any definite word, please tell me.

I'm looking forward to being with you, whenever it might be.

Please write me, too.

With much love,   Sonoko

Poston, March 5, 1943

Dear Shigezo san:

There is a bowl of fresh wild flowers in our room today. Children and I went across the little stream to the empty field for a walk and found these yellow daisy-like flowers growing in a strip near the water. Their leaves are dainty—like cosmos leaves.

You know, I was thinking today that time marches on and if I'm to keep up, we should bury the past and always look toward what's coming.

Our photograph albums were all confiscated and since I had taken the trouble to mount almost all of the pictures, there's not a single family picture left—except for our wedding picture. . . . I wrote to the F.B.I. asking for the albums and other things like my notebook with defense Savings Stamp Book and Baby Account Book, but they said they didn't take the things into their possession. I felt so bad about it and wanted to ask just who could tell me where the confiscated things are, but upon second thought decided that perhaps such a sentiment is something of the past that I should bury. Then again, I think that perhaps if I persist I could locate those things valuable only to you and me.

By new military order, Poston has become part of free zone. Even if we were free to go out from this camp, the nearest town is Parker, about 19 miles away, and even that is about like the town of Coachilla.

Many are willing to relocate themselves outside but are without means. This will be given consideration, it is hoped.

Love, Sonoko

Shigezo received notification in a letter from the Department of Justice dated April 15, 1943, that he was eligible to be reunited with his family. However, the letter indicated that the transfer was subject to delay. After a brief period in Santa Fe, he was allowed to travel to Poston early in July 1943, where the family was reunited. The last letter Sonoko wrote to Shigezo was dated July 2, 1943.

Poston, July 2, 1943

Dear Shigezo san:

I'm sorry that I have not written for a while and had you worried. . . . When people have been coming home suddenly, I keep wondering perhaps you might come home today or tomorrow and I must prepare the house and welcome you to an orderly place, and in doing various chores, the time passes away quickly. But it has already been nearly a month. I wrote you a letter to Lordsburg and enclosed children's pictures, but I presume you have received them. . . .

Am hoping you could return before Masahiro's birthday. Misao and Miki are waiting, too. Miki seems to remember you. She looks at your picture and points and says "Daddy" and also says you are far away. Masahiro remembers the time you were taken away and tells me to 'phone and have you come home quickly.

Everyone is fine. Please don't worry. I'm washing curtains, doing the windows and keeping the house in order. We look forward to your return. . . .

Good luck, Sonoko

Following the war, the Iwatas relocated in Seabrook, New Jersey, a community where many other Japanese-Americans also lived. They had one more child. Both Sonoko and Shigezo worked for the Seabrook Frozen Food Company until their retirement in the early 1970s. Shigezo died in 1986. Sonoko continues to live in Seabrook where she is actively involved in church work. She has ten grandchildren.

After Pearl Harbor, support for the war effort was virtually unanimous. However, a small minority of Americans opposed the war because they were pacifists. Of the more than 34 million men who registered for the draft, an estimated 72,000 applied for conscientious objector status. Approximately 6,000 persons were denied CO status and imprisoned.

John Kellam was one of the conscientious objectors in the United States who was imprisoned during World War II. He and his future wife, Carol Zens, met in the early 1940s while attending the Florida Avenue Meeting of the Friends Meeting of Washington, D.C. John, who had graduated from the University of Minnesota in 1938 and had done graduate work the following year at the Massachusetts Institute of Technology, was a city planner for the state of Maryland. Carol worked as a secretary in Washington, D.C. After a three-year courtship, they were married on August 30, 1944. Shortly after their marriage, the newlyweds moved to Toledo, Ohio, where John had been hired as a city planner.

Both Carol and John had grown up in traditional Protestant households. However, their affiliation with the Society of Friends helped to convince them to embrace the tenets of pacifism. When the United States entered World War II, John, who had not yet formally joined the Society of Friends, applied for conscientious objector status. His request was turned down by his draft board. In the fall of 1944, John refused induction into the Army. On Christmas Eve 1944, he was arrested by the FBI for violating the 1940 Selective Service Act. In January 1945, John was convicted and fined $1,000 and sentenced to five years in prison.

Carol, who was pregnant, returned to Washington, D.C., to live with her mother. She worked as a secretary for the United States News until about a month before their daughter, Susan, was born on August 30, 1945. Carol's letters to John provide an intimate look at the ways in which a small group of Americans, who were out of step with the mainstream, also survived "the duration."

Washington, D.C., Jan. 31, 1945

Dearest:

I've received two swell letters from thee, but have been so busy and consequently so tired, this is the first chance I've had to write thee. I didn't know what the rules were, anyway. Thee says thee is permitted to write two letters each week. I think thee can write three. At least, it says in item 13, "Instructions to be followed in correspondence with prisoners." "13. Inmates are permitted to send 3 letters per week, and to receive a total of 7. Letters in excess of 7 in any week will be returned to the writer." Let me know how many I should write to thee each week. And when thee needs more money. . . .

Gee, Johnny, the Calverts [who befriended the Kellam family] have been so swell. I don't know how to thank them. Money would be an insult, although I thought of sending $5 to the Toledo Friends Group. Should I? The Calverts took me in, and fed me, helped me pack, and took me to the station. They're wonderful Friends. How does thee suggest I thank them? . . . .

I received the box from the prison. . . . Thy shoes and coat are being repaired. The suit is being cleaned and pressed, and I think I shall give it to the Friends. It's not worth keeping for thee, especially when less fortunate people can make good use of it. I gave a good many of thy old clothes to the Friends group in Toledo. Mrs. Calvert said they could cut up the old pants and make little skirts and pants from them.

I miss thee terribly, my dearest. All my love to thee. I feel fine except a little bit sickish now and then.

Carol Z. Kellam

Washington, D.C., Feb. 6, 1945

Hi Dearest:

. . . I'm writing this at work (my second day) as it's early (8:10) and I have no work to do as yet. I was sort of tired yesterday when 5 p.m. came (quitting time) although the work is very easy. I'm doing stenographic work with the Bureau of National Affairs, a publishing company headed by David Lawrence and affiliated with the United States News. . . .

Oh, I work from 8:15 a.m. to 5 p.m. five days a week—no Saturday work. Lunch is from 11:45 to 12:30 and I eat with Nelda [a close friend] and some other girls at a canteen in a church nearby—where whites and Negroes eat together!! I believe the denomination is Southern Presbyterian—it's called Church of the Pilgrims. . . .

My girl friend, Ree, is going to have a baby in September—we think our baby will come earlier, however. She asked me how I felt and I told her fine except once in a while. She said she felt fine once in a while. . . . I haven't been to a doctor yet. I'll write first to the University of Chicago to see if they can recommend a doctor here who believes in the principles of natural childbirth. . . .

One of the girls in the office here just now showed me a picture of a boy friend of hers who is a conscientious objector working in a mental hospital in Marion, Virginia. She says he is a swell fellow, and she sticks up for him through the criticism she has received for going out with him. People here have all been very nice—no raised eyebrows. And I can work as long as I want to. . . .

I am wearing thy watch and think about thee every time I look at it. I hope thee can find work to do there, cause thee'll be happier, but that's up to thee and the authorities.

All my love, Thy Cary

Washington, D.C., May 6, 1945

Hi Darling:

. . . I wonder, is pacifism moral, or logical? Is democracy moral or logical? The logical end to militarism, where people are allowed to live only if they are useful to, or in complete agreement with, the military government, is one person only left alive in a devastated world. Look at the horrors now being uncovered in German concentration camps to see what happens when the military mind gets in control of a government. . . .

All my love,   Thy Cary

Washington, D.C., May 22, 1945

My Darling:

Practically ten days since my last epistle to thee! Gosh! But the weather was so hot, and I was so tired, that I just couldn't write. It's cooler now, and I feel much better, although Sunday I fainted in Meeting. It was only temporary, and I was greatly embarrassed, and people were quite concerned. I really think it was caused by lack of air, as thee knows how I suffer in close spaces even without Junior to provide for, and if he takes after me in his oxygen requirements, I really have to have quite a supply. . . . I wonder if I should attempt Meetings any more. The books say to avoid crowds, but I don't know if I should go to that extreme. . . . [A neighbor] has said his car was available at any time, day or night, that he was there to drive me to the hospital. He thought it would be impossible to get a taxi. I'll ask the doctor about that when I go to see her next week. . . .

Time . . . tells about Pastor Neimoller [a well-known, German, anti-Nazi activist], briefly. Says he "became an anti-Nazi the hard way." He was a staunch early-Party member. But when he saw how the wind was blowing he stood up in his Dahlen pulpit and denounced Hitler's mumbo-jumbo racial theories. He also refused to put the will of Der Fuhrer above the will of God. . . .

All my love to thee, Johnny.

Hope All's well.   Thy, Carol

Washington, D.C., June 4, 1945

Johnny Dearest:

Just a short note to thee. I'm so tired I just have to go to bed early, even though I know I haven't written to thee since May 30. I was worried about not hearing from thee for so long. I didn't know whether thee was getting my letters and I was getting thine, and I didn't want to write for public consumption only, and besides, working keeps me tired—I'll be quitting at the end of this month and can take a rest in the mornings and afternoons, as I'm supposed to. Today I was very happy to receive thy letter of May 28, with nothing erased except its number (which was erased on the envelope too). This letter told me of the label they had put on thy cage, and of the thoughts brought out in thee by thy group meeting concerning the importance of the mind and the spirit and the unimportance of the body as a means of coercion. Thee has wonderful thoughts, and thee's right. But so many people can't or aren't taught to control their bodies so as to bring themselves true happiness. They find it so much easier to put their bodies to destructive use. It's up to thee, and people like thee, to show by example how much more satisfaction and real living we can get from life when we live for ideals instead of bodily comfort. Then the body cannot be used for punishment, whether by incarceration or torture or mere hampering of movement. . . .

To go back to bodies, I really regard mine with an exaggerated sense of importance, no doubt, these days when there is a child developing in it. Well-born children should be a country's greatest asset, and a country should strive to see that its children are well-born, and, if they were worthy of the trust of their citizens, should see that children in the whole world over are well born, instead of starving them and dropping fire bombs on them. . . .

All my love, dearest from, Carol

Washington, D.C., July 19, 1945

My Dearest:

. . . The Friends had a shower for me at the Meeting House, Sunday afternoon, July 8. I received many lovely gifts for the baby. . . . The Meeting House Friends are giving me a high chair and more than enough money for the doctor's bill and for two months' diaper-washing service. Allen said there was no collection taken—that people had been asking him if they couldn't help in some way, so he had just let them know about the shower. So thee sees that our Friends are thinking of us. I was amazed at their generosity toward us, and didn't know what to say, but I appreciate their thoughtfulness very, very much.

I had this letter from thy Mom, dated July 12: "Thank you, thank you, for relieving my mind about John. I knew that something was very wrong and I kept thinking that perhaps he was being a 'guinea pig' of some sort, and it was driving me crazy. Please don't encourage any more 'sacrifice,' will you? He has an immediate duty to you and me and to his child, which is more important than any so-called sacrificial expression of Spirit. I warned him about hunger strikes or other demonstrations of martyr complexes, before I left him. . . . I shall continue to pray that he be kept safe and well in body and mind and spirit. . . ."

I didn't think it would do much harm to tell her of thy hunger strike after it was all over and thee was recovering so nicely. I didn't expect her to be so concerned, but I can understand why she should be. Does thee think thee can write to her and Alex?

All my love to thee, darling, Thy Cary

Washington, D.C., Aug. 11, 1945

Hi Dearest:

Still no signs of Junior's debut. I think he's waiting till the war's over and people stop officially murdering each other. I hope that news comes any minute now, although I shan't celebrate "victory"—It's been too horribly costly. I don't know what it will mean to the two of us personally and the others in our positions—that depends, I guess, on how vindictive our government is. Yesterday, the boy next door had his radio on listening to the "man in the street" program, from various large cities all over the U.S., on the Japanese surrender offer. I surely was surprised at the many bloodthirsty people who said we should continue fighting until the "Japs" surrendered unconditionally, or until all were killed, and the emperor bagged for a war criminal. I heard only one lady (I didn't listen to the whole program) who had a son fighting in the Pacific, say that we should accept the surrender terms, and as for the emperor, why, in the words of Jesus, "What is that to thee? Follow thou me."

. . . As I look out of my window and see the beauties of God all around I am made to wonder why is there so much sin in this beautiful land. The tall stately hollyhocks are lovely in all their different colors and the roses have been lovely with their pink, red and yellow clusters and this morning I can see the gladiolus begin to throw out their long spirals in all colors. . . .

Well, darling, I guess thy eyes are getting tired, not to mention the poor censor's. [This was a typed, single-spaced, six-page letter.] If this comes back, I'll send it to thee piece-meal, unless I'm in the hospital. But I haven't had any letter-writing instructions from Lewisburg. [John had been transferred to the Lewisburg Federal Prison in Lewisburg, Pennsylvania.]

All my love to thee,   Thy Cary

John was released from the Lewisburg, Pennsylvania, Federal Prison in November 1946. He and Carol were reunited, and he met his fifteen-month-old daughter, Susan, for the first time. A second daughter, Wendy, was born in 1947. The Kellams moved to Providence, Rhode Island, in 1950 where John worked as a city planner for thirty-one years. Carol died of cancer in 1967. John lives in Providence and remains committed to pacifism and is an active member of the Providence Meeting of the Society of Friends. He has four grandchildren.

He's _Sure_ to get
V···-MAIL

Safest Overseas Mail
U.S. ARMY POSTAL SERVICE

Chapter *8*

The Price of Victory

DURING WORLD WAR II, BETWEEN 15 AND 20 MILLION MILITARY personnel died throughout the world. Twenty-five million individuals were wounded. In addition, the civilian death toll has been estimated at close to 40 million. Of the more than 16 million Americans who served in the military, nearly 300,000 were killed in action and another 700,000 were wounded in battle. Over 105,000 American citizens were prisoners of war.

When dreaded telegrams from the government arrived, loved ones were required to draw upon an inner strength that many did not know they had. For some, there was still hope. Those who were "missing in action" might be found. Prisoner-of-war camps would eventually be liberated. During the agonizing weeks and months when information about loved ones was insufficient and fragmentary, letter writers wrote heartrending letters of love.

Assuaging sorrow and dealing with the loss of a loved one took much effort. Mothers, wives, fiancées, sisters, and friends continued to pray for loved ones who had sacrificed their lives for the war. For many of these gold-star citizens, the "duration" has not yet come to an end. The price of victory is still being exacted.

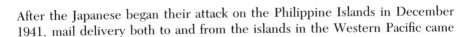

After the Japanese began their attack on the Philippine Islands in December 1941, mail delivery both to and from the islands in the Western Pacific came to a virtual standstill. As the Allies regained control of occupied territory, delivery of the mail resumed. However, the mail arrived only sporadically in those areas which remained under enemy control. In fact, there was virtually no communication with the men left on Bataan and Corregidor until the end of the war.

Upon his arrival in Australia in March 1942, General Douglas MacArthur established a unit in his headquarters which was directed to devise replies to the many letters which were sent to him. Included among the letters which MacArthur received were hundreds of queries concerning persons who were missing in action, who were prisoners of war, and who had been unable to communicate with their families and friends.

MacArthur and his staff answered all of the letter writers with grace, offering as much information as was possible at the time. They were, above all, responsive to the need to supply information, often very unpleasant information, to those who wrote to the General.

The following letters are examples of the wide variety of concerns generated by the traumatic events of World War II which were expressed by American women when writing to General MacArthur. The letters have been reproduced exactly as they were written.*

Kilgore, Texas, Nov. 24, 1944

Our Sincere friend, General MacArthur:

So true are those words, for you are the treasured friend we mothers look to—look to you as God guides your worthy heart and mind. And to those of us who have sons hidden in the Philippines since those days of long ago, that seems like centuries, when Bataan had "too little, too late" and sheer courage could not hold out against the might of the enemy—our beloved sons were left marooned to—I dare not ponder on what may been their fate. But *some* are sure to be in the hills awaiting liberation! So long our hearts have yearned for this moment when Old Glory again proudly ripples in the breeze over The Islands—we've prayed so earnestly for it— have *pushed* with you and with every fiber of our being!

Why do I write this? Because it is my only hope. I have written hundreds of letters to every possible source trying to gain information regarding my son, but he was never declared a prison-of-war. But, oh, General MacArthur, he may come out of the hills—head high—but so in need of word from *home*—the home he loved—and no word for *years*. Others can now write in care of the Red Cross to be delivered to their boys upon liberation—but I can't. I have no prison camp number. But I know your heart shall so rejoice as each one is liberated that your understanding of what they have endured will prompt you to save this letter I enclose and see that my

---

*The letters written to General MacArthur are located in the MacArthur Memorial Archives and Library, Norfolk, Virginia, Record Group 3: Southwest Pacific Area, Commander-in-Chief Correspondence. Reprinted by permission of the MacArthur Memorial Archives and Library.

Ralph gets it. . . . I'd like for you to read the letter I've written him. He is all I have.

I do so deeply thank you—and may God guide you in every move you make. I feel He does! Each night I pray for your guidance and protection.

In appreciation, Sincerely,   Mrs. Anna B. Apperson

Bronx, New York, Early Summer, 1944

Dear General MacArthur:

I am a mother left alone with a broken heart. My son Angelo Castelli fell in action with your troops at Hollandia on April 23. I was not notified of his death by the government. Oh! General MacArthur, doesn't a mother count at all? He was married Dec. 23, 1943 and I did not know it. His wife had him as a married man for 24 hours. He was called back to serve on Dec. 25 Christmas Day and that was the last I saw of him. His wife notified me bluntly over the telephone. His allotment to me stopped in Jan. I did not think it strange because sometimes those things happen. Please General he was a good boy, wasn't he? Did he die a hard death General? Oh! Please won't you drop me a line and tell me if he suffered long or not. My mind is so uneasy. I want just a few words of my boy General if in kindness you will do this for me. General MacArthur was his idol. May the grace of God be with you in your every step.

Sincerely,   (Mrs.) Doris Castelli

Seagraves, Texas, July 21, 1943

My Dear General MacArthur:

You are such a busy man and have so many perplexing problems, but I have arisen every morning, for three weeks, with such increasing desire to write you, that I am, at last, doing it.

My only son, Buford Cooksey, who with the 200th C.A. (A.A.) formerly of Ft. Stotsenburg and who was later taken prisoner, when Bataan fell—died in prison in Osaka, Japan on the 11th of June.

The questions I want to ask you—did those boys ever know it was impossible to get help to them—or did they harbor bitterness all of that seeming eternity—thinking their country figured the risk was too great—while Buford was drafted into the Army (he went in first draft) he was a very Patriotic boy.

Oh, this Bataan situation is almost more than we can stand.

Please disregard this last—for we are still America's mothers.

Most Prayerfully

I wait an answer, if you ever have time.

Mrs. B. D. Cooksey

Blountsville, Ala., May 14, 1944

General Douglas MacArthur:

received your letter telling me about my son O how sad it was. to her it ws mor than i can tell he left his home August 11, 1941 got to come back home and stay two days with me he was ready and willing to Do his part

Still that dont fill his vakon place at home my husban Died after my Son went to service i have a Son in the Hosptille has been in thir all most twelve monts. I Sint Maxwell a fountinpen he rote to me he had a watch i would like to have his knife and watch and pen if thy are eny way foreme to get them to keep. Please sind them to me if you Can All i can do is do the best i can and some Day i meet him again my prayers is for all the boys Mexwell rote me he had Some money out thir he put in the Bank. He didnt Say, how much. i want you to please See a Bout it and help me to find it if you can i sure do thank you for the letter i got Hoping i here Frome you.

Mrs. Jennie Denney

Lowell, Mass., July 30, 1943

Dear and Brave General MacArthur:

Before you read any further, please ask yourself this question, "Am I General Douglas MacArthur?" If you are an assistant or mail summarizer, you need not read any further. I am sure that you are doing your best in trying to help the greatest man God ever created, but if your answer is "no" to that question, please deliver this letter *right away* to General MacArthur because this letter is very important—make sure that *he* gets it right away.

Dear General, by this time you must have my letter, and I beg you, please do not tear it and throw it in the waste basket. Because, in this letter, I want to pour out my heart to you—my own life, I think, could never equal the value of what this letter can perhaps do, so you see how much it means. I know it is very bold and forward of me to write to you—a great General— but my heart is pushing the pen right along and will not let it stop. So, if you don't think you have time right this minute, then put it aside until you do find a few moments,—but please read it. . . .

My childhood sweetheart and fiance, *Staff Sgt Joseph Roland Dennis Simoneau,* enlisted in the Army in 1939. Brave, wasn't he? He lied about his age because he wanted so much to be helping his Country. But, he turned 18 two months later. I will never forget that night—5 years ago young as we were—I was in my first year of high school—I was fourteen years old—he was seventeen, but we knew our hearts. He said to me, "Lou we are too young for love—we must pass the stage of growing up before we can really appreciate what love is; you must continue to be a good girl and I must make a man of myself—we must learn not to be selfish. I want and desire you so much, Lou, and I will work so hard. I will go to school and study hard, and become someone, and I will do everything my Superiors in the Army request of me." And, with those words, he left me. . . .

And now I am putting in 48 hours and sometimes 55 hours a week working in a War Plant, I still use every minute of my spare time praying for him. He was reported "missing in action" shortly after the surrender. And, I lived in doubt until three weeks ago when he was reported a Jap[anese] prisoner at a Java camp, by the Japanese Red Cross. . . .

But it is for him I am fighting for. I do not care if he never wants me when and if he does ever return. All I want is mercy for him. I want him to come back in good health and all in one piece, so that he might enjoy his share of freedom for which he fought. When I hear about how the Jap[anese] treat their prisoners, I can't help but think that *something can be done*. I ask this of you because I have done everything else I could, and I know you are the only one who can do something. . . .

I will be 19 in just a few weeks, but please do not think I am a child, because I really am not. I would give my life to save this Country or to save the life of one who fought for it. . . .

On my part, I place myself in your full command—anything you ask of me will be obtained—to the last drop of blood I have and my life itself, if you request it. Anything I possess that might help you to get these men out of Java is lying at your feet. *Don't let the Jap[anese] torture these men.* . . .

With deep respect, anxiety and love, I am at your command—God Bless you.

Lucille DesCoteau

Atwater, Calif., April 1943

Dear General MacArthur:

Did you know my father Lt. George Gilbert Soper he was in Manila. He was at General Hdq. Philippine Dept and was assistant adjutant. If so will you please tell me if he was wound or killed. If you find him when you go back to the Philippines will you tell him that we have a baby bother named for him. He is one years old. Would your little boy like a puppy. My dog have six of them. I am in the fifth grade in Mitchell School Atwater California. My teachers name is Mrs. Colburn. My bother David is in the second grade his teachers name is Mrs. Daggs. We have moved from San Jose to Atwater California. My mother is collecting fat for the war. I am eleven years old. We have a little calf and we going to get some ducks. I live in the country and go on the first bus. I live with my mother and two bother and grandmother. I wish I could see you but I hope this letter will do. My room is collecting silk and nylon stockings for the war. We have giving to the Red Cross and Chinese relief and to the Greek relief. We buy defense stamps too.

Elva Ruth Soper

Chicago, Ill., Jan. 1945

Dear Sir:

This is the first prayer of nineteen forty five, that our boys come home safe and sound. It is written on the first minute of the new year and if God ever listened to a prayer I hope it is this one. . . .

This is a hard letter to write because we people of Scandinavian descent hardly ever ask favors. We are stoic and stubborn and usually take whatever life decides to hand, on the chin. I have thought for two days now, and for months before that whether I could get up courage to write. I am sorry I did not have such courage before now but had to start the New Year with it. . . .

I wanted to help my son so desperately, yet of course I realized I had no right to interfere. But cant a mother have some right even if there is a war and in this case it is not only best for the boy for it seems to me he is not being able to do his best in the condition he is in. I know his physical condition so well that believe me I really do know what I am talking about. Please show this to the medical officer at the hospital where he is at. . . .

Please take care of my boys, let Robert get well, let him stay in the hospital till he is, let him get into work in the hospital where he can be of real help, And please God hold your healing hand over the mind and the spirit and the physical well being of all the soldiers in the Philippines and all over the world, for if each one of them has a mother or a wife whose prayer joins with mine this first hour of 1945 I am sure the strength of it, the strength of all the combined prayers of this day will be able to move mountains. . . .

Very Respectfully,   Mrs. Nels Neslund

Army chaplains, government officials, and Red Cross workers also received heartrending letters from women seeking information about loved ones who were classified as missing in action or prisoners of war. Captain L. E. Cousins was an Army chaplain with the 314th Infantry Regiment in Europe who received hundreds of letters inquiring of the whereabouts of MIAs and POWs. Here are three such letters.

Mt. Airy, Md., Feb. 23, 1945

Dear Chaplain,

On February 8th, I received a telegram from the War Department informing me that my husband—Private Leonard L. Burke 33889596—of Co. H. 314th Inf. 79th Division had been reported missing in action in France since the 20th of January. Since that time I have received no word of any kind. You realize, I am sure, how awful the suspense is when you are not able to do one thing about it. If only I could know that he is alive. I thought perhaps you could tell me something about what happened and if you think he could be a prisoner of war.

I have two small children and the strain I am under is telling on my nerves.

If you could tell me anything whatsoever, I would certainly appreciate it.

Yours truly,   Mrs. Hazel M. Burke

Wheeling, W. Va., Feb. 19, 1945

Dear Chaplain,

I am writing to you in regard to something that means a great deal to us. If you can possibly help us in any way, we will be very grateful to you.

On February 6, we received a telegram from the War Department stating that S/Sgt. Philip T. Hess was missing in action somewhere in France on January 20th.

We would like to know if you could find out anything about what happened to him for us. Maybe you could find one of his friends who might know something about him. Could you tell me if many prisoners were taken from the 79th Division that day? Anything you could tell us will be greatly appreciated.

Phil and I have been engaged since July. We went together all during high school. I love him very much and I hope and pray that he is all right. I know God will watch over him for me.

I know that there are many others in the same situation that I am and I only hope that this war will end soon so that the men can come home and live a peaceful, normal life as before.

Thank you Chaplain, for your trouble and I want you to know that we will appreciate any information you can give us.

Yours very truly, Virginia Jackson

Philadelphia, Pa., March 23, 1945

Dear Sir:

I hope you will pardon my writing you, but wondered if you could possibly give me any information concerning one of your men? It is Fred C. Adler 3317273.

I am anxious about him as well as the church members of the church he belongs to. I have 79 of our "Boys" on my list that I have written to for the last three years, and as their adopted mother, I have their welfare close to my heart.

His parents were informed he was missing, but I felt perhaps by now, you may have some news of him.

I would sincerely appreciate any word from you of him.

He is very much loved by everyone who knows him, and he never neglected writing me faithfully.

For any news I would be eternally grateful.

Very respectfully yours, Mrs. L. Weber

———————— ✍ ————————

It was sometimes left to the "rank and file" to respond to requests about the death of loved ones. Private Gel Long was killed during the D-Day invasion of Normandy on June 6, 1944. His mother, Alice Long, wrote to his good friend and Army "buddy," Corporal Gordon Leech, and asked for details about her son's death.

[?], Oct. 27, 1944

Dear Cpl. Leech:

I know you think I am ungrateful for any favors. On the contrary, I have been so broke up I have not had the strength or ambition to write other than a letter or two to Irene [her deceased son's wife] and my other boy.

Thanks for writing and I would love to have a picture of the spot where he is laid if you will. He was my "Baby Boy" and such a youngster when he enlisted. I had a letter from the padre, which was very touching.

Could you tell me just where he was wounded? I mean the place. If you are not allowed to now, would you be so kind as to bear this in mind and tell me later when it is not a military secret. Also just where he is laid to rest and if it is in a permanent burying place or if he will be moved later.

Well there is so little I can say. Only that I again thank you for writing. And it is a mother's prayer you will be spared to your mother and friends.

All the best   Mrs. Alice Long

Thirteen-year-old Charmaine Leavitt of Kalamazoo, Michigan, wrote the following V-Mail to Private Justin J. Slager, a family friend and neighbor who was stationed in North Africa, shortly after learning that he been declared missing in action. Later, Private Slager's family and friends learned that he had been killed.

Kalamazoo, Dec. 29, 1943

Dear Justin,

I don't know whether you will get this letter or not but I hope that you do. This morning your mother got a telegram saying that you were missing in action. I sure hope that you are O.K. and I also would like to know where you are. Everybody is worried about you around here and so am I. . . .

Do you take pictures from planes?

I sure will hate to go back to school again. Now if I was old enough I would join the SPAR (?) or something like that. Maybe I could be a mascot or something.

Charmaine

Myra A. Strachner, a student at New York University, wrote more than 300 letters to her nineteen-year-old boyfriend, Private Bernie Staller, who was killed in action on March 18, 1945. Bernie had sent all of Myra's letters home so they could be reread in later years. Although Myra learned in early April that Bernie was missing in action, she continued to write to him for the next two weeks. What follows is the last letter she wrote to him. The day after Myra wrote this letter, the War Department informed Bernie's family that he had been killed.

Bronx, N.Y., April 18, 1945

Darling—

I was at your house tonight. They showed me some pictures of you taken in your high school class room and track team. The one I liked best was the one where you and another fellow were ready to start running. I looked at you, and this is what went thru my mind.

That hair is cropped close, but still is curled around my finger as if it were grasping it. I've kissed those lips. That expression I've seen so often. These legs were pressed against mine. I've held those wrists with my fingers. My hands have been in those hands. My fingers have touched those sides and both touched lightly and dug into those shoulders. My lips have kissed that throat.

And I know you had to be alive because you're so alive! Do you know what I mean?

Someday when we have long night hours before us, I'll tell you all about this—how I felt and what people said.

Today I cried again. I haven't since the day the president died. I was lying on my bed in the afternoon today and I found my lips forming the words, "It's too hard! It's too hard!" over and over again, and when I realized what I was saying I started to cry very quietly. Then I went into the den and played some of the songs that mean something to us and I cried hard for a little while. . . .

Darling, come to me in a dream tonight and tell me that you're alive and safe. Please! I know you want to tell me. Maybe somewhere in a prison camp tonight you're saying to yourself that tonight you're going to try to tell me that you're alive. If there's anything good in the world, they'll let you tell me.

Now to sleep, and to wait for your message. I'll love you till I die.

Myra

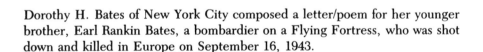

Dorothy H. Bates of New York City composed a letter/poem for her younger brother, Earl Rankin Bates, a bombardier on a Flying Fortress, who was shot down and killed in Europe on September 16, 1943.

New York, Dec. 19, 1943

DEAR BROTHER

What of past enjoined session
Heralding the expense of forbearers?
Why, today, the cadence echoed, with the march,
While Time, by your acceptance, has chartered
Your purpose, your dignity, your courage?

WAR DEFIES MANKIND

I escape the peopled city with its myriad worlds
To tarry where the road circles the old pond's edge,
Here, where the omnipresent is manifested in the face of nature,
I search acceptance of the inevitable.
Here, I may think of all our days together,
Ever so carefully, choosing from those hours,
Gathering memories, to cast like pebbles we threw yesterday.
Phantoms skim the surface of THIS day. . . .
I watch them sink into the depth of ALL tomorrows.

Often have I pondered . . . waiting
What portion time held for me;
Thoughts were it would be I, as the older,
Who would go before.
We were to lock hands again,
I leaning against your youth, was to have ignited,
With my loneliness, the eager fires of its imagination;
To claim strength against that age
Which, barked by harsh trials
Recognizes stilled passions and submits of fears.

Forgive me
If at times my heart will weigh like a swollen plum
Suffering a pain so sharp as to sever it from reason.
Do not leave me for long
That I should wander alone in those days
When my heart will be frozen
Like the waters at whose edge we stand.
Just as the piquant, haunting nostalgia of wood smoke
Awakens the heart of the country born
Are the needs of our comradeship wafted over my senses. . . .
Right against the laughter of my courage it comes
And I find little reserve in years of maturity.

I hear the air beat down.
Overhead pass the age old flight of wild duck.
Their wings echo your silence.
BROTHER, this shall be my watch with them,
The seasons to recognize both,
Knowing you and the silent host of your Sky Armada
Will bide with vigilance.

D. H. B.

———————————————

The following letters were found in the effects of Lt. Major Mooney Messick,
of Gassville, Arkansas, after he was killed in action on May 5, 1944, in the

South Pacific. He was pilot of a B-24 which did not make it back from a mission. The writer, a young Hawaiian woman, apparently met Lt. Messick when he visited the club where she worked. She knew him as Lt. Patrick Merrick.

Honolulu, Spring 1944

Dear Sweetheart:

I received your nice letter a few days ago.

It's exactly 3:40 p.m. now and thought I had better write to you.

I miss you very much, and hope you'll come home and see me again.

Honey, Bobbie hasn't told me about you coming over often. She hasn't said a word to me.

And what's more I like you to come over, honey and see me.

Alright, Sweetheart, I'll allow only my old friends to walk home with me instead of soldiers.

Some of them have asked to take me home. And asked me once or twice to go to the La Hula Rhumba with them, but mom is very much against it, so my answer to them is generally no.

Gee, Sweetheart, I didn't know it was time for me to go to work, so I'll have to close now and honey, I'll be thinking of you.

Love,   Gwen

Honolulu, April 5, 1944

Dear Pat:

I received your letter and was glad to hear from you.

You don't have to worry about me taking anyone serious because I'll wait until I'm twenty. I know it sounds silly, but I'll try.

Sorry you had to wait so long, but I'm still sick and still going to work every day. I have been working eight hours lately and when I come home I just jump into bed.

Well, Pat, I'll say "Aloha" and best of health to you.

Yours,   Gwen (Nell)

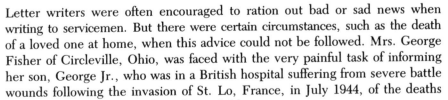

Letter writers were often encouraged to ration out bad or sad news when writing to servicemen. But there were certain circumstances, such as the death of a loved one at home, when this advice could not be followed. Mrs. George Fisher of Circleville, Ohio, was faced with the very painful task of informing her son, George Jr., who was in a British hospital suffering from severe battle wounds following the invasion of St. Lo, France, in July 1944, of the deaths of his wife, Josephine, and newborn child.

Circleville, Sept. 1, 1944

My darling—

Yesterday was your birthday. Mother wishes so much she could tell you what a wonderful birthday present might have been yours. Instead I have not words that can begin to tell you the sorrow that has come to us all. Josephine was taken to Grant Hospital Wednesday night in Loring Hill's ambulance to a baby specialist. She began to get worse soon after arrival. After noon yesterday the doctor forced labor to bring the baby—a little tiny girl weighing 4 lbs. 12 oz—hoping that after the baby came he could stop the poison which had set in Josephine, but to no avail. After being in a coma for over 24 hours, our dear girl slipped away to join the baby you both wanted so much, in heaven. She hadn't known anything nor been in any pain thru it all. We are all so heartbroken. Trouble seems never to come singly, but bear up, dearest, and trust in God. . . .

Darling, everything was done for her that the best baby doctor in Columbus could do for her but when that acute toxemia sets in it is hard to save either one. We will always remember our Jo as the dear sweet girl and wonderful wife that she was. . . .

Now dearest, I hope you will have some one write us as often as you can. We all have appreciated the letters that have been written for you and hope you will keep them coming. We will be so glad when you are back over here and we will come wherever you are sent. We hope it will be close so that we can come often and that you will soon not need to stay in a hospital. We'll be so glad to have you home once more. We're hoping there will be some word from you . . . tomorrow. Keep pulling my dearest and pray.

Your Loving, Mother

George Fisher, Jr., never recovered from his battle wounds. His family later learned that a sniper's bullet had almost severed his spinal cord, paralyzing him from the neck down. He died on July 25, 1945.

—————————— ✍ ——————————

Patricia O'Brien, who had grown up in Iowa, was an eighteen-year-old student at the University of Maryland in July 1940 when she met her husband-to-be, A. S. "Big Al" Aiken, who was twenty-three. He had recently qualified as a pilot in the Army Air Corps. Soon after they met, in October 1940, he was sent to Texas for advanced training. After graduation in March 1941, he was stationed at Selfridge Field, near Detroit, Michigan.

Lt. Aiken was at his home in Maryland to attend his father's funeral when the Japanese attack on Pearl Harbor occurred. After hearing the news of the attack, he reported back to his base immediately. The couple had planned to be married the following May. However, the day he returned to his base, he was sent to Alaska, and they were forced to postpone their wedding date.

Patricia began working for the military in Washington, D.C., during the summer of 1942. In October 1942, she was selected, with eight other young women, to travel to Alaska to work for the Army Air Corps. On her way to Alaska, during a stopover in Seattle, she received a telephone call from her father telling her that her future husband was concerned about what life would be like for an unmarried woman in "Seward's Icebox." She returned to Iowa, and in January 1943, she and Al were married at her home. After spending a month together, he returned to Alaska. She went back to Washington to another Army Air Corps position in the newly constructed Pentagon.

In addition to writing to her husband, Patricia also wrote regularly to many war brides. Although her letters were generally upbeat, there were times when circumstances forced her to let her guard down.

Greenbelt, Md., April 24, 1943

Hi, Joe:

I've about reached my low point so according to the Dorothy Dix's, I shouldn't be writing to you and lowering your morale—but as I always say, what the hell's a husband for. Yesterday I got a letter from Peg Murray, the girl I liked the most in the bunch who went to Alaska. We had a lot of fun together since most of the other gals were on the watch and we were both engaged. He was an Air Corps man too, and in India, sailed from Bolling on 5 hrs. notice about a month after you first left the country. Anyway, he was killed on the 21st of February and as she says, she doesn't much feel like ever coming home again. Then Mrs. Matthews answered my letter today. She had a baby 2 days after she got the telegram. It's a boy named R.D., Jr. It was a pretty bad letter, but I'm sure I don't blame her for going to pieces. She's stuck in North Dakota probably for the rest of her life and says instead of 23 she wishes she were 73. I get what she means. Then on top of that, you write that you won't be home in July—altho' I thought that was coming—still you could have picked a more convenient day to tell me. On thinking the whole thing over—I wish some kind soul would blow the whole damn world to hell—and I'd be glad to be among the missing.

I think it would be better to be in Poland or Greece where they kill all the family instead of just one person and leave the others grubbing around trying to make a life out of nothing, like those two kids will have to do. I can't even feel good about us—if we do get out of it, we'll probably be fat, frightened and always running around trying to save our own necks like most of the people around here. . . .

Evelyn Matthews wants me to write anything you told me about the circumstances. All I can remember is that he made two passes, one of them unnecessary and I hope to God he knows how much he's done to her. If I ever heard you'd done anything like that and hadn't got away with it, I'd hate you for the rest of my life. He didn't have the right to be heroic. . . .

You ought to be here where I could weep on your silly shoulder instead of so far away I can't even remember what you look like. Anyway, stall as long as you like and I hope you have a helluva good time.

Pat

A. S. Aiken remained in the Air Force after the war, retiring in 1966. He continued to work as a civilian pilot until 1972. He then took an office job, retiring a third time in 1984. Patricia is active in local politics. The couple has two children and one grandchild. They have lived in Annapolis, Maryland, since 1966.

Edith Anson Howard was born on December 2, 1921, in San Angelo, Texas. She was the daughter of a younger son of British nobility who had moved to Texas to establish a ranch there in the late 1880s. Her mother, Louisa Goddard Van Wagenen, was a graduate of Smith College. Edith lived much of her childhood in England. She was educated in France, England, and Switzerland as well as at the Chapin School in New York before attending Smith College from 1940 to 1943. She left Smith to marry Alfred Ryland Howard. He was a graduate of Rice Institute and had a law degree from the University of Texas. As a member of the Texas National Guard, he began his active service prior to Pearl Harbor.

Edith and Ryland were married on August 15, 1943. He was sent overseas in early 1944 and was part of the invasion forces in France in June 1944. He served as a forward artillery spotter in a "grasshopper," a small unarmed plane which directed artillery fire on the enemy. He was shot down and killed on July 4, 1944. He had recently been promoted to Captain. Edith was pregnant with their son, Ryland, who was born November 16, 1944.

These letters are selected from the very few which were found in the effects of Captain Howard. The letters deal with Edith's life as a young war bride while she waited out her husband's time in combat. Many of the letters were written after Ryland was killed, but before Edith had been notified by the War Department.

San Angelo, June 26, 1944

My Own Sweet Darling—

. . . My dear Ryland, I don't have to say this to you, for you know and feel it all anyway but I want to. Keep something inside of you clean and shiny and beautiful no matter what goes on around you. When Everything seems horrid and black remember the thing inside of you, turn to it and cling to it, and know that someday it won't be just that way inside you, but all around you. And remember that it won't be too many years before you will have to teach this to your children. Be aware of it and understand it so that you can explain it to them. . . .

Oh my sweet, you can never know what it means to me now to know I'm to have your child—I'm lonely for you, but never alone. You can't imagine how much of my thoughts are taken up with Cuddles. Just think, you aren't *one* person any more but *two*—And that second one, small as it is, is with me. . . .

Gosh, Darling, I never cease to thank God that we married—Imagine if I had to go and be gay with a lot of stupid men—I just couldn't have stood it. . . .

All my love always and always—Cuddles makes me so hot—I'm practically dripping on this letter—

P.S. You can eat oysters in France in summertime. And try some mussels or "moules"—They're delicious—

"Edie The Gourmand Gourmet"

San Angelo, June 30, 1944

My darling Ryland

. . . HEY, you know what? I felt Cuddles for the first time today. It's very faint, not a kick, but more like a feeble stretch. It's the oddest sensation, rather pleasant. Oh, there I go again. You have the earthiest wife. I don't know what you are going to do with me. . . .

I adore you. Can't help repeating and repeating. And miss you.

Oh, gee.

Edie

San Angelo, July 3, 1944

Darling Ryland,

. . . If you are away for two years or more, I'll expire with loneliness. I just could not stand it. I miss you so now that I am miserable. Sometimes there is so much hate in my soul against the Germans that I can't take it in. I loathe every butcher and baker and hausfrau. And I hope that when the Russians get to Germany they kill every man, woman and child as wantonly as they have been taught to by those teutonic fiends. Hope they torture them too. I'm afraid I will never be able to travel in Germany. I'd be arrested for Murder in the first few days. I really want to fill one of them anyway with Buckshot. I wish one of the prisoners escaping from Abilene would care to stick a nose on my ranch. I'd cripple him good and proper. Killing is much too good for them.

There's no news, that's why I'm wasting time blowing off steam like a ten-year-old. I don't care. I get so furious with People here. They talk stupidly against the English and Russians. They think the war in Europe will be over by Christmas. It took 4 years to drive them off French soil the last time and as far as I can see it will take a good two this trip as far as the English and Americans are concerned. The Russians will probably hit Berlin long before you do. And I certainly hope so. And despite all this pessimism I still think *you* will be home by Dec. 2nd. Illogical? yes, but I just know it. . . .

All my love,   Edie

Although Ryland Howard was killed in action on July 4, 1944, Edith continued to write to him until late July, when she received official notification of his death.

San Angelo, July 6, 1944

My most precious Darling Ryland.

. . . Oh, the most wonderful news!!—Anne Tweedy Ardery's Phil is coming home from England any day now. . . . Isn't it marvelous? I'm just so happy and excited for her—And our turn will come when it's time— Won't it be heavenly to have your arms around me and your sweet head pressed down on mine—And if it's next winter around baby time you'll be so absolutely tender and gentle—I know so well how you'll touch me, and how you'll look at me—I think your eyes will be shiny and proud too—Will they? Will you be a little proud about being a Daddy?—Of course you will.

Ryland? I wonder if I'm wrong. What do you think? But it's the oddest thing but all the people Mumny's age make me a little unhappy, and disappointed—and embarrassed—Maybe it's because they are all very unhappy inside—But they all seem to be acting brittle and frivolous and over-gay—They talk about the war in a way that doesn't seem intelligent—I don't include Mummy in this—Because fundamentally she has no illusions about the gravity of our task. But most of the others have an over optimism that shocks and frightens me. And it embarrasses me and my friends when they talk about *us*. It isn't true, Ryland—We aren't brave—We live from day to day as normally as we can, for that is human nature—People don't weep and wail—And life, though it truly does and can have tragic moments, yet it isn't possible for tragedy to be with you 24 hrs of the day—No matter how low things seem, nevertheless, there are immense pleasures—and very real ones. Babies, Friends—Even food and sleep are pleasures as *you* do know. For the *first* time in my life I'm happier with my own contemporaries—And that pleases me. I'm still growing up, and maybe that's a process that never really stops. . . .

I love you so much darling, darling, DARLING Ryland. And missing you is *awful*. Come home safe soon. You can't know what hell I do go through every minute knowing what it is for you in that God Damn Nazi Inferno. Oh I hate so awfully to have you have to go through this—What can I say to help or comfort you—I'm so useless to the person I love more than my life.

Edie.

Edith Howland gave birth to a son, Ryland, on November 16, 1944. After the war, on April 15, 1947, she married a childhood friend, Ford Boulware. He had served in the Army as a battalion commander during landings in Africa, Sicily, Italy, and Normandy. He was promoted to Lieutenant Colonel after the African landings. Since their marriage, the couple has devoted most of their time to managing their ranch in San Angelo. They had no children, other than Ford's stepson, Ryland.

————————————————

Natalie Mirenda, a second generation Italian-American from New York City, married Frank Maddalena on June 23, 1940. They had two children: a son, "Frankie" Jr., born in December 1941, and a daughter, Maria, born a year later. In February 1944, Frank, then 29 years old, was drafted. After six months of basic training at Camp Blanding, Florida, he was sent to Europe where he joined thousands of other replacement troops who were engaged in the fierce fighting following the D-Day invasion of June 1944. Private Maddalena was killed during the Battle of the Huertgen Forest on November 22, 1944.

Natalie had remained in New York City during Frank's basic training. Throughout this period, the couple wrote to each other daily. In addition, Frank occasionally telephoned Natalie, and he made two brief visits home before being shipped overseas.

After Frank was sent to Europe in September 1944, Natalie's life in New York City revolved around caring for their two young children, looking after her parents who lived on an upper floor of her apartment, and meeting with and consoling other war wives in the neighborhood. Eleven girlhood friends, all living within two blocks of her apartment, received dreaded telegrams from the government during the war.

On December 5, 1944, Natalie learned that her husband was missing in action. A year later he was declared dead.

Natalie's letters to Frank are filled with information about their two young children, her longing for him, and her concern for his safety.

New York, April 16, 1944

My darling,

This is another Sunday gone by without you. The day has been so long and it rained until late this afternoon. . . .

Honey, from the way things look, I don't think that there can be a very quick finish to this awful war (I hope I'm wrong) cause even if it lasts another week that week will be an eternity just as long as we're not together.

I'll close now as I want to go to bed. Good night, darling and pleasant dreams. I love you.

Always, Natalie

New York, May 8, 1944

Dearest,

. . . So you hit the jackpot. This crazy mail. . . . I know it's hard to appreciate three letters in one day as going without mail so long must be heartbreaking. And especially since you had such a lousy week too. . . .

Frankie is really a rascal and there are times when I'd like to wring his neck. Like today, I had him in the park and he climbed all over the benches, jumped up and down and yelled like Tarzan, and I'm all worn out from keeping after him. Maria's not so bad as I wouldn't mind anyway because she's such a little doll. . . .

This morning I said, "Frankie, be quiet. I'm reading Daddy's letter." He stuck his little nose under mine and said, "Daddy come home now, finish work." But with such feeling. He's so anxious for you. I persuaded him that you couldn't come yet so he said, "O.K., mommy," just like a little man. . . .

I guess I'll get those pictures this week from you. . . . So darling, till you're all mine forever and a day.

I'll always love you, Natalie

New York, July 27, 1944

Dearest One,

Today I got your letter of Monday. The children just got up from their naps, but I couldn't take them out as we are having a thunderstorm, but good. The heavens just opened and forgot to close. At first baby was frightened, but she saw Frankie imitate and laugh at the thunder and she changed her tears to laughter.

I'm glad you enjoyed my two letters. You asked if I got along on the money that I get. Well the truth of the matter is that I've started to use our savings. I've already had to take $100. Up until now, I had so much in the house that you bought before you went away, plus what you left and you've sent home, I was able to manage for awhile. But now I have to go to the bankroll. When that's gone, well, we won't eat, that's all. . . .

Both the children are on the floor and raising a racket. The call of the wild, I call it. . . .

Gee, honey, if you could only hold me forever, your happiness would be shared by me. I miss you and love you so very much.

I'll close now with a million kisses just for you.

Always, Mommy

P.S. How's the heat? Still bothering you?

After Frank was sent to Europe, Natalie's letters took on a new sense of urgency.

New York, Oct. 11, 1944

My dearest one,

What can you be thinking now? I mean my not writing so often. It's just that I'm so disgusted with this life that I'm beginning to lose courage and faith. Ten years ago, I was such a happy carefree person, daring and so full of the joy of living. And yet today, I'm so burdened with responsibilities that I fear my shoulders can't carry them all. I could and would want to if I had you here with me to help me.

The kids are fine and today I took Frankie with me and put a deposit on a coat for him. It's a very nice one, brown background with a salt and pepper tweed. He really looks adorable in it. . . .

I'll close for now, and I'll love you always.

Natalie

New York, Oct. 17, 1944

My darling,

Today I got your letter of the 9th in which you said you had missed writing for a few days. . . . Oh God, I think I'll go nuts. I see you everywhere—in the chair, behind me, in the shadows of the rooms. Everyplace I go you are always with me and in the back of my mind. I seem to have a continuous headache because I'm so worried about you. It doesn't look like this war is coming to an end. I've stopped listening to the radio and reading the papers as I only eat my heart out knowing that it will keep you away from me all the more. I see that a 1st Army infantry censor is reading the mail. I hope that I'm not jumping to conclusions but I guess that means you'll be with the 1st Army.

Frankie is fine and tonight asked Pop where you were. He's a lot like you and tries not to show how he feels. That must be the reason he hasn't been asking for you very much. Maria is cutting more teeth and is a little cranky and has lost her appetite for awhile. It's always something!!

I love you my dear, so very much and I just can't see life for me with anyone else but you.

Always, Natalie

New York, Nov. 19, 1944

Dearest One,

Today was endless as I've had no mail from you since Monday. Frank, my dearest, what is happening to us? We were going to grow old together. Enjoy and raise our children. The thought that you may be at this very moment fighting is maddening. I suppose that you are with the 1st Army as most of the letters have been censored by a 1st Army censor. I read in the papers that there is a lot of snow and sleet in northern France. Oh, Frank, take care of yourself. You know you catch cold easily. Take care of yourself also as we need you home so much. . . .

Mom had a letter from my uncle in Rome. He says that the Italian people are all sick from hunger and also that they are in rags. He wanted to know if we had anyone in Italy. I wish I might have told him that you were there. Then I'd be sure that you'd be safe for awhile. . . .

I love you my dear and pray that God keeps you well and safe.

Always, Natalie

Natalie wrote the following V-Mail letter only hours before learning that her husband was missing in action. It is the last letter which she wrote to Frank.

New York, Dec. 5, 1944

My dearest Frank,

Still no mail from you. I really don't know what to think anymore. The kids are fine and so adorable. Right now, I put colored handkerchiefs on their heads and they are dancing and singing. If things were right, you'd just be getting home from work and how happy the kids would be to see you. Frank, when I walk alone, I seem to feel you sneaking up on me and putting your arms around me. I turn around and you're not there. I guess I'm just wishing in vain. Gee, soon it will be Xmas. Well, for me it's just another day, but for the kids I'll do my best to make it merry. If only I could hear that perhaps the war was soon over and then you were to come home. I'd be so relieved. I love you and miss you and my life is incomplete and useless without you. Remember, I can't appreciate our kids without you. All send their best.

    Always, Natalie

(Everynite at 10 I miss you and love you.)

Natalie Maddalena devoted the next forty years to raising her children and providing for her aging parents. She also assumed primary responsibility for her younger brother, a disabled veteran, who lost an eye during the Battle of Leyte Gulf. At first, she supported her family by doing hand embroidery. After her children entered school, she worked as a medical secretary for an opthamologist. She has also been a very active member of Gold Star Wives of New York. She did not remarry. She lives in Valhalla, New York, not far from where she and Frank conducted their courtship, and works part-time as a secretary for a local optometrist. She enjoys traveling with her two grandchildren and taking courses at Westchester Community College.

Marjorie Dalquist and her future husband, Rowland Gaunt, grew up together in the same neighborhood in Cranston, Rhode Island. After a courtship of several years, they were married in August 1943, the same week that Rowland received his navigator's wings from the Army Air Corps. She was twenty-three and he was twenty-two. In November 1943, Lt. Gaunt was sent to England where he served as a navigator on a Flying Fortress with the 305th Bombardment Group. During the war, Marjorie worked as a legal secretary for an attorney in Providence, Rhode Island.

Their marriage was cut short on February 22, 1944, when Lt. Gaunt was killed while flying on a mission over the North Sea off the coast of Denmark. Marjorie received a telegram from the War Department in early March informing her that her husband was missing in action. The letters which she wrote to Rowland during February and March were returned to her by the Post Office and stamped "Missing in Action/Return to Sender." These letters are a moving testament to the sacrifices many were compelled to make during the Second World War.

                                      Cranston, Feb. 12, 1944

Dearest mine—

    I love you so, darling. I'd give everything I own if I could spend a few moments with you to feel and reassure myself of your love and to give you of mine. I realize that in that deep, dark period after the news that you were already flying, my mood got into my letters and I'm very sorry. I'm fine now—my pride and joy in you is a shining armor and as a general rule, I'm gay. . . .

It gives me the strangest feeling to know you have taken part in battles I have read about. Sometimes I wonder if I should clip out the accounts and save them for you, but when you come home you'll have had enough of war. . . .

Darling, I do love you so—oh, just thinking about it overwhelms me. You're everything I love and desire. I know it won't be too long before you are home again and it will be so joyous an occasion.

We had a beautiful soft snow storm last night and today about 8 inches fell. It's a real old fashioned snow, and it fell beautifully and silently ever so long. It looks so fresh and white. I love snow. I love you.

Be good to yourself, sweetie.

I kiss your hands and your lips, and I worship you as always.

Marjorie

Marjorie wrote the following letter on the day that Rowland was killed. In the letter, she referred to a newspaper article which described a bombing raid in which fifteen planes were lost. What she did not realize was that Rowland was the navigator of one of those planes.

Cranston, Feb. 22, 1944

Dearest—

I've been thinking about you all day today. . . . Something bothers me, sweetie. In a couple of letters you have said, "Don't be hard on me." Have I darling? I haven't meant to be. I think you're wonderful the way you write. I live for your letters, of course, because they are my only link to my dearest possession. I'm sorry if I've been demanding. Forgive me. It's only because I miss you so much and worry about you. I'm not in danger, but you know how you'd feel if I didn't write. Write as often as you can—V-Mail or otherwise. I don't expect more than that. Your letters are my life bread.

I suspect from the newspapers that you have been very busy of late. Tonight's paper tells of a big raid—1500 planes with only 15 lost. I think of you and pray, darling, but I know you're fine. . . .

Oh, golly, I miss you—physically. I miss being able to hold your hand, and feel the roughness of your clothing, and the warmth of your lips and firmness of your teeth underneath. Oh, I'd better not dwell on it too long. Sometimes I'm content to love you "spiritually," but other times my mind just screams with loneliness for your presence. I adore you so. I love you with every atom of me. Do a good job quick and hurry home to my arms.

Love, Marge

Cranston, Feb. 25, 1944

M'love:

. . . No letter again today. I hope I get one this afternoon. The poor postman, he hates to come without a letter. He never looks my way when he hasn't got one. I can tell by the way he says "hello" whether he has or not.

You must be getting real British cycling around and dining in tea rooms. Do those places look like you expected them to look? When you write those things, I have a definite picture in my mind. . . .

I love you darling. You pop up all over in my memories. Was there anything that either of us did, that the other didn't do? I still can't believe you're true, even after all this—and heaven too—cause you did make a personal little heaven for me on earth—the heaven of your heart and love. I adore you, sugar.

Button me close in your pocket when you fly won't you? Right over your heart? Mmmmmm⸱

Marge

Cranston, March 7, 1944

Rowlie, honey:

My lil heart is kind of sad, not having had its spirits lifted in quite a few days. In other words, no letter yet.

Golly, Moses, but they have been keeping you boys busy. Every day that I read the papers the news grows greater. I feel though as if I know so very little as far as you are concerned. I'll just have to have patience and wait. . . .

I love you so much, darling. I get all tongue-tied when I try to tell you. When I go into Grace Church these noontimes, I kneel and I start to pray and I can't explain the feeling that comes over me. You and God and love are all mixed up, and my heart and mind are talking to you and God. It's such a strong feeling, it just surges out of me and wraps itself around you wherever you are and whatever you are doing. My mind usually sees you in a plane, and I can feel myself putting my arms around you, standing beside you while you are seated, and cradling your head on my breast and protecting your body with mine—my spirit really I guess. It's so real to me. I love you so, and miss you so. Be strong and have faith, won't you dear. It will be such a thrilling day—golly, I hope it comes soon.

God Bless you, Darling. I love you.

Marge

After learning that Rowland was missing in action, Marjorie wrote scores of letters to the War Department, the American Red Cross, the families of Flying Fortress crew members, and even the Danish Underground in an effort to learn more about the details of her husband's fate. While awaiting further news of Rowland, she clung to the hope that he was still alive.

Several months after Rowland's plane was shot down, Marjorie received a package from a shop in London which contained a small, antique music box. Since she had a special fondness for music boxes, Marjorie, at first, held out hope that this was a message that Rowland was safe. Upon writing to the London shopkeeper, however, she learned that her husband had put a deposit on the music box and had promised to return the following week to pay the balance. Unfortunately, his ill-fated mission over the North Sea intervened. It was Rowland's fellow officers who had paid the balance and had had the shopkeeper send the music box to Marjorie.

By the fall of 1944, Marjorie was becoming reconciled to the fact that Rowland would not be coming back. In November she wrote a long and heart-rending memorial letter to her husband.

Cranston, Nov. 8, 1944

My dear husband:

No couple ever had a harder start in marriage than we did, darling, and yet no couple ever had a more beautiful start. I love you so desperately and I've longed for you so these many months that you have been lost in the wide, wide, world. I know in my heart that you are safe and that God is caring for you, but it has been so very hard to live with this terrible uncertainty.

I'm so proud of you. To me you are everything fine and clean and beautiful in the world, and without you everything fine and clean and beautiful seems to have vanished. I keep thinking about the injustice in the world. You, who are so good and kind, you, the kind of person the world needs, why must it be you who has to suffer, when so many, many boys who do not seem to amount to anything, live on for themselves alone.

Wherever you are, I know you must feel my love for you. My love has grown stronger each day and it is just bursting for expression. I've told you many times how much I love you, and I am so thankful for that now. I'm thankful too, because I feel that we did share a beautiful love; it was so beautiful perhaps that is why the memory of it aches in my heart. I have felt that our short time together as man and wife was perfection in every way. I think you feel as I do, and I'm so glad because the promise of it must sustain you wherever you are. Please, darling, think on those things, keep your eyes uplifted and trust in God. I've prayed continually for His protection over you and His guidance during these long trying months. I pray for Him to give you patience and to bless you and make you strong. Oh, that I might bear it for you. I would gladly die that you might come back to those that love you and live gloriously to serve humanity and God. It is so very hard to understand. My mind is constantly in turmoil—why, why, why, going round and round and round. People say I'm brave and a brick, and all sorts of things, but I'm not. I'm hating and fighting every moment that you are lost. I do go on working and reading and talking, but honestly I don't know how or why I do it. The way I feel, time stopped for me last March when that hateful telegram arrived. I just can't believe it is November and almost a year since last I saw you. Oh, sorrowful year, that took away my love and cast him on the mercy of unseeing men. Darling, I know what you are going through is hell, just as I am in hell, but darling if only we can have the faith and strength to endure it, paradise must be on the other side. I love you so. . . .

We are not truly separated from one another, for spiritually we are very close, but how my heart aches for the physical things—just the touch of your hand, the rough fabric of your coat, and the smoothness of your clean white

shirt, but those are minor things compared to how I long for your arms and
your lips and your blessed eyes. Oh, darling, please come back to me soon
and may God keep you much as you were when you left. Please, dear, don't
grow bitter and cynical. God help you keep that joyous youth, that vibrant
energy, that clean mind and courageous spirit that you bore when you left.
May God bring you proudly back to my arms, and soon, please God.

Be strong, my darling. May God give you courage, patience and strength
that will carry you triumphantly through your ordeals to lasting peace,
gentleness and love.

Here is my hand and my love, darling. Hold to it tightly as I will yours
and surely ours will be a glorious victory.

I love you,   Marge

On October 16, 1945, Marjorie received word from the War Department that
Rowland had been declared dead. Two and a half years after Rowland died,
Marjorie married his brother, Arthur, who had served in the Marines with
the Night Fighters in the South Pacific during the war. Marjorie and Arthur
had three children. Arthur died of a heart attack at the age of 42 on February
23, 1962, eighteen years and one day after Rowland had died. For the next
twenty-two years, Marjorie worked as a secretary for the Cranston, Rhode
Island, school department.

Marjorie Gaunt lives in North Kingston, Rhode Island, and is a docent at
the Museum of the Rhode Island School of Design as well as an enthusiastic
member of the Appalachian Mountain Club. She also enjoys traveling and
taking creative writing courses.

Alice and Leo Unker and their infant son, Eliot, were living in New York City
when Leo was drafted, early in 1944, at the age of 35. During the war, Alice
was employed as a clerical worker at the Army Port of Embarkation in Brooklyn. She later became a courier for the Army. After basic training at Camp
Blanding, Florida, Leo was immediately sent to France as a replacement in-
fantryman. Ten days later, in October 1944, he was wounded when a faulty
hand grenade exploded in the pocket of his greatcoat. He spent the remaining
five months of his military career in hospitals in France, England, and the
United States. Alice's letters to Leo convey her kaleidoscopic feelings upon
hearing of his wound.

Brooklyn, Nov. 1, 1944

My Dear Warrior:

Where did they get you? Or is that too a military secret. This morning
at 11 a.m. I received a telegram from the Adjutant General saying you were

slightly wounded in action on the 17th of Oct. in France. Also, that I would be advised as reports of your condition were received. Bubs, what happened? How are you feeling? Please try to answer all the questions you know are in my mind. Bubbie, darling, what now? I guess as soon as you're better they'll send you back. All I can say, is don't rush back like a martyr as you did when you were at Blanding. Boy [their son] and I are expecting you back safe and sound when the war is over, so do your part. I sound slightly idiotic—even to myself.

The last letter I received from you was Friday, Oct. 27th, and it was written on the 12th of Oct. You said you were expecting to see action shortly, or were you hiding the truth. Anyway, I'm hoping to get mail from you so that I'll know how you are and what happened.

It's now already two weeks and a day since you were wounded. How long are you going to be hospitalized? I beg you, don't keep me in the dark. . . .

Love   Alice

Brooklyn, Nov. 5, 1944

Dearest Bubs:

Nothing new. Eliot is supposed to be napping, but of course he's not. It's about 2 p.m. and I'm expecting your Mom. We are going to the Botanic Gardens and the Zoo. I hope your mother feels like going or we'll be obliged to stay home. I haven't told your mother that you were hurt. Am waiting for your letter. Anyway, everyone is so sympathetic, for example, Ida came running to Brooklyn today to stay for a few days, and keep me company. Inda and Newt brought me a box of candies, and when I left Esther's this afternoon she gave me another box. Bubolu darling, what are the chances of your not going back to the front. Foolish of me to ask but that's the way I feel.

It'll be a great relief to get a letter. I'll be able to write a little more sensibly.

Love,   Alice

P.S. I have been thinking the matter over and I've decided to call your sister Lil and tell her. I'm afraid your mother may get a telegram, too. In that case she'd find a note in the door, when she gets home. So, I'll tell Lil to get there first. In case she decides to tell your Mother, she can tell her gently.

Wish I could bring you some flowers, magazines and kisses. If you've got a pretty nurse, ask her to do it for me.

Yours,   Alice

Brooklyn, Nov. 8, 1944

Dear Bubbie:

Your first letters since your accident arrived today. No need telling you how amazed I was. It was nothing short of a miracle that the damage wasn't much greater. I suppose everything is relative. But since receiving the telegram, I've been so upset that learning what your injuries were helped pacify me somewhat. It must be pretty bad, anyway, if you've been hospitalized and given all those injections. I hope (please, try to understand) you won't have to go back. You must have been knocked silly when it happened. Was there anyone with you at the time? I know I shouldn't ask questions because you'd tell me of anything that wasn't forbidden. But I was wondering where you were. I imagine you're with Gen. Patton's 3rd Army, 80th Division, below Luxembourg and Belgium at Metz or Nancy? What hospital are you in, you're not in Paris, are you?

Oh, well, what am I supposed to tell your mother? Have you written to her? You mentioned that you'll be going back into combat. Are you leaving the hospital and when? Maybe, I'll get another letter tomorrow that will say more. Don't think I don't appreciate your ten page letter. I could never do anything like it. But, I've turned into a selfish and gluttonous wife and want more, more, more. For instance, in the last letter you write dated Oct. 27 (it came with the ten pager and another V-Mail letter dated Oct. 26), you say you might go to Great Britain. Now I wonder why. Is it to recuperate? Or special treatment? I wish you had told me how soon you'd be walking around. Bubbie, I think I've become a nag in my old age. One might think we didn't even have an election yesterday. Anything I might say on the subject would be old stuff so I won't say that all of us are mighty pleased with the results. . . .

I love you,   Alice

I'll write tomorrow. You don't leave my thoughts for a minute. Boy is wonderful.

Brooklyn, Nov. 10, 1944

Hello, my Bubolu Darling:

. . . I still can't get over the long letter (the only one) written in the hospital in which you described the circumstances of your accident. I must have read it a hundred times. At present, it's getting the once over by your mom. I took the two V-Mail letters and the big one and the telegram with me to the Bronx yesterday to prove that you were well enough to write. Even she admitted that it took a pretty sound mind and body to produce such a beauty. You see, Lil and I decided not to tell your mother anything until we had word from you. Much to my relief, she reacted beautifully and for the first time in weeks has a little peace of mind. We're all so thankful. I hope I don't hurt your feelings, no doubt you've been in great pain, but Bubs, darling, we imagined every thing under the sun, now at least we know. I would imagine you'd write to me every day. Maybe you'll tell me later you haven't, not even while you are in the hospital. . . .

Bubs, I'd feel lots better if I could get more mail. As it is, I'm feeling fine, and can't complain. Be well.

Love,   Alice

Alice was able to visit her husband two times while he was recuperating at a military hospital in Valley Forge, Pennsylvania. He was discharged from the service in the spring of 1945. After the war, the couple had another child. Leo was killed in an automobile accident in 1949. Alice married a second time in 1952, and her second husband, Benjamin Feld, adopted the two children.

Alice ran a student travel and study agency in New York City for twenty years. She received her bachelor's degree from the State University of New York in 1975 at the age of 60. Her first child, whom she often referred to as "Boy" in her World War II letters, is the founder of the Feld Ballet. Alice and her husband live in New York City.

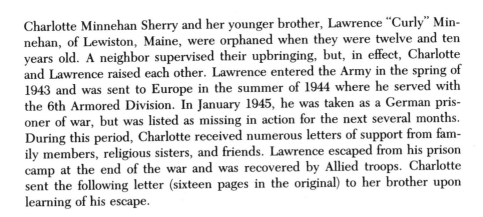

Charlotte Minnehan Sherry and her younger brother, Lawrence "Curly" Minnehan, of Lewiston, Maine, were orphaned when they were twelve and ten years old. A neighbor supervised their upbringing, but, in effect, Charlotte and Lawrence raised each other. Lawrence entered the Army in the spring of 1943 and was sent to Europe in the summer of 1944 where he served with the 6th Armored Division. In January 1945, he was taken as a German prisoner of war, but was listed as missing in action for the next several months. During this period, Charlotte received numerous letters of support from family members, religious sisters, and friends. Lawrence escaped from his prison camp at the end of the war and was recovered by Allied troops. Charlotte sent the following letter (sixteen pages in the original) to her brother upon learning of his escape.

Lewiston, April 23, 1945

HI!!!!
Dearest Lawrence:

The dark clouds have lifted, and at long last, we've received the letter we've looked for on the average of three times a day—and a peek in between times—with many a wistful look at the clerks at the P.O. with each errand at that building. Just haunted them! But it paid dividends—and then some!

My goodness—where to begin! About a week ago, some of my old letters started coming back from France, dated October, November, December, so I don't doubt that you're way behind on news. But, I can hardly sit long enough to concentrate on the past, what with everything so wonderful again and such bright prospects ahead! Where shall I begin? I knew I should have kept a diary!! When that—wire caught up with us on Saturday, January 27th—"Life's Darkest Moment." Jim [Charlotte's husband, who was in the Navy] and I both said we'd keep on writing and mail our letters all at once as soon as we'd heard from you, but we were sissy and kept away from newspapers—radio commentators—newsreels, because they didn't have the news *we* were looking for and not being posted on much news—didn't have much to talk about—except how hard we were all praying—the Masses and Novenas and candles that were being offered for your safe return.

Boy, what a great day when your letter arrived last Monday. . . . When I opened the letter and saw Repatriation Center, my French came in handy and I screamed, "Curley's coming home!" Everyone went w-i-l-d!. . . . I've been spinning like a top ever since. More people have written notes and called words of happiness for us. To top it all, Jim chose *that very day* to call because he said, "I've got the funniest feeling you've heard from Curley." Isn't that a coincidence? Old killjoy, I couldn't even surprise him, but you can be sure he was much relieved! He was in Puerto Rico then, but he's since than left for Trinidad. . . .

This is in itself a day of historic tinge—the eve of meeting of the relief armies, the eve of the San Francisco Conference—and—who knows what else might happen. Aren't you shocked by the death of President Roosevelt? We are "mourning" for thirty days, and there has been a lot of Memorial Services. Seems so odd to say "President" and follow it by Truman. Wonder what he'll be like—big shoes he has to fill. . . .

It was impossible to keep Jim from worrying about how I was reacting. He kept calling and calling—so—with help from our *very* good friend, Dr. Kay, and the Red Cross, Jim came home for 12 days, plus travel time (Feb. 19–March 4) on Emergency Time. He came home to boost my morale and— I boosted his, instead! I'd be getting a meal in the kitchen and suddenly Jim would break his neck to get to the radio to shut off the news—all the time I hadn't noticed it was on, even. Can't you just picture him!! Poor Jim, he did *more* worrying! We were in Lewiston for a week, spent two duty bound days in Danvers [in Massachusetts with Jim's parents], and a week in N.Y.C., far away from everyone we knew. What a help to get away from all the well-meaning but over-sympathetic neighbors.

Let's see, what's for news? . . . Gee, you won't like the Purity [a local soda fountain]. It's been sold again and they've put booths where the fountain was and where the booths were opposite where you sat evenings—is a fountain and bar the length of the room. It's nice, but so *darn differ-ent!*. . . .

It sure is perfect sitting down and gabbing away with you after all these months. Every nite I'd say, "Please take care of him, and let him *know* everything is okay at home," and now it is so wonderful to be saying so many "Thank-yous" now. . . .

More in a few days. I'm watching for mail, too!

Lots and Lots of Love,   Charlotte

Following his discharge from the Army in the summer of 1945, Lawrence, with the help of the GI Bill, attended Bowdoin College. After graduating, he secured a position as an engineer with the Bell Telephone Company in New Jersey. He died fifteen years ago. Charlotte and Jim were reunited at the end of the war and settled in the Lewiston area. They had no children. Charlotte has been confined to a nursing home for a number of years.

George L. Cockerham of DeQuincy, Louisiana, served in the Army Air Corps in the Philippines during World War II. In April 1942, he was taken prisoner on Bataan. He survived the Bataan Death March, was transported on a "hell ship" to Japan, and served as a laborer in a copper mine in Osaka for the remainder of the war. Ressa Jenkins, an Army nurse who escaped from Bataan on a submarine, brought some of Private Cockerham's personal effects (watch, ring, and wallet) with her and eventually sent them to his parents. His family did not hear from him until the end of the war. George was liberated on August 20, 1945, his twenty-fifth birthday. The following letter, written by Christine Cockerham, George's mother, describes the relief and joy which she and other family members and friends felt upon learning that he had survived the war years.

DeQuincy, Oct. 1, 1945

My Dearest Son:

Just received your letter and you don't know how happy we were, for you see it has been 4 years next month since I had your letter telling me you had arrived in Manila. I don't just know where to start telling you about all that's happened:

Betty Jo [George's sister] is entertaining the Tigerettes now and I can't hear myself think. As you know this is her last year in school. She's still fat and happy. The baby [Glady Faye] is in the eighth grade and fatter than the other three girls.

Biddy [George's sister] and Fred were married three years ago last May and he has been in Europe ever since, but is back in the states now and will be home any day now. Emily Lou [George's sister] married Tom Ellis in Jan. 1944 and he is at present in Yokohama, Japan, with the 11th Airborne Troops—and was looking for you—hoping he would see you first. He was in the Philippines till it was won—Ernest Perkins is there too. He saw them bringing the prisoners out of Cabanatuan #1 [a notorious Japanese prisoner-of-war camp] and just knew every one that passed would be you, as that's where we thought you were. I have written everybody that I could that had escaped trying to get news of you. But they were all sorry they couldn't tell me anything. I have your watch. Miss Jenkins sent it to us. Her sister was liberated at Manila from Santo Tomas [a Japanese internment camp for enemy civilians and military nurses]. So much for that.

Our old school house burned down in 1942 and now we have a new one and it sure is pretty. We are working on our house—have the bedrooms fixed and are going to build two more rooms on the back. Thought we would have it done by the time you came home, but we couldn't get the lumber—but they are going to release it soon. Then we can finish up. . . .

I am enclosing some snap shots of the kids. We sent you a bunch at different times but I don't suppose you ever got them.

Daddy has twelve days vacation due him and he has been waiting—hoping you would get to come home and you all could go camping. He's already planning. We have our [railroad] pass to San Francisco to come meet you—that is, if they will let us know in time.

Glady Faye can play the piano real well and is taking lessons again now.

Mother is so excited and nervous I can't think of anything to write. Did you get my letter I sent through the Red Cross in August—also a cable?

Everybody is well and so happy about our hearing from you. Mrs. Van Winkle got her letter from Jesse at 7 a.m.—telling about seeing you on Okinawa. The whole town was like wild fire—the phone rang all the time to see if it was true.

Will stop so Uncle Dade can mail this on [train] No. 9 for me—looking every day for a phone call or telegram from you that you are in the states and are home.

Everybody sends their love.   Your loving Mother

George was reunited with his family in late October 1945. He was given a tumultuous "welcome home" by the townspeople of DeQuincy—most of whom had gathered at the railway station to greet his train. Shortly after returning home, George met Mildred Eastham, a recent graduate of Louisiana State University, who had been hired to teach in DeQuincy's newly constructed school. They were married on George's twenty-sixth birthday—August 20, 1946—exactly one year after he had been liberated. The following year, their only child, George Milton, was born. George Sr. worked for the Continental Oil Company for twenty-three years. He died in 1984. Christine Cockerham devoted the remaining years of her life to homemaking and caring for her grandson. She died at the age of 74 in 1973.

In 1943, Josephine Keutman, a fifty-three-year-old widow living in the Bronx, New York, reluctantly gave her youngest child and only son, Charles, then eighteen years old, permission to join the Army Air Corps. He received his commission as a second lieutenant shortly after his nineteenth birthday. In August 1944, Lt. Keutman was sent to Spinazzola, Italy, with the 460th Bombardment Group where he served as a bombardier on B-24 Liberator bombers. On September 13, during his ninth mission, he and his crew were shot down over Poland. He was captured by the Germans and taken to Stalag Luft I—a POW camp composed of Army Air Corps officers. For six weeks, Charles was listed as missing in action. During this period, Josephine Keutman wrote to her son almost every day. These letters were returned to her with the comment: "Missing, Return to Sender." The pain and heartache she experienced throughout this very difficult period are poignantly reflected in her letters.

Bronx, Oct. 2, 1944

To My Darling,

Just a line to let you know that we received a wire from the War Department stating that you were missing. The shock, I don't need to tell you was something which cannot be explained, but I am sure that it won't be too long before I hear from you as you know God is with you and watching that nothing should happen. In Him we have to place our trust and confidence.

This letter is really very hard to write, but honey I know you are going through the same torture that I am and also your sisters. Everyone is so kind to us in offering up prayers for your safe return, but that ache in my heart does not seem to ease.

Sissy Flyn had an announced Mass for your safe return. I went up to Father Foster and you were prayed for in all the Masses on Sunday, October 1st. I cannot name the different churches or friends who have lit candles for your safe return. In any case you may be held as a prisoner of war, which I know will take at least a couple of months before we are notified. I will keep up as I am so sure that some where you are under someone's care, and God is watching over you. So I hope that you are praying as hard as I am. . . .

Honey, I hope you are well and in good hands and at the present time we too are well. I will continue to write for I am sure that you may even get back to your base, so may the blessings of God be with you all.

With all my love,   Mom

Bronx, Oct. 5, 1944

Darling,

Oh, how hard it is to be kept in the dark, if only in some way, we could receive some information regarding the welfare or safety of you and your crew. Honey, I want to tell you not to worry about me at home. We are all well, but very much upset concerning you. It is for you that we are worrying about, as to where you are being kept. I have prayed day and night and I feel that you and all are safe and hope that you keep well with the help of God.

We have written to quite a few people as to who could help us out with any bit of news, but it all centers around "secrecy." We have been told it would take 3 months before we hear any news. Your commanding officer is supposed to convey some news concerning that mission. The War Department informed us to that effect, but so far nothing has been heard. We don't know if the whole crew was on that "mission" or not, if only someone in the group or Squadron would write to end this suspense. God only knows.

I have endured a week of I don't know how to explain, but it was *hell* in plain words, but I have prayed as I never prayed to the God above to watch over and protect and send you home to me safe. I am sure that my prayers will be answered. If only you are not being tortured, especially in mind. If it is in any way possible for you to write, I know you will do it, but I also know that you can't for certain reasons even if it were possible.

I want to confide in you I have a feeling and it is very strong that I will be seeing or hearing from you soon. God will give me the strength to endure it. Hope to hear the end of this slaughter soon. May God protect and watch you all.

I miss you so much.

Love, Mom

Bronx, Oct. 25, 1944

To My Darling (where ever you are, come back to me.)

Today is exactly 6 weeks that you went on that fatal mission. Maybe some miracle or gift of God has happened that will enable you to come back to your base or maybe home. God only knows how I am worrying about you so far away from home and maybe being tortured or sick or even wounded. Oh how I need you. Maybe God is listening to my plea as I keep praying day and night for your safe return. No matter who you meet will say, "Oh, he will be back." I don't want you to think that I have no confidence in you, so I put my trust in "Him" and "Blessed Mother."

Yesterday I did receive the pieces of lace you sent to me and I do think they are the grandest doilies that I ever saw. I surely will value them above everything, especially to think that I was in your mind. Thanks so much son. . . .

While I am writing I am being blinded with tears which are running faster than the pen is writing. Oh God, please help send you back to me soon. I have nothing else in life, but you. I will close now and will keep my fingers crossed, like we did when you went to school. God always answered my prayers and I'm sure he will not forsake me now. So hoping to see or hear from you soon with all my love and hope it will find you well. May God be watching and protect you from all harm. I miss you much, my heart is broken.

Love, Mom

Late in October 1944, Mrs. Keutman received a telegram from the War Department stating that Charles was a POW in Germany. She now began writing letters to her son on special POW stationery and addressed his mail to Stalag Luft I, Germany.

Bronx, Dec. 22, 1944

Dear Charles,

Oh what a joy it is to write and tell you that I received your first card today dated September 18. Oh darling, just to see your writing was a stimulant to me. Oh, I can't tell you. I guess you feel the same as I do. It was grand to hear that you are well. In fact, we have heard from some of your crew's next of kin. I guess we have everything to be grateful for in knowing you were safe. . . .

This is the best Christmas present to me—only to be home would be still better. My prayers and them of all your friends were answered. You have no idea of the amount of people who are concerned about you. . . . The radio is full of Christmas cheer and also that you POWs will have all the festivities of Christmas. I hope it is true. I myself will not be home. There is too much missing now that you are not here. Last year I had a telephone call, but I am so happy knowing you are safe! . . . I cannot say happy holiday to you now, but you know my thoughts are with you always.

All my Love, Mom

Russian troops liberated Stalag Luft I on May 1, 1945. On May 13, Lt. Keutman was flown to one of the many "Tent Cities" in France where former prisoners of war awaited passage to the United States. Lt. Keutman returned to New York in June 1945 where he and his mother experienced a joyful reunion. Following the war, he made a career with the Air Force. He received his pilot's license in 1952 and retired as a lieutenant colonel in 1969. Josephine Keutman died in 1952.

After retiring from the Air Force, Charles worked at several civilian jobs which involved operations research analysis and technical editing. He retired in August 1988 and lives in North Stonington, Connecticut, with his wife and two college-aged daughters.

Chapter 9

Why We Fought

MUCH HAS BEEN WRITTEN ABOUT THE MEANING OF THE SEC-
ond World War. It has been called "the good war," but it has also been
described as a stupid and sadistic venture.

To the majority of Americans who lived from 1941 to 1945, however, the
war seems to have had real purpose and meaning. That purpose was defined
as "fighting to save the American way of life." Many slogans were created
during the way which offered short, pithy sayings designed to further refine
this idea. Ultimately, though, the citizens of the United States probably knew
why they went to war as well as any sloganeer.

Americans fought because their country called them. Once called, they ex-
plicitly defended the Constitution, the Bill of Rights, and what Franklin Roosevelt described as The Four Freedoms. Women on the home front expressed
their support for these same ideals in many of the letters which they wrote.
Finally, in August 1945, the war was over. In their euphoric victory and
homecoming letters, American women reaffirmed their views on the meaning
of the war.

It was now time to come home. It was also time to renew the loving ties
which had been kept alive by the billions of letters which had bridged the
distances of separation.

There were many ways in which American women promoted the war effort. One of the more interesting involved the work of a Mississippi woman, Mrs. J. T. Leggett, the wife of a former pastor of the Hattiesburg Methodist Church. The first of her endeavors came when she sent small bags of soil from her "Victory Garden" to her son in the 7th Army Air Corps to drop over the Marshall Islands. Her project grew to include bags with soil from the capitol grounds of the forty-eight states, which she sent to General Douglas Mac-Arthur and other high-ranking military figures. She labeled her bags of soil, "For This We Fight."*

Hattiesburg, March 14, 1944

Dear Gen. MacArthur:

Enclosed you will find three Victory Bags, filled with good old U.S. earth. Having an invalid husband there is so little I am able to do. I am making and sending these little bags to boys in all the war zones. My son, who is a Cpl. with the 7th Army Air Corps, says he is having a wonderful time dropping these bags over the Marshalls and Carolines.

We are particularly interested in the men from your way, since so many were trained here at Camp Shelby. There, too, there are quite a number of our home boys with you. One of your Chaplains, H. M. Vaughan, is a cousin of mine.

We pray, daily, for you and your men. God will take care of you and guide you as you make your return trip to the Philippines. May it be soon.

God Bless you is the prayer

of

Mrs. J. T. Leggett

Use these as you like.

Hattiesburg, Sept. 26, 1944

Dear General MacArthur:

In February I sent to Admiral Nimitz several bags of "US" earth. I asked that the small bags, "For This We Fight" bags, be placed under the flag poles of the conquered islands and the large "For This We Fight" bag, be placed on the foundation of the Government building in these islands. Our son is in the Seventh Air Force, so I asked that he be allowed to place this soil on this foundation.

. . . The idea of putting soil, from the entire United States, on every island caused me to write every Governor asking for three or four tablespoons full of soil. This is to be taken from the grounds of their State Capitol. . . .

I am sending several of the small bags to you to place under the flag poles wherever you like. The larger ones are to be placed where you want

---

*The letters written to General MacArthur are located in the MacArthur Memorial Archives and Library, Norfolk, Virginia, Record Group 3: Southwest Pacific Area, Commander-in-Chief Correspondence. Reprinted by permission of the MacArthur Archives and Library.

them. I am sending two extra pretty ones. They are for Corregidor. I hope to be able to send enough of these bags to go on every island.

We are all very happy over the progress you are making on your return trip to the Philippines. May God be with you all the way.

With all best wishes, I am

Very Sincerely,   Mrs. J. T. Leggett

Hattiesburg, January 9, 1945

Dear General MacArthur:

The wonderful news of your return to Luzon, is coming in over the radio. . . . This soil comes from the 48 states. . . . I ask that you give one [bag of soil] to President Osmena, and that you two place it where you think best. And that a picture be taken of your placing it. In this I am sending a small bag. It is the largest I can send air mail. . . . Our son was under fire. May God bless and protect you and your men is the earnest prayer of

Mrs. J. T. Leggett

As the following letters which were written to General MacArthur demonstrate, citizens throughout the U.S. had come to an understanding of "why we were fighting" the Second World War.

Kankakee, June 3, 1942

Dear Sir:

You will find enclosed a money order for $100.00.

Compliments of Beauticians sorority, the Ke Cite Chapter of Beta Beta Lambda, Kankakee, Illinois.

This money is placed at your disposal to be used at your discretion among a few American boys in service.

Thanking you in advance.

We are Sincerely yours,

Karma Lee Harshbarger, Secretary

Wichita, November 10, 1942

Dear Sir:

You may wonder why I am writing and who I am. Well to begin with I saw a piece in the paper that said a little boy of nine wrote to you. That gave me the same idea, so that is why I am writing to you. You may want to know what I look like so I will try my best to describe myself. I am twelve and about 5 foot 1 in. I have brown eyes and brown hair. I am in the seventh grade at school and I like all of my teachers, which is quite unusual. I supposed you would like to know what we at home are doing. My mother saves grease for bullets. I also buy a war stamp every time I get a quarter. We save paper, all kinds of metal and rubber. I have a bicycle but I don't very often ride it to save rubber tires. One of the mill company's has organized a club for children called "The Junior Commandos," and they are doing a great job. We Girl Scouts are doing our bit by taking care of small children so that the parents may work in war factories. We are also running errands for people. I thought you might like to know that we here at home have a picture of you hanging on our front room wall with an American flag over it. I have five uncles in the army and one cousin in the marines. One of my uncles is in a camp in Mississippi. I have another uncle somewhere near Australia. As far as I know he is in New Caledonia but I think he has been moved. I am writing this letter in hopes you will get it, because I don't know your exact address. By the way, if you would like my school mates to write to you I would be glad to tell them so. Well it is about time for taps so I had better be closing this letter.

Yours Truely

Miss Joan Dooley

P.S. If you can find a little time to answer my letter I would feel it a *great honor*. . . .

We all know what a great job your doing over there, and I know we'll all try to do our part.

Florida State Department of Education,
Vocational Training for War Production Workers,
Jacksonville, Nov. 22, 1943

Dear General MacArthur:

I am writing you on behalf of my "girls," women from 17 to 60 who are in training here now and the ones who have completed their training and are now working in war production lines, at Army Air Force service depots and sub-depots, in machine shops, in shipyards and in factories.

You see, they have brothers and sweethearts and husbands and cousins and sons with you and other military leaders on the fighting fronts. Some of them have had loved ones whom they shall not see; others have seen the ones they love return, bearing the injuries, the scars, the permanent disabilities resultant from fierce and bitter battle.

Many of these loyal women have expressed themselves to me as disturbed by rumors that our fighters do not believe they are being adequately backed up by the home front.

So I am writing this for them . . . to say that *they* are backing you and your men up to the limit of their abilities. This is to assure most deeply that as far as American womanhood, represented in these girls, is concerned, you and your men not only have their love, their prayers and their tears, but also all of the materiel with which they can provide you through sweat and grease and grime and the strength of their minds, bodies and spirits. No matter the fortunes of war they are with you all the way.

Sincerely,   C. L. McWilliams, Supervisor of Women, Jacksonville Vocational School

Terre Haute, Ind., July 19, 1942

Dear General MacArthur:

I am Mrs. Henry of 911 So. 10th St writing you this letter. I gave birth to a baby boy at the Union Hospital on July 10, and named him Patrick

McArthur. His grandfather Henry named McArthur after you hoping you gain our country for us. Most all the babies that were born were boys but none of them named them after you. They were about 38 boys with acception of 3 girls I think were born too while I was there. Hoping this letter will gain our country and for our General to keep up his good fight.

Answer if will.

Sincerely,   Mrs. Raymond Henry

Carbondale, Pa., Dec. 12, 1942

My Dear General MacArthur:

Under separate cover I have mailed to you a package containing a pair of wool sox for you, a pair woolen mittens for your wife and two pair for your boy, which I have knitted personally, from start to finish and hope you will have much comfort wearing the same—incidentally I am 83 years of age, born in this city, and this present war is the forth under which I have lived, but earnestly praying night and day for the success of the Allied forces and that peace and comfort will come to the world with the extermination of that Maniac Hitler and his partners. May the thoughts of a United Nation for peace ever more be realized.

Yours truly,   Mrs. Emma Messenger

Lucile Wilson, a school teacher from Everett, Washington, wrote regularly to her only child, Private Herrett S. Wilson, who was stationed in the Pacific throughout much of the war. In a letter written in June 1944, she provided a provocative response to the question, "Is it all for naught?"

Everett, June 27, 1944

Dearest Son,

. . . I can see why you ask the question, "I fought and killed so that the enemy might not invade our land and I ask is it all for naught when red, white, and blue fascists drive Nisei about like coyotes and plague the fathers, mothers, and relatives of our colored comrades that fight by our side." There are many things that will make you ask yourself this question, "Is it all for naught?" from time to time. I've asked myself this question for you many times. I'm sure every mother has done the same. . . . Millions of veterans and home folks intelligently asking this question may bring great post war changes. This is the hope of the *future*.

Jefferson gave us a goal in the Declaration of Independence and the American Bill of Rights. In the 150 years past we have made strides and have widened the base of Democracy. At first only property owners could vote and in some sections as New England only church members and property owners. So we can see visible changes in our scope of Democracy, but you are right we have great strides to make *here* in our own country. You suggest I raise my voice. In other words through enlightenment, social pressure etc. further strides can be made. The 14th Amendment (right of Negroes to vote) is a farce in many Southern states. Mrs. Roosevelt is hated in the South because of her racial viewpoint. People who visit the South say they begin to understand better the Southern viewpoint and problems although they do not agree entirely with them. . . .

I will be anxiously awaiting further news of your condition, homecoming, or what have you?

Much, much love, Mom

The following "victory" letter, written by Doris J. Winiker of Brooklyn, New York, to her Army husband, Corporal Walter Winiker, stationed with the Central Pacific Command Base Headquarters in Hawaii, provides a first-hand commentary about the victory celebrations in New York City. The letter expresses the ebullience felt by many people throughout the United States upon learning that peace had finally been declared.

Brooklyn, Aug. 16, 1945

HURRAH! V I C T O R Y HURRAY! YIPPEE!

My Darling Sweetheart—Wally,

Of all times to delay my letter writing to you—is these past few days— but to tell you the truth angel, I've been celebrating so much that I just can't put it all into words. I'm drunk with joy and happiness because at least we're definitely on the path to our Utopia and our reunion that we've spent almost two years of our life waiting for. Darling, I'm on top of the world! You know how I've been writing you about your homecoming these past few weeks. I guess you must have thought I was pretty desperate to keep continuously asking you when you were returning home—Well, to tell you the truth I was. There seemed to be no hope for the immediate future and the waiting and hoping and wanting was really getting the better of me. Your answers were quite discouraging and I really had begun to resign myself to an extremely long waiting period—and just as I was trying to adjust myself to another few years of loneliness—the war was over—how wonderful! Angel, can it really be true! We're free! Well,—almost. We won't really be free until you're in a good ole draped civilian suit again. . . .

Well, baby, I think I'll start telling you about the celebrating on the home front. . . . Let us go back to this past Tuesday when the radio announced Japan's acceptance of our surrender terms. About four o'clock in the morning mother and dad came into my room and excitedly woke me up to tell me the WAR WAS OVER! Well, I never got out of bed so quickly, even though I suspected that I must still be dreaming. There in the dark of night, just before the dawn of another day, the whole world suddenly became alive with excitement. Cars were riding through the dark street with their horns blowing. People outside were dancing in the streets with their nightgowns and pajamas on. Children from one year and up were running through the dark street banging pots and pans, blowing horns and ringing bells. There are some young boys on East 3rd Street that have a small band of music and they began to play in the middle of the street as every one danced. People shouted from their windows and small bon-fires were started all along the street. Victory! Glorious Victory! How good it felt! Of course, many stopped to pray for our lost boys and many a tear was shed. . . .

Tuesday night . . . Mother and Dad and I sat in the living room talking things over. We naturally spoke of your homecoming, which at that moment of excitement seemed to be in the immediate future. Mother and Dad started making promises which I won't hold them to because of the excitement of the moment—but if they do remember those promises—it would be nice. They said that when you became a Civie again they would purchase your *complete* Civilian outfit and get me a fur jacket. After that I walked over to Bea's house. Florrie, Sara and lots of other people were sitting outside. They had a bridge table full of goodies set out on the sidewalk and all along the block there were parties going on. We talked of the future and thrilled at some of our plans. Bea and I were guessing at when you boys would be home—but all we can do is guess. There are so many factors to consider and we decided to wait for some further word from you boys.

Yesterday, at about 4:00 p.m. Bea, her sister, Libby, and I went to the city [New York] to celebrate. Darling, if you haven't seen Broadway during the Victory Celebrations then you've really missed one of the most thrilling and most unbelievable sights in the whole world. It's very difficult to put into words. First of all the gutters were jammed with people, mostly servicemen, packed in tightly from curb to curb—some walking eight and ten abreast, singing, laughing, and blowing horns. Confetti and streamers were ankle deep and were being sold at every street corner and even in the middle of the gutter. Policemen and M.P.s lined each side of the gutter shoulder to shoulder, but took no heed of the goings on like the sailors and soldiers standing in the gutter and grabbing every woman and girl in their arms and passionately kissing them in spite of kicking, screaming, and protesting. People sat on the curbs of Broadway and Times square right in front of the cops and necked—but most violently! Soldiers and sailors climbed on the hoods of passing cars and police and M.P.s just stood there smiling. A sailor started after me and wouldn't give up even though I ran and ran all over the street and finally took refuge in back of a cop—but when I asked him to protect me—the cop offered to kiss me too—so unable to help myself any longer—I got kissed! (against my will—of course). Can you forgive me sugar? It was a very disturbing experience because I had forgotten what it's like to be kissed—but I didn't enjoy it—it only made me all the more lonesome for you, baby. . . .

But that was only a small part of our evening. First we went for dinner to the Brass Rail. It was tres enjoyable. Then we went to the Strand to see Erskine Hawkins in person and "Christmas in Connecticut" on the screen. Very, very enjoyable. Then we went to a cocktail lounge for a drink—I had a Tom Collins and had Bea and Libby in stitches. Really, I don't know what makes me so humorous. But Bea actually had to tell me to stop before she got sick from laughing. From there we went walking through the crowds watching the amazing sights which only a day of Victory could have brought forward. Then we went to Child's for a sandwich and another drink. This time I had a Rum and Coke. Whoppee! No, I wasn't drunk. Just gay! We all agreed that we had a really good time. Now I'll be able to tell my children (our chillun) the thrill of watching Broadway's V.J. Day's Celebrations! Now, you'd better get your story ready for the kid's bedtime tale. . . .

I hate to leave you, sweetheart, but perhaps, very soon our good nites will be said in bed, facing each other as we lie in each other's arms in our dimly lit bedroom on our cool blue sheets—ah heaven—we'll have it—won't we angel darling? I love you more than life itself. You are my whole life and I adore you, my precious husband. Come home for our 5th Anniversary. Please! I love you with all my heart and soul. Here a few sample kisses for here, there and everywhere—and if you want some more—come and get it.

Always your very own,
Doris

Betty Maue's "victory" letter to her fiancé, Ario Pacelli, who was serving with the Army in Italy, captured the excitement and joy felt by many of the citizens of Hazelton, Pennsylvania, at the conclusion of the war.

Hazleton, Aug. 15, 1945

My Own Beloved Sweetheart: x x x x x x x x x x x x x x

Good morning, my dear, and how are you this morning after celebrating the good news. I pray you're fine and that you have good news about coming home soon, too.

Last nite I hurried to finish that letter I started at noon so Dotty could mail it. And, I expected to write more but the excitement and the noise was just too much. Cars kept passing the house and every one tried to think of a louder noise than the other. They had old dish pans, wash tubs, and oil cans tied on the back of cars and bicycles and wagons and the horns must be about worn out because they kept them blowing constantly. I drove Dotty down to the post office just to witness Broad St. Never ever did I see such a crowd on our own little Broad Street. Traffic was awful and confetti and papers had the streets and pavements white. Oh, it is so wonderful to know it is over, and all praise to God that He has given us victory.

As soon as the news came over the radio, Mother, Sarah and I had a private thanksgiving and praise service and all had a good cry for joy. God has wonderfully cared for you and Russel and Harry and oh how we thank Him.

We even forgot to eat supper (Mother was eating as the news came) and we all went out and sat on the porch until after 11 p.m. . . .

It was after twelve when we retired and what a sleep I had, the best in months, it seemed. . . . About 7:15 my alarm went off and it was so quiet and peaceful. It seemed as though all of Hazleton was sleeping. The President declared a two day holiday, but I came out to the office, so I thought I'd write you. I'll be on call today. . . .

As I passed people coming to work, everyone has a smile and seems so happy. It's so wonderful.

At seven tonite we're to have a parade and 8:15 church service. It was to be our Public Health Nurses' meeting too so I don't know what we'll do about that. . . .

All my heart's true love to you alone.

God bless you, dear.

Your Honey,   Betty

Twenty-one-year-old Frances Ricica worked as a nurse's aide in an Ann Arbor, Michigan, hospital during World War II. At the conclusion of the war, she wrote two provocative letters to her future husband, Rollin "Pete" Zilke, who was stationed with the Army in Europe.

Ann Arbor, Aug. 11, 1945

Hi, Darling:

Half a minute away from the other letter. In case you don't get them at the same time, this is Wed., Aug. and eleventh, and this is just continuing a letter. What do you think of the atomic bomb dropped on the Japanese the other night? Powerful, isn't it? I don't like it one bit tho. It's too powerful, and it won't be long before other countries discover how to make it, and if even there's a disagreement, I hate to think of what will happen. I wish it hadn't been ever discovered. Tonight came the news that Russia has declared war on Japan. It's alright in a way, I guess, but it seemed to me as if we were getting along quite well by ourselves. Only an "off the side" reason. Russia will own an awful lot of territory if we let her have Japan (I'm sure we don't want it). But I guess I'm just thinking too much and gathering too many conclusions, None of them good. . . .

Love,   Fran

Ann Arbor, V-J Day [crossed out]

Not yet. Guess can call this "Surrender" day.

My Own Darling:

Are you celebrating tonight too? Everybody everywhere is and I've never seen anything like it. Uptown Ann Arbor is a riot, streamers, confetti, papers flying through the air. The streets are so jammed with people that even traffic lights didn't do any good. They turned them off. Policemen on every corner but they've decided long ago [not] to try and keep order. They're just leaning on lamp posts and letting the people do what they will. . . .

It's so good to have this war all over. No more war. Just think, darling, what it all means. It covers so much, no more killing, all the boys will be home (and if not home, at least safe), no more shortages of any thing and most important of all to me, is that maybe you'll be coming home sooner than Jan. Do you think so? I hope so, so very much.

It's almost too good to be true, isn't it? Especially since we've had false alarms. Sunday, it came through, and every one began celebrating and people felt let down because it really hadn't. This morning it came through again, and people became excited, extras came out, radios buzzed, and again, it was false, and all afternoon was glum. Then tonight, we were all waiting for seven o'clock to come around because the President was to speak.

I went to the grocery story just before, hoping I'd get there before seven, and I almost made it. From one of the houses, I heard the announcement, really official this time, and I fairly flew to the store. There wasn't much more to be heard, but I was so excited I couldn't remember every thing I was supposed to get. Nick (one of the proprietors) was having himself a bottle of beer and tried to coax me into having some. I told him I didn't drink the stuff, and every other reason I could think of, but when he said "Then, let's Toast Victory!", well, I drank, not much, tho'. He only poured a little for me. Well, all felt so good. Don was there too, and we all but danced around the store. He said it was excusable tonight to hug the customers and right after he flicked off his apron and said he was going home. They closed the store right after I left so I didn't get there any too soon for tomorrow's groceries.

On the way home I could hear uptown cars and whistles blowing and as soon as I got in, I told the kids too, "Let's go up." They dressed as fast as they could and we walked fast, but already there were jams. It's all so exciting. Oh, Darling, I wish so much that you could be home now, everything would be perfect then. I miss you so much when something big comes up, something that means a lot. I don't want you to miss any of it, and I guess, I want you there for myself. I can't even really enjoy myself without you. If you could be here tonight, if we could share the wonderfulness of V-J together. What would we do, go to church and then paint the town red? Do you ever get tired of hearing me say, "I wish you were here"? It seems as if I say it so much. I can't put this feeling on paper that I could if I were talking to you. It's the same when I say, "I miss you so much" or "I love you, my darling!" I'm going to say, "I wish you were home," again cause maybe I'd have tomorrow off and what couldn't we do with a whole day!! I'll probably dream half the night about it. I love you, Peter, I love you. I love you so much that sometimes I don't know what to do with myself. I think so much about us, nothing in particular, just being together, imagining what it's like to have my arms around you, to feel you close to me. I think of what we did when you were home and how you looked on different occasions—the time you pretended you were going to sleep, when you were packing your bag to return to camp, how you looked at the train depot, where you were sitting beside me on the back step, and when you were listening to "Peaceful Valley" and so *many* other different times, I'm thinking of you all the time.

Must go, honey
Goodnight
Love,   Fran

Rose McClain of Snoqualmie Falls, Washington, wrote her impressions about the coming of peace in a letter to her husband, Charles McClain, who was serving with the Navy in the Pacific.

Snoqualmie Falls, Aug. 14, 1945

My Darling:

The whole world is full of joy and expressing it in some way or another this evening. I know it's the ending of great suffering and pain of war. Darling, I can't celebrate remembering the one I know can't come back [yet]. Maybe it will be all washed away when you are home again. Anyway, we can start counting our 180 days backwards and know before the end of that time, God willing, we will be together again. For all our lives, we can be together again. Today I cried and thanked God for the end of this war and I shall continue to pray this shall be the end of war for all time. That our children will learn kindness, patience, honesty, and the depth of love and trust we have learned, from all of this, with out the tragedy of war. That they shall never know hate, selfishness and death from such as this has been.

I don't suppose I will be able to mail this letter for two days as everything is closed and people are going mad, but then, why not. . . .

All my love and kisses,

Your wife and sweetheart,   Rosie

Even an event as momentous as the end of World War II did not put an end to farm chores. Sarah E. Stout of the small farming community of Tipton, Iowa, wrote the following "victory" letter to her nephew, Donald F. Stout, a corporal with the 7th Combat Cargo Squadron in the Pacific.

Tipton, Aug. 21, 1945

Dear Donald,

Well, how do you feel now? Things look brighter, don't you think so? I am anxious to hear from you and learn what your reaction was to the news about Japan. Of course, I realize that we have a long way to go yet, but one phase of it is over now. . . .

We canned 18 pints of sweet corn yesterday. I want to make some peach preserves tomorrow. I'll be glad when I get the fruit jars filled. Tomatoes aren't ready to can yet. I usually can about 40 quarts of tomato juice as well as 50 or 60 quarts of tomatoes. . . .

I had a card from Dorothy [Donald's wife] since she came home from Chicago. You can imagine how pleased she is now. In fact we all are very happy that at last brighter days are ahead.

No fishing news to report. Your Uncle Ralph hasn't had much free time lately. The rush will soon be over and then perhaps he will spend some time fishing.

Here's hoping I'll hear from you soon. Perhaps letters will travel faster now. We really can't complain about the mail service, can we?

No more now as it is time to do the evening chores. That task comes regularly.

Keep well and happy. See some of the sights whenever you can.

Love,   Aunt Dick

Bethel Upthagrove of Casper, Wyoming, expressed great joy and relief upon learning that her fiancé, Sergeant Allan Herdman, who served for two and a-half years with the Army in Iran, was finally on his way home.

                                                        Casper, April 12, 1945

My dearest, darling Allan,

Dark clouds moved rapidly overhead carried by a strong north wind as I made my way to work this morning. As I turned onto Wolcott St., the sight of an airman and his girl walking arm in arm served only to accentuate my own feeling of loneliness and I pulled my coat more closely around me trying to shut out the cold.

As is my custom, I stopped at the post office to check my box for mail. Awaiting my eager fingers was that familiar airmail envelope bearing your APO number. Opening it my eyes immediately fell on those three beautiful words. *"I'm Coming Home!"* wow! The glow I felt could light up a whole city block! Yes, we are both walking on air.

This morning was quite a contrast to that morning in October 1942 when you put your stripes in jeopardy by leaving your area and coming to the back door of PX 5 for one final embrace as you told me you were leaving. As I stood mute before you, trying to control the sobs I could feel welling up inside me, you tenderly reminded me of the words of the song, "good bye little dear, I'll be back in a year," and all I could do was bob my head up and down. Once back inside the PX I made a dash for the store room and there among the paper cups and jars of syrup, I let the tears flow. That was the unhappiest day of my life. . . .

I think the plans we made several months ago are still the best—when I receive your telegram I'll grab the first train east. It will take me about four days to reach your home, giving your family some time with you before I claim your undivided attention.

Yes, I'm still in favor of a simple ceremony at the parsonage. The words and their meaning are the same wherever spoken. We can make our own music. My heart will sing, "I love you truly," and yours will answer, "truly dear."

In the midst of my personal joy, I was shocked to learn that President Roosevelt died suddenly this morning. How tragic that he couldn't have lived to see the end of the war. He is the only president that I can remember. . . .

My darling, the hour is late and I find myself dreaming of the time soon when we can go to sleep in each other's arms. Until tomorrow, dearest, know that I will love you.

Forever,   Beth

Carma Froemling of St. Louis, Missouri, was elated upon learning that her husband, Corporal Albert Froemling, who served with the Army in Europe for sixteen months, would be returning home.

St. Louis, Feb. 14, 1946

My darling husband,

Words just can't express how happy I am darling. I guess you can well understand why. Yes dear, I received your wonderful telegram tonight and on all nights, Valentine's night.

Al, every word was correctly spelled and I'm sure I'm not dreaming when it read you would be leaving about March 9th. Oh it is just the medicine I needed. I'm so happy darling. This is something I have hoped and prayed for many a day now and at last my Al is coming home to me.

I've sure had the best Valentine present I could ever have.

Darling, I guess you will be able to write me more definite plans from time to time. Oh it seems so long since I last had a letter but darling this wire tonight has made up for everything. Be sure and let me know when you are sailing and when you think you will arrive in New York. Oh how happy I bet you will be to see good old New York. . . .

Darling, just to know I will soon be seeing you makes me so excited. By the way do you still have that mustache? I'm sure hoping it is gone by now because I want to see my Al just like he left. An old mustache will get in my way when I want to kiss my husband.

Well darling, now we can look toward our happy life together. We sure have been apart just plenty long enough. I guess though the Lord knew that and is keeping us.

Al, I just called Mom a few minutes ago and told her the good news. I know all your folks will be happy to hear the news. Mom is leaving Saturday for Hot Springs so I know she will enjoy her vacation knowing you will soon be on your way. . . .

Well dear, I guess this will be my last letter to my Al until he sees his wife. So please take good care of yourself. It sure will feel strange not writing each day after writing most every day for three years. It has been a great joy though and I won't forget a single letter. Al your letters sure have meant the world to me. . . .

Well dear, I must close now. I'm just so very very happy. Just think darling you will soon be a good old civilian again. Isn't that wonderful?

Once again a real safe voyage home and may it be real real soon. I can't wait now. If only you could be here for your birthday. I'm hoping darling.

Until I *see you* always remember I love you more than anyone and miss you so dreadfully.

All my love and kisses are my Al's alone forever.

Your Carma

Laura Lee Gibby of Pocatello, Idaho, reflected on the meaning of the end of the war after she received a telegram from her husband, Paul, announcing his return home. He was with the Army in the Phillippines when the war ended.

Pocatello, Jan. 1, 1946

Dearest Darling Sweetheart:

. . . Yesterday the mailman drove up in the field and honked repeat-
edly. I figured Daddy would answer him as he . . . was out by the mailbox,
but he didn't. He didn't know who it was. The mailman turned around and
drove back out to the road. I hurried out and guess what was in the box. A
telegram! It rather gave me a funny feeling. Boy, I would have been scared
if it'd been in war. Thanks, Honey for it. I, at least, knew you were all
right. . . .

Honey, really, you've had an experience, a very broadening experience
by being in the Army and travelling around. As a discussion of habit in
Thoreau's *Walden* says, "I left the woods for as good a reason as I went
there. Perhaps, it seemed to me, that I had several more lives to live, and
could not spare any more time for that one. . . ."

Sometimes I rather wish I had the opportunity to learn something different and broadening. . . .

Good night, my sweet,

Love Always,   Laura Lee

Marjorie Haselton, of Athol, Massachusetts, wrote a powerful letter about the
meaning of the war to her husband, Richard, who was part of a guerrilla Navy
unit operating behind enemy lines in China. Her sentiments were shared by
many other Americans.

Athol, V-J Day—Aug. 15, 1945

My Darling,

I'm listening to the radio and I have a feeling that somewhere, right
now, you are listening, too. Bing [Crosby] is talking to our hearts, as only
he can do it, and the top talent of the U.S.A., is contributing its bit. The
songs they are singing have me alternating between laughter and tears. I'm
so glad, Dick, that we have loved to sing together. Since you've been away,
my greatest comfort has been in hearing and singing the songs we've
loved. . . .

You and I were brought up to think cynically of patriotism—not by our
parents, but by the books, plays, movies and magazine features written by
the bitter, realistic writers of the twenties and thirties. They called patriotism a tool of the demagogues, a spell binder to blind our eyes to the "real"
truth. We thought they were right—at least, I know, I did. I hated everything in music, books, movies, etc. that stressed love of country. That was
for the yokels. The uninitiated, but not for anyone who really was in the
know. Maybe I was right—I don't know. One thing I *AM* sure of—a thing
this war has taught me—I love my country and I'm not ashamed to admit it
anymore. Perhaps I am only thinking along the lines the nation's propagan-
dists want me to think. But I know I am proud of the men of my generation.
Brought up like you and I, in false prosperity then degrading depression,
they have overcome these handicaps. And shown the world that America

has something the world can never take away from us—a determination to keep our way of life. Underneath what the Jap[anese] and the Germans believe to be a "what-the-hell," decadent attitude—you boys proved that you had a fighting spirit and team work that couldn't be beaten. Call it Yankee ingenuity or whatever you will, it still is the one force that won the war—the thing the enemy never believed we had. That is why, tonight, I am proud to be an American, and married to one of its fighting men. None of you fellows wanted the deal life handed you—but just about every one of you gritted your teeth and hung on. "Do the job, get it over with, and get home again" was the by-word. You proved that Americans may look soft and easy going, "spoiled" by the highest standard of living in the world, yet when the hour of need came you showed them we could take it—*and* dish it out.

I think the President sounded tonight as if he felt that way, too. Proud enough to bust. And, Gee, what other country in this world would let an insignificant *Private* introduce over the air, the head man of the country? Thank God for letting us live and bring up our family in a country like this. It's not perfect, I know, but it's the best there is—and away ahead of the rest!

I've been up on my soap box, but I meant it—every word!!! . . .

I've been hoping your special assignment is one that the surrender will make unnecessary. Wouldn't it be grand if you were heading *home* right now! I know that's too much to expect, but I hope I get a letter Tuesday with real news (day after Labor Day) cause I want my chance to show you in person how much.

I love you. Me

Marjorie Elizabeth and John Larson experienced a very long war. He was inducted into the Army in early January 1941 and was not discharged until five years later. During that period, he was engaged in fierce combat in Europe. The couple had originally planned to devote this time to missionary and church work.

When the war was over in Europe, John returned to the United States for a brief furlough before being sent to the Pacific to be part of the second wave of troops to invade Japan. However, the war had ended before he reached Japan. He served with the occupation troops for several months, returning to the United States in early 1946.

Throughout the wartime period, Marjorie and John Larson had readily understood why the war had to be fought. They accepted their place in the war effort without bitterness or feeling unduly sorry for themselves. They were sustained by their love for each other and their postwar hopes. As the war came to a conclusion, Marjorie wrote her husband a moving letter discussing their contributions in the light of the sacrifices of others.

Chicago, Aug. 19, 1945

My Dearest Precious Lamb:

It is 8:45 and I am writing thee, for I have some little talkings for you. . . .

I stayed for church and we had a guest pastor. He was very good and his sermon was on "Peace." Inner peace and world peace. . . . Everyone asked if I wasn't expecting you home soon. Well, I had to tell them no, not unless the orders were changed. Well, the truth and reality sank deeper and deeper into my heart and soul and caused a huge rock in my stomach. . . . My heart became even more uneasy, to say nothing of missing you, so it all netted me a lovely headache and it was really bad. I rested 'till about 6 when I was so hot I couldn't rest anymore up here and I went down and ate supper. . . .

Your mom called me this afternoon, and asked if I would like to come over to say "Hello" to the folks, but I didn't say yes or no, for I was so low. Your mom asked me if you had said anything new. I have never told her you must go, for in case you don't she will be spared.

All day I have been thinking of what I could say to you of my heart, on the subject of your going overseas again now after waiting almost 5 years for the war's end, and release. I have a lot of deep tho'ts, and one thing from way back. That is, that if I didn't believe in it (the war) and your service, perhaps death would have been in my eyes, just a sacrifice to the fact we can not get along with our fellowmen.

However, there is one thing I feel that could be no different, and that is that I'd not want you home, I'd want you in it, *because* you were standing shoulder to shoulder with the finest young men our side could muster. Men have died, been buried beneath white crosses across the globe in strange lands, killed in the same fight you fought in. Others have been maimed and wounded, and suffer much of physical and spiritual pain. Others too have spent many of the best years of their lives and lost sometimes, what they were fighting for, their wives, homes and families. None of them wanted this, any more than you did enjoy all the years of your service. All of them wanted to come back and whole to their loved ones. But, there is no justice in this thing. You and many millions did come back, whole and to their loved ones, thro' no fault of your own either, but by the grace of God. There are many thousands, even millions, who will still serve now in this big thing—the aftermath of this hell we call war. Many of those who will serve will have given even more than you, and many will have given less, but that cannot always be helped. I know I would rather feel in my heart and I know you would too—feel that you did more than your share rather than less.

It won't be too much longer, just a year perhaps, and there will be no fox holes for you to sit in, day in and day out, in water where your head and knees only stick out. You will not be shot at. The worst is over and done with. The waiting will be hard and long, and it will take a different kind of courage, and patience, and stamina than fighting does, but with God behind you, you cannot fail. . . .

And, Johnnie, at the end of the time, be it long or short, this is the road home to the dreams you have lived on for five years, and I'll be there too, my heart always yours, my dreams yours, our love one.

It is easy to write all this perhaps in one moment when we can be truly great. It is harder to live up to the great moment as the long lonely days drag by, but in so doing we are building the character and personalities we want to be, also to pass on to our babies. It is for these great things in you that I love and admire you and will find life dull till you return, and bad should you not. It isn't easy to be great, but therein lies the greatness and the beauty of your character, in facing the hard things, it comes out like the diamond under the jeweler's polishing.

You are a great person to me, John. We have gone thru a lot together, and have always been given strength for the task. We'll make it thru this time too.

I think so much of the gold stars on our service flags over the country, and what the gold stars mean in the hearts of those who loved and lost. I think too of those boys broken and maimed in mind and body. All this we have been spared, not that we deserve it. Surely, if more time and separation is expected of us, we can give that with chins up, and eyes on the hills. . . .

I feel that there are many who have not given half as much of themselves as you have, but that is really their hard luck. Then, on the other hand, many have given more and so as long as any of them stick the fight, we can too.

I love thee, dearest, my own beloved husband, my life, my all, and you are worth waiting for, till Doomsday, and there I am, at Doomsday. . . .

Me

Thy own.

Monday Morning P.S.

Oh, Johnnie. I am praying it will be right and fair for you to come home and that it works out that way. I was so sure you would get out, that today, realizing you may not has me at the bottom of the well, but I still believe what I wrote yesterday.

Me. *I Love Thee.*

In her "victory" letter to her future husband, Donald C. Swartzbaugh, who was in the Army Air Corps and stationed in India at an RAF base, Constance Hope Jones of Kirkwood, Missouri, remarked that perhaps "the biggest job is yet ahead."

Kirkwood, Aug. 18, 1945

Donnie:

Here I am again. How'd you celebrate the great news of the Jap[anese] surrender? I'll never forget how things happened around here. Pop got out his 45 and his 38 and blasted away his long saved shells. He was just like a kid playing with a new toy! (They tell me that *men* are always little boys, anyway, and I believe it.) In addition to that the church bells rang, whistles blasted loud and long, kids got out drums, pots and pans, flags, etc. and paraded the streets, people let loose of their tires and gas and paraded thru the streets until well into the night. Thousands crowded the streets in St. Louis. At Memorial plaza, 40,000 kissed and danced their way on the streets all night long. The next day everything was closed up tight. Today, most of the war plants are closed up and people are wondering about jobs.

. . . I've been neglecting you but not on purpose. I've just now caught my breath from all the work and excitement. I guess the war's end means you'll be home again sometime within the next six months. I hope so. After all, it's been a long time, hasn't it?

I think our family has been lucky in that both of our "warriors" are safe and sound. There are thousands of families not quite so lucky.

Tonight I'm invited to a party celebrating the return of an old friend from the WAVES. . . . I believe in every man having an equal chance in getting jobs. Just because a man was an officer in the army does not in itself entitle him to a choice job in civilian life. . . .

Now, I suppose Pres. Truman and Congress really have a big job of getting things and people adjusted to peace time ways of hiring and doing! Perhaps, the biggest job is yet ahead.

Over the radio yesterday (I can *hear* even tho I can't *read*), I heard the starting of another war! All about how the U.S. was developing new and secret weapons and how we should keep our secrets from the Russians! One was Winston Churchill; another was the head of the Army Air Forces! Talk like that is a betrayal of those who died or were wounded in this war and of those who are working to make it possible for nations to live in peace with each other! . . .

Till later,   Connie

CHRONOLOGY OF WORLD WAR II EVENTS

September 1, 1939	Germany invades Poland. Hostilities begin.
October 3, 1939	United States declares neutrality.
April 9, 1940	German forces invade Denmark and Norway.
May 10, 1940	Germany attacks the Netherlands, Belgium, and France.
May 26–June 4, 1940	Dunkirk evacuation of over 300,000 French and British troops.
July 10, 1940	Battle of Britain begins.
September 3, 1940	U.S. exchanges 50 destroyers for bases in British territory.
September 16, 1940	Compulsory military service adopted by U.S.
September 27, 1940	Germany, Italy, and Japan sign Tripartite Pact.
November 5, 1940	FDR re-elected for third term.
March 11, 1941	U.S. Congress passes Lend-Lease Act.
May 27, 1941	FDR declares unlimited state of emergency in U.S.
June 22, 1941	Germany invades Russia.
July 1941	U.S. forces occupy Iceland and Greenland.
August 14, 1941	Atlantic Charter proclaimed.
September–December 1941	Undeclared naval war in Atlantic.
December 7, 1941	Japan attacks Pearl Harbor.
December 19, 1941	Britain begins conscription of women.
March 28, 1942	Free mailing privileges extended to U.S. forces.

April 1, 1942	Internment of Japanese-Americans on West Coast begins.
April 9, 1942	U.S. forces on Bataan surrender.
April 10, 1942	Lanham Act for emergency assistance to communities hardest hit by war passed. Funds extended to day-care centers in 1943.
April 18, 1942	U.S. aircraft raid Tokyo.
Spring 1942	Rationing begins in the United States.
May 4–8, 1942	Battle of Coral Sea.
May 14, 1942	Women's Army Auxiliary Corps created; followed by establishment of other women's military units.
June 3–7, 1942	Battle of Midway.
June 22, 1942	First V-Mail sent.
June 23, 1942	Servicemen's Dependency Allowance Act passed.
August 7, 1942	U.S. forces land on Guadalcanal.
September 6, 1942	Battle of Stalingrad begins.
September 15, 1942	Prices and wages frozen in the U.S.
November 7–8, 1942	Allied forces land in North Africa.
January 14–24, 1943	Casablanca meeting of FDR and Churchill.
February 8, 1943	Soviet Union wins battle of Kursk.
May 13, 1943	Axis forces in North Africa surrender.
July 1, 1943	Rent levels frozen in the United States. Withholding of income taxes from wages begins.
July 10, 1943	Allied forces land in Sicily.
August 3, 1943	Emergency Maternity and Infant Care program for wives of enlisted men begins.
September 9, 1943	Allied forces land in Italy.
September 14–16, 1943	Major Allied victories in New Guinea.
November 28–December 1, 1943	Teheran Conference.
January 31, 1944	U.S. forces land in Marshall Islands.
March 25, 1944	U.S. forces invade Hollandia in New Guinea.
June 4, 1944	Allies enter Rome.
June 6, 1944	D-Day invasion. Allied forces invade Normandy.
June 22, 1944	Congress passes comprehensive G.I. Bill of Rights.
July 18, 1944	Allies capture St. Lo and break out in France.
September 13, 1944	Allied forces cross German boundaries.
October 24–26, 1944	Battle of Leyte Gulf.
November 7, 1944	FDR re-elected for fourth term.
December 16, 1944	Battle of the Bulge begins.
February 4–24, 1945	Manila liberated.
February 4–12, 1945	Yalta conference.
February 13, 1945	U.S. forces cross Rhine.
February 19, 1945	U.S. forces land on Iwo Jima.

April 1, 1945	U.S. forces land on Okinawa.
April 12, 1945	FDR dies; Harry Truman becomes President
April 25–June 26, 1945	San Francisco U.N. Conference.
April 27, 1945	U.S. and Soviet troops meet at Torgau on the Elbe river.
April 30, 1945	Hitler commits suicide.
May 8, 1945	V-E Day.
May 11, 1945	Point system to determine time of return of enlisted military personnel to U.S. put into effect.
July 17–August 2, 1945	Potsdam Conference.
August 6, 1945	A-bomb dropped on Hiroshima.
August 8, 1945	Russia declares war on Japan.
August 9, 1945	A-bomb dropped on Nagasaki.
August 15, 1945	V-J Day. Japan formerly announces surrender.
October 24, 1945	U.N. Charter activated.

FOR FURTHER READING

The millions of letter which were written during World War II remain un-
derutilized by historians. This is especially true for the letters written by women.
However, some attention has been given to letters written by women who
served in the military. Two contemporary works are Alma Lutz, ed., *With
Love, Jane: Letters from American Women on the War Fronts* (New York:
John Day Company, 1945), and Auxiliary Elizabeth R. Pollack, *Yes, M'am:
The Personal Papers of a WAAC Private* (Philadelphia: J. B. Lippincott, 1943).

Recent publications which have used letters written by service women include Anne Bosanko Green, *One Woman's War: Letters Home from the Wom-
en's Army Corps, 1944–1946* (St. Paul, Minn.: Minnesota Historical Society,
1989); Blanche Green, *Growing Up in the WAC: Letters to My Sister, 1944–
46* (New York: Vantage, 1987); and June Wandrey, *Bedpan Commando: The
Story of a Combat Nurse During World War II* (Elmore, Ohio: Elmore Publishing, 1989).

Two books which use letters written by women on the home front during
World War II are Judy Barrett Litoff, David C. Smith, Barbara Wooddall
Taylor, and Charles E. Taylor, *Miss You: The World War II Letters of Barbara Wooddall Taylor and Charles E. Taylor* (Athens: Univ. of Georgia Press,
1990), and Judy Barrett Litoff and David C. Smith, eds., *Dear Boys: World
War II Letters from a Woman Back Home* (Jackson: Univ. Press of Mississippi, 1991).

Several personal accounts and memoirs appeared during and immediately
after the war which contain valuable insights about the impact of the war on
American women. They include Guiliema F. Alsop and Mary F. McBride,

Arms and the Girl (New York: Vanguard, 1943); Susan B. Anthony III, *Out of the Kitchen—Into the War* (New York: S. Daye, 1943); Keith Ayling, *Calling All Women* (New York: Harper and Brothers, 1942); Laura Nelson Baker, *Wanted: Women in War Industry* (New York: E. P. Dutton, 1943); Margaret Culkin Banning, *Women for Defense* (New York: Duell, Sloan and Pearce, 1942); Constance Bowman, *Slacks and Callouses* (New York: Longmans, Green, 1944); Herbert Burstein, *Women in War: A Complete Guide to Service in Armed Forces and War Industries* (New York: Service Publishing, 1943); Augusta M. Clawson, *Shipyard Diary of a Woman Welder* (New York: Penguin, 1944); Elizabeth Gurley Flynn, *Women in the War* (New York: Worker's Library, 1942); Nell Giles, *Punch In, Susie!* (New York: Harper and Brothers, 1943); Elizabeth Hawes, *Why Women Cry or Wenches with Wrenches* (New York: Reynal and Hitchman, 1943); Barbara Klaw, *Camp Follower: The Story of a Soldier's Wife* (New York: Random House, 1943); Ann Pendleton, pseud. for Mary Trask, *Hit the Rivet, Sister* (n.p.: Horvell Soskin Publishers, 1943); Jean Stanbury, *Bars on Her Shoulders: A Story of a WAAC* (New York: Dodd, Mead, 1943); Eleanor Stevenson and Pete Martin, *I Knew Your Soldier* (Washington, D.C., and New York: Infantry Journal Publishers and Penguin, 1945); and Josephine Von Miklos, *I Took a War Job* (New York: Simon and Schuster, 1943).

Three contemporary guides for wartime women are Clella Reeves Collins, *The Army Woman's Handbook* (New York: Whittlesey House, 1941, rev. 1942); Clella Reeves Collins, *The Navy Woman's Handbook* (New York: Whittlesey House, 1942); and Ethel Gorham, *So Your Husband's Gone to War* (New York: Doubleday, Doran, 1942).

Over the last decade a number of secondary works have been published which pay special attention to the impact of World War II on the lives of women. Important books include Karen Anderson, *Wartime Women: Sex Roles, Family Relations and the Status of Women During World War II* (Westport, Conn.: Greenwood, 1981); D'Ann Campbell, *Women at War With America: Private Lives in a Patriotic Era* (Cambridge: Harvard Univ. Press, 1984); Susan M. Hartmann, *The Home Front and Beyond: American Women in the 1940s* (Boston: Twayne, 1982); Sherna B. Gluck, *Rosie the Riveter Revisited: Women, the War and Social Change* (Boston: Twayne, 1987); Margaret Randolph Higonnet, et al., eds., *Behind the Lines: Gender and the Two World Wars* (New Haven: Yale Univ. Press, 1987); Maureen Honey, *Creating Rosie the Riveter: Class, Gender and Propaganda During World War II* (Amherst: Univ. of Massachusetts Press, 1984); Sally Van Wagenen Keil, *These Wonderful Women in Their Flying Machines* (New York: Rawson, Wade, 1979); Amy Kesselman, *Fleeting Opportunities: Women Shipyard Workers in Portland and Vancouver During World War II and Reconversion* (Albany: State Univ. of New York, 1990); Ruth Milkman, *Gender at Work: The Dynamics of Job Segregation of Sex During World War II* (Urbana: Univ. of Illinois Press, 1987); Leila Rupp, *Mobilizing Women for War: German and American Propaganda, 1939–1945* (Princeton: Princeton Univ. Press, 1978); Elfrieda Berthiaume Shukert and Barbara Smith Scibetta, *War Brides of World War II* (Novato,

Calif.: Presidio, 1988); and Mary Martha Thomas, *Riveting and Rationing in Dixie: Alabama Women in the Second World War* (Tuscaloosa: Univ. of Alabama Press, 1987).

For more general works about life on the home front, see John Morton Blum, *V Was for Victory: Politics and American Culture During World War II* (New York: Harcourt Brace Jovanovich, 1976); David Brinkley, *Washington Goes to War* (New York: Knopf, 1988); John Costello, *Virtue Under Fire: How World War II Changed Our Social and Sexual Attitudes* (Boston: Little, Brown, 1985); Ross Gregory, *America 1941: A Nation at the Crossroads* (New York: Free Press, 1989); Mark Johnathan Harris, Franklin Mitchell, and Steven Schechter, *The Home Front: America During World War II* (New York: G. P. Putnam's Sons, 1984); A. A. Hoehling, *Home Front: USA* (New York: Thomas Y. Crowell, 1966); Roy Hoopes, *Americans Remember the Home Front—An Oral Narrative* (New York: Hawthorn, 1973); Lee Kennett, *For the Duration: The United States Goes to War: Pearl Harbor–1942* (New York: Charles Scribner's Sons, 1985); William Kenney, *The Crucial Years, 1940–1945* (New York: McFadden, 1962); Richard Lingeman, *Don't You Know There's a War On? The American Home Front, 1941–1945* (New York: G. P. Putnam's Sons, 1970); Geoffrey Perrett, *Days of Sadness, Years of Triumph: The American People, 1939–1945* (New York: Coward, McCann Geoghegan, 1973); Richard Polenberg, *War and Society: The United States, 1941–1945* (Philadelphia: J. P. Lippincott, 1972); Donald I. Rogers, *Since You Went Away* (New Rochelle: Arlington House, 1973); Archie Satterfield, *The Home Front: An Oral History of the War Years in America, 1941–1945* (Chicago: Playboy Press, 1981); Studs Terkel, *"The Good War": An Oral History of World War II* (New York: Pantheon, 1984); and Alan Winkler, *Home Front, USA: America During World War II* (Arlington Heights, Ill.: H. Davidson, 1986).

Index